Criminal Law in the Age of the Administrative State

Recent Titles in

Studies in Penal Theory and Philosophy

R.A. Duff, Michael Tonry, General Editors

Popular Punishment
On the Normative Significance of Public Opinion
Jesper Ryberg and Julian V. Roberts

Just Sentencing
Principles and Procedures for a Workable System
Richard S. Frase

Punishment, Participatory Democracy, and the Jury
Albert W. Dzur

Retributivism Has a Past
Has It a Future?
Edited by Michael Tonry

Taming the Presumption of Innocence
Richard Lippke

Sentencing Multiple Crimes
Edited by Jesper Ryberg, Julian V. Roberts and Jan W. de Keijser

Playing Fair
Political Obligation and the Problems of Punishment
Richard Dagger

Hate, Politics, Law
Critical Perspectives on Combating Hate
Edited by Thomas Brudholm and Birgitte Schepelern Johansen

Criminal Law in the Age of the Administrative State

VINCENT CHIAO

OXFORD
UNIVERSITY PRESS

OXFORD
UNIVERSITY PRESS

Oxford University Press is a department of the University of Oxford. It furthers the University's objective of excellence in research, scholarship, and education by publishing worldwide. Oxford is a registered trade mark of Oxford University Press in the UK and certain other countries.

Published in the United States of America by Oxford University Press
198 Madison Avenue, New York, NY 10016, United States of America.

Library of Congress Cataloging-in-Publication Data
Names: Chiao, Vincent, author.
Title: Criminal law in the age of the administrative state / Vincent Chiao.
Description: Oxford [UK] ; New York, NY : Oxford University Press, 2018.
Identifiers: LCCN 2018013395 | ISBN 9780190273941 (hard cover) |
ISBN 9780190920838 (epub)
Subjects: LCSH: Criminal law—Philosophy. | Criminal justice, Administration of. |
Public law. | Administrative law. | Welfare state. | Criminal procedure.
Classification: LCC K5018 .C53 2018 | DDC 345—dc23
LC record available at https://lccn.loc.gov/2018013395

Contents

Introduction

> We do not live in society in order to condemn, though we may condemn in order to live.[1]

What is the criminal law for? One influential answer is that the criminal law vindicates pre-politically rights and condemns wrongdoing. On this account, the criminal law has an intrinsic subject matter—certain types of moral wrongdoing—and it provides a distinctive response to that wrongdoing, namely condemnatory punishment. This understanding of the criminal law sets the stage for familiar debates in the philosophical literature on punishment, and informs the methodological framework in which that question is pursued. The philosophy of criminal law is, from this point of view, essentially an exercise in applied moral philosophy. Its concepts and preoccupations are familiar from interpersonal morality: desert, wrongdoing, excuse, blame, and so forth.

I defend a contrasting account. The criminal law and its associated institutions are, I claim, subject to the same principles of institutional and political evaluation that apply to public law and public institutions generally. The criminal law is a public institution that has a profound impact on people's lives. It therefore seems appropriate to see how it stacks up under familiar principles of political justification, particularly those that pertain to the role of public institutions in shaping life chances. Criminal law is public law, whether or not it also vindicates private rights.[2]

---

1. H.L.A. Hart, *Punishment and Responsibility: Essays in the Philosophy of Law*, 2nd ed. (Oxford University Press 2008), 172.

2. The "public law" label is not original to me; I draw here upon the important work of Malcolm Thorburn. See "Criminal Law as Public Law," in R.A. Duff and Stuart Green, eds., *Philosophical Foundations of Criminal Law* (Oxford University Press 2011), 21–43; and "Justifications, Powers and Authority," *Yale Law Journal* 117 (2008): 1070–130.

A public law conception starts with an account of punishment as a means of fostering social cooperation, an idea familiar from game theory, evolutionary biology, and classical sociology. Punishing rule-violating conduct fosters social cooperation by assuring those who are willing to cooperate that they will not be taken advantage of by those who defect. Punishment promotes the development of attitudes of reciprocity and willingness to engage with others on shared terms of social cooperation. It is not that punishment terrifies people into doing things they would not otherwise be inclined to do, as classical deterrence theory would have it. Rather, by stabilizing cooperative attitudes, punishment makes cooperation not just reasonable, but rational as well.

The cooperative basis of punishment provides a fresh vantage point on the project of justifying the criminal law. The cooperative basis of punishment suggests that the justification of criminal law cannot be separated from a justification of the forms of cooperation that the criminal law fosters. By the same token, our reasons for valuing social cooperation provide a normative platform for evaluating the criminal law. After all, that cooperation is valuable and worth supporting does not imply that just anything goes so long as it promotes cooperation. The means we select for fostering cooperation should themselves be consistent with our reasons for valuing cooperation in the first place. What this suggests is that a normative theory of the criminal law should live up to a fully political standard of justification: the same values and ideals that explain our reasons for valuing social cooperation under law apply to the moral evaluation of the criminal law.

Criminal law as public law thus stands at some distance from the highly individualistic account of rights and wrongs that motivates most forms of contemporary retributivism, whether of a moralistic or a Kantian strain. The criminal law is a means to an end, not an end in itself. It draws its value from the value of the public institutions and practices it supports. The value and justification of punishment cannot be drawn directly out of our everyday norms of interpersonal morality. The relevant concepts and principles of interpersonal morality carry weight in the justification of criminal law only insofar as they are incorporated within a broader account of justice in public law and public institutions.

Criminal law as public law is consistent with a wide range of approaches to normative political theory. It is not my aim in this book to defend any one approach over all others. I do aim, however, to illustrate how the demands of a fully political standard of justification can be met. I do this by considering a form of democratic egalitarianism, and unpacking how an account of social and political equality along those lines might be extended into the context of the criminal law. Drawing on work by Phillip Pettit, Elizabeth Anderson, and Niko Kolodny, I sketch an egalitarian ideal of "anti-deference"—an ideal of a society of peers in which, in Pettit's evocative phrase, each person can look every other person in the eye without fear or deference.[3] I give a particular interpretation to this idea, one that is democratic, egalitarian but not equalizing, and centered on a form of freedom—effective access to central capabilities—as its currency of evaluation. Public institutions should strive to protect each person's effective access to a range of central capabilities, where a central capability is one that is required, in a given social context, to live as a peer among peers. Access is effective when a person is able to exercise those capabilities without having to show undue deference to another.

An important feature of this conception of social equality is that a person does not lose her standing as an equal by virtue of having committed a crime. Were it otherwise, the category of criminal wrongdoing would in effect be given a pre-politically significance that limits our commitment to social and political equality. But this is to look at matters the wrong way around: from a public law perspective, the category of criminal wrongdoing is analyzed in terms of basic political values, not vice versa. The question is not to determine how criminality limits our commitment to equality, but rather to determine how a society of equals should appropriately respond to crime. This suggests that the central question for an egalitarian theory of the criminal law is to explain the conditions under which a society equals may reasonably rely on punitive measures to sustain egalitarian social relations. While egalitarian institutions might sometimes punish people for committing crimes, they should not for that reason consider a person's basic equality to be waived or defeated.

Punishment under the criminal law is most consistent with a commitment to social and political equality when it gives those who are subject to it an equal opportunity for influence in defining the law and setting policy, and, subject to that constraint, when it optimally protects effective access to central capability for all. The equal opportunity for influence principle is grounded in the thought that for some to have the unilateral power to call the shots when it comes to making criminal justice policy—what

3. Elizabeth Anderson, "What Is the Point of Equality?," *Ethics* 109 (1999): 287–337; Philip Pettit, *On the People's Terms* (Cambridge University Press 2013). Nico Kolodny, "Being Under the Power of Others," in *Republicanism and Democracy*, eds Y Elizar and G Rousselière (Cambridge University Press forthcoming).

kind of conduct to criminalize, which neighborhoods to police, whom to search, whom to prosecute, and what counts as an appropriate punishment for a crime—is for those people to have unjustified social power and authority over others.[4] This power and authority gives them a status that others lack, and is prone to generate objectionable patterns of deference. Perhaps this might be less problematic in areas of public policy that are less overtly coercive, or where the possibility of opting out is more realistic. But the criminal law is both highly coercive and mandatory. Allowing for equal opportunity for influence over the criminal law meliorates the concern that the criminal law boils down to gussied up bullying, however fair and effective it may otherwise be.

Subject to this constraint, capability-impairing policies of enforcement and punishment should be a last resort, employed only when no other reasonably available cooperative strategy does as well at protecting effective access to central capability for all. Since egalitarians should not view it as easier to justify a criminal law intervention simply because those who bear the brunt of its force have committed, or are suspected of having committed, criminal acts, a decision to rely on criminal sanctions to enforce a legal norm must be justifiable to all, victim and accused alike. By the same token, the criminal law should not be used, even as a means of protecting central capability, in ways that reflect humiliating judgments about those who are subject to the law. Doing so would be plainly contrary to the commitment to social equality that lies at the heart of anti-deference as a political ideal.

These concerns occupy the first half of the book (Chapters 1, 2, and 3). The remaining chapters are devoted to applying the egalitarian theory of criminal law to a range of important problems in contemporary criminal law and policy. In Chapter 4, I consider the phenomenon of mass incarceration. Starting in the 1970s, the United States has experienced unprecedented growth in incarceration rates, to the point where it currently houses 20 percent of the world's inmate population despite constituting only 5 percent of the world's population. Although most retributivists bemoan current incarceration levels, I argue that standard forms of retributivism—focused exclusively on the moral liability of individuals to punishment, and expressly marginalizing the significance of the social costs and benefits of punishment—have a difficult time explaining

4. Niko Kolodny, "Rule Over None I," *Philosophy & Public Affairs* 42(3) (2014): 195–229; "Rule Over None II," *Philosophy & Public Affairs* 42(4) (2014): 287–336.

what is wrong with mass incarceration. I argue that, from an egalitarian point of view, social investment in punishment becomes excessive once the marginal gains to universal and effective access to central capability are overshadowed by the losses (including opportunity costs) to that same egalitarian value. It is plausible that the current rate of incarceration in the United States significantly exceeds any reasonable estimate of this value.

Chapter 5 considers questions of criminalization. I criticize the prevailing "subject matter" approach, which treats the criminal law as centered upon a pre-politically specified subject matter (*mala in se*, pre-political rights, etc.). From the point of view of a public law conception, the criminal law does not have an intrinsic subject matter. Or, at least, any specification of the criminal law's subject matter rests on a political judgment about when social cooperation is preferable to private ordering. When should some type of conduct actually be criminalized? I argue that we have good reason to criminalize conduct if doing so is essential to promoting each person's ability to securely and effectively exercise basic capability. In contrast, I argue that the fact that conduct is morally wrongful is neither necessary nor sufficient for criminalization. In other words, we should reject moral wrongfulness as a principle of criminalization.

Chapter 6 turns to questions of criminal procedure and constitutional law. The United States Supreme Court has consistently adopted a formalistic approach to defining criminal law: a law is "criminal" if it does not merely seek to discourage, prevent, or otherwise regulate conduct, but rather is intended to condemn it by means of expressive punishment. Because many procedural rights—for instance, access to a lawyer, the ban on double jeopardy and retroactive application of a law—are limited to people facing criminal prosecutions, the result is to sharply limit the scope of those procedural rights on the basis of a court's judgment as to whether a legislature intended to punish when it enacted some law. Drawing upon the concept of a central capability familiar from the work of Amartya Sen and Martha Nussbaum, I suggest that a law that has the effect of burdening a person's effective access—access on terms befitting a peer—to central capabilities should be treated as effectively a criminal law. Whether such laws are "truly" criminal law should play no role in regulating access to procedural rights, particularly in an era in which legislatures have been attaching increasing numbers of ostensibly non-criminal "collateral" consequences to a criminal conviction. From the point of view of public law, the central question remains one of determining what kind of process is due. That question should be resolved on the basis of what kinds of capabilities are actually in jeopardy, rather than an estimation of a legislature's potentially punitive motives.

Finally, in Chapter 7 I turn to questions of responsibility. Equality may seem to be at odds with responsibility, and nowhere more so than in the criminal law. The egalitarian theory of criminal law that I articulate in this book may give the impression of denying that people are responsible for the choices they make. Taking responsibility seriously implies respecting the choices people make, even when they are poor ones. That seems, in turn, to suggest that when people engage in conduct that is ill-considered, culpable, or blameworthy, we have powerful, responsibility-based reasons to blame and punish them for doing so. In contrast, I argue that we can have responsibility without resentment: taking responsibility seriously does not inevitably require blaming and punishing people for their wrongful acts. I suggest that one way of taking responsibility seriously is by strengthening the social, emotional, and cognitive conditions under which responsible agency is developed and exercised. Instead of punishing people for crimes once they are committed, public institutions can instead develop initiatives (such as early childhood education and youth employment) that prevent crime by developing the capacity for responsible agency. Since neither criminal punishment nor social programs of this kind are self-executing—both consume scarce resources and political attention—a principle of distributive justice is required to adjudicate between them. Hence, rather than denying responsibility, egalitarian principles can help navigate a responsibility-responsibility trade-off.

In a nutshell, in this book I defend the claim that we should look beyond individualistic notions of responsibility and desert for guidance about the design of criminal justice institutions and laws. Instead, I propose drawing from a conception of democratic equality. Looking at the criminal law in this way suggests that "because you deserve it" is neither a necessary nor sufficient basis for a public institution, including one engaged in the administration of criminal law, to deny you access to the basic rights and prerogatives of civic membership. I interpret those basic rights and prerogatives expansively, including not only rights of equal political participation but also access to the range of capabilities required in a given society to lead a life as a peer among peers. The banishment of desert is not based on a doubt that people can deserve things, or that people can be responsible for what they do. It arises, instead, out of the application of a fully political standard of justification of the criminal law coupled with a democratic and egalitarian conception of justice in public institutions.

These values, I claim, prohibit treating people, even people who commit crimes, as excluded from a society's major institutions. That kind of exclusion is fundamentally inconsistent with the ideal of a society of peers, one that is devoid of the patterns of power, authority, and deference that are characteristic of hierarchical societies.

The public law approach I defend in this book is not sui generis. The ambition and, in many ways, the conclusions that I defend in this book flow out of David Garland's *The Culture of Control* and, especially, John Braithwaite and Philip Pettit's *Not Just Deserts*. Like Garland, I emphasize the connections between criminal justice and the welfare state, both in terms of how the criminal law was once understood to be part of a broader panoply of state-provided services, social insurance programs, and welfare-oriented policies, and in terms of its interpretation as a retributive, moralistic, and condemnatory institution as the welfare state has been rolled back. Like Braithwaite and Pettit, my ambition is to develop a comprehensive approach to criminal justice, one that is sensitive to its inevitable trade-offs and uncertainties while nevertheless being protective of basic rights. And, like Braithwaite and Pettit, my preferred framework draws upon republican ideas, particularly as they have been developed by Pettit in his subsequent political philosophy. Other important political theories of punishment include the contractualist and Rawlsian theories developed by Matt Matravers and Sharon Dolovich, respectively; Lindsay Farmer's historicist account of criminal law and civil order; Malcolm Thorburn's Kantian constitutionalism (from whom the label "criminal law as public law" is borrowed); and, most foundationally, H.L.A. Hart's efforts, in *Punishment and Responsibility*, to show how the philosophy of criminal law could avoid a moralistic retributivism without falling into an oppressively technocratic conception of crime and punishment.[5]

Hart's central insight in *Punishment and Responsibility* was that the criminal law could be interpreted from the point of view of basic political values, rather than the thick norms of interpersonal morality. However, despite Hart's stature in the field, the last generation of

5. Matt Matravers, *Justice and Punishment: The Rationale of Coercion* (Oxford University Press 2000); Sharon Dolovich, "Legitimate Punishment in Liberal Democracy," *Buffalo Criminal Law Review* 7(2) (2004): 307–442; Lindsay Farmer, *Making the Modern Criminal Law: Criminalization and Civil Order* (Oxford University Press 2016); Malcolm Thorburn, "Criminal Law as Public Law"; H.L.A. Hart, *Punishment and Responsibility*.

English-language scholarship has been dominated by the steady growth of retributive theories of punishment and, more generally, of highly individualistic theories of criminal law. Although social scientists have generally appreciated the institutional character of criminal law and criminal justice—its trade-offs and uncertainties, its relation to other types of social policy, the significance of institutional design and incentives, and its role in entrenching patterns of deprivation and subordination—among philosophers and legal theorists, institutional approaches have remained a decidedly minor literature. That tide now seems to be turning. After a generation of attempts to explain why people who have committed crimes have no reason to complain when we punish them for doing so, and after a generation of unremitting and ultra-harsh penal policies, the place of criminal justice institutions in a putatively liberal and democratic society is finally beginning to receive serious attention from a wide range of political philosophers. My hope is that this book will, in some small way, contribute to furthering that conversation.

This book grew out of numerous eye-opening conversations with Danny Priel about the common law, distributive justice, and legal theory in the context of modern welfare states; this book, in effect, seeks merely to memorialize those conversations, and to pursue them to their natural conclusions. I am additionally grateful to Elizabeth Anderson, Corey Brettschneider, Mark Dsouza, Antony Duff, David Enoch, Lindsay Farmer, Talia Fisher, Leora Dahan Katz, Chris DiMatteo, Chad Flanders, Erin Kelly, Adam Kolber, Chris Kutz, Veenu Goswami, Miri Gur-Arye, Alon Harel, Adil Haque, Zach Hoskins, Matt Matravers, Sandra Marshall, Simon Palmer, Arthur Ripstein, Alice Ristroph, Emma Romano, Re'em Segev, Jonathan Simon, Matt Steilen, Simon Stern, Hamish Stewart, François Tanguay-Renaud, Malcolm Thorburn, Kit Wellman, Javier Wilenmann, and Ekow Yankah for detailed comments on portions of the manuscript, in its various stages of disarray. I am grateful as well to James Cook and the editorial staff at Oxford University Press for their support throughout this process. In addition, I have benefitted from numerous conversations about the arguments presented in this book from audiences at Berkeley Law School, the University of Buffalo School of Law, the City University of Hong Kong, the University of Glasgow School of Law, Hebrew University, the London School of Economics, Loyola Law School, the University of Michigan School of Law, the Nottingham Criminal Justice Research Centre and Centre for Normative Political Theory, Osgoode Hall Law School, the Oxford Jurisprudence Discussion Group, the University of Surrey School of Law, the Faculty of Laws at University College London, and my home institution, the University of Toronto Faculty of Law. The *Jerusalem Review of Legal Studies* was kind enough to sponsor a workshop on a nearly final draft of the manuscript, in which numerous errors were pointed out to me. I owe a special debt of gratitude to the Israel Institute for Advanced Study, where, in the company of a wonderful group of scholars, many of the central ideas of this book were first developed. If there is a more conducive environment for academic inquiry, I have yet to discover it. Portions of Chapter 1 (Section 1.3) draw from "Two Conceptions of the Criminal Law," in Chad Flanders and Zach Hoskins, eds., *The New Philosophy of Criminal Law* (Rowman & Littlefield 2015). Portions of Chapter 2 draw from my paper, "What Is the Criminal Law For?" in *Law and Philosophy* 35 (2016): 137–63. Chapter 4 is a slightly revised version of a paper first published in *Criminal Law and Philosophy*. I am grateful to the publishers for permission to reprint those texts. Finally, I owe an enduring debt to Margaret, Max, and Niko, who tolerated the intolerable—an aspiring author.

Criminal Law in the Age of the Administrative State

1

Criminal Law as Public Law I

CONTEXT

1.1 Introduction

On a late winter day in 1984, a father brought his unconscious four-year-old son to the emergency room. The boy had suffered injuries that were sufficiently severe to require emergency brain surgery, including the removal of large sections of his skull. Although the boy's life was saved, the right hemisphere of his brain was destroyed, leaving him partially paralyzed and severely mentally disabled. Afterward, the surgeon reported finding bruising and internal bleeding consistent with a prolonged pattern of severe physical abuse. Members of Wisconsin's Department of Social Services had known that the boy was potentially being seriously abused for over a year. On a prior occasion, he had been brought to the hospital with a three-inch abrasion on his forehead as well as "numerous" other injuries across his body. At that time, the boy's father and his girlfriend were interviewed by medical staff, social services workers, and a police officer, but the boy was left in the couple's custody for lack of sufficient evidence that the injuries were due to abuse. Over the course of the following year, the boy's caseworker documented mounting evidence of such abuse. This included two further admissions to emergency rooms for bruising and lacerations, a corneal abrasion, reports from neighbors and family friends who had witnessed separate incidents of the boy being knocked to the ground by the couple, burn marks on his body that appeared to have been caused by a cigarette, and a pattern of physical violence between the father and his girlfriend, resulting in the police responding on six separate occasions to reports of domestic violence at the household. Nevertheless, the boy remained in the father's custody until one day he was brought to the hospital so severely injured that brain surgery was required to save his life.

Doctors and police rejected the father's claim that the boy had sustained his injuries by falling down the basement stairs. It was more likely, they concluded, that the massive brain damage had resulted from physical abuse. A warrant was eventually issued for the father's arrest; after some negotiations, he entered an Alford plea, refusing to concede that he had abused his son while nevertheless conceding that the state had amassed enough evidence to convict him. He ultimately served two years in prison.[1]

In the meantime, the boy's biological mother filed suit, arguing that the state had failed in its duty to protect the boy while he was in his father's custody. The case, *DeShaney v. Winnebago County Department of Social Services*, eventually wound up before the Supreme Court of the United States.[2] Over the dissents of Justices Brennan, Blackmun, and Marshall, the Supreme Court ruled in favor of the state, reasoning that the boy was not entitled to expect the state to protect him from his abusive father. The due process clause, the court held, limited only the *state's* ability to deprive people of life, liberty, and property. It did not require the state to go further and affirmatively protect its citizens from harm inflicted by others. In dismissing the case, the Supreme Court echoed a panel of the Seventh Circuit that had come to the same conclusion. The Seventh Circuit reasoned that although the state's social worker had been "ineffectual" at protecting the younger DeShaney, she had not actually caused his injuries herself. Since the Constitution, in the view of the Seventh Circuit, was a "charter of negative rather than positive liberties," and since the state had not itself caused the boy's injuries, it could not be held responsible for merely failing to prevent someone else from doing so.[3]

DeShaney raises a wide-ranging and intensely controverted question: What role should public institutions play in the lives of those who live under their jurisdiction? The Court's answer was austere. Perhaps the various officials who were involved in the case should have done a better job of protecting the boy than they did. But, like the imperfect moral duty

1. This account is drawn from Lynne Curry's book, *The* DeShaney *Case: Child Abuse, Family Rights and the Dilemma of State Intervention* (University Press of Kansas 2007), especially chs. 1 & 3.

2. 489 U.S. 189 (1989).

3. 812 F.2d 298, 301 (1987).

of charity, the moral expectation that the state will protect and promote the welfare of its citizens is discharged at the state's discretion. Neither the boy nor his mother had a legitimate expectation—a legally cognizable claim—that the state's social workers, medical personnel, or police officers would intervene to rescue the boy from his situation. The *DeShaney* court understood public institutions to be bound to respect people's rights as against the state, but no more.

Of course, Wisconsin *did* do more. For one thing, it convicted and punished Randy DeShaney for abusing his son. But following the logic of *DeShaney*, the state need not enforce the criminal law at all, at least insofar as the point of doing so is to protect people from being beaten up, killed, raped, or otherwise victimized. Those are wrongs that befall some people at the hands of others, not wrongs committed by the state acting through its agents. To be sure, there is a sense in which enforcement of the criminal law might be morally required, even under *DeShaney*. While the state might not have had an obligation to protect the younger DeShaney from violence at the hands of his father, it might still have an obligation to recognize the wrong that was done. However, from this perspective, the state had acted faultlessly. After all, it *did* ultimately prosecute the elder DeShaney for abusing his son. In doing so, it mobilized its criminal law to express public disapproval of the wrongdoing and to call the elder DeShaney to account for that wrongdoing. True, that disapproval was not worth very much to the boy, as it failed to protect him from being beaten by his father. But in the Court's view, public institutions are not required to prove their worth. They are just required to respect rights.

Seen in this light, the Supreme Court's judgment in *DeShaney* marked a thoroughgoing rejection of the penal welfarism that dominated Anglo-American thinking about the criminal law until the waning decades of the twentieth century. "Penal welfarism" is the view that, as David Garland has characterized it, "penal measures ought, where possible, to be rehabilitative interventions rather than negative, retributive punishments," and in which "the standard response to problems of crime and delinquency . . . [is] a combination of social work and social reform, professional treatment and public provision."[4] To the contrary, *DeShaney* suggests a view of the criminal process as purely reactive—as providing condemnation *ex post*

---

4. David Garland, *The Culture of Control* (University of Chicago Press 2001), 35, 39 (emphasis removed); see also Garland's earlier book, *Punishment and Welfare* (Gower 1987).

rather than protection *ex ante*. Seen in this light, retributive justice is the moral remainder left by the rollback of the social welfare state.[5]

This book defends a different view of both the criminal law, and of the significance of public institutions more generally. *DeShaney* notwithstanding, we now live in the age of the administrative state. We have created public institutions that have sweeping mandates to devise, promulgate, and enforce legal rules over incredible swaths of individual and social life. Public law regulates the product safety standards for the cradles in which we place our newborn, and it specifies the health and zoning regulations that govern how we bury our dead. The institutions and substantive legal rules they promulgate are oriented toward the public welfare, and in that sense the modern administrative state is a welfare state. Crucially, the moral authority of the welfare state does not flow from *noblesse oblige* flowing from a society's elites toward its huddled and clamoring masses. The political morality of the modern administrative state bottoms out on a principle of equal respect and concern. It bottoms out on the idea that those who live under their jurisdiction have claims—"as of right," as lawyers put it—to being treated as an equal. Hence, a person's access to crucial social services—healthcare, social security, unemployment and disability insurance, police protection, education, and so forth—is not predicated on establishing that she has led a morally blameless life and hence deserves our charity. Public law does not rest on a principle of moral desert. It rests on a principle of universal entitlement, as a matter of basic political equality.

From this point of view, Wisconsin's public institutions—including its criminal law—failed in their obligations toward the younger DeShaney. They failed to secure for him the prerogatives of a life lived as a peer, and left him exposed to the violent domination of his father and the father's girlfriend. This does not necessarily mean that anyone should have gone to prison for that failure. What it means is that the law governing when and how the state can intervene in private relationships potentially needed to be reconsidered. They should ensure that no party to a private relationship is under the thumb of any other party. Insofar as the criminal law is

5. How anachronistic was *DeShaney*? David Garland comments, of the British Children Act of 1908—a full eighty years prior to *DeShaney*—that the legislation "established the 'revolutionary' principle . . . that the problems of family 'failure' were to be administered not solely by charity and voluntary social work but through a series of public channels, presided over by the specialist juvenile court." *Punishment and Welfare*, 222–3.

required to make that the case, then the criminal law can have a legitimate role to play in backstopping family law. Perhaps, for instance, it would have been reasonable to empower the caseworker, knowing what she did at the time, to have removed the younger DeShaney from his father's custody. If so, it might perhaps also have been reasonable to enable the state to enforce that decision through an escalating series of sanctions, including sanctions of a criminal nature.

What is the place of the criminal law within this picture of public law and public institutions?[6] The criminal law is a means to an end, and that end is: to help secure the rule of stable and just public institutions. The basic principle of public institutions, in turn, is to extend the equal protection of the law to all—that is, to promote the common good on terms befitting social and political equals. In this sense, criminal law rests on the same principle of universal entitlement that animates public law more broadly. Of course, what terms are fair and equitable is a controversial question. I shall, in due course, suggest an egalitarian principle of fair cooperation: cooperation that protects, as far as possible, each person's ability to live a life as a peer among peers. Under this principle, the criminal law must satisfy a more demanding standard than merely acknowledging wrongs after they occur. We should expect more from public institutions, including the criminal law. We should expect it to contribute to making peoples' lives go better than they otherwise would. And we should expect it to do so on the basis of each person's status as an equal, not on the basis of moral desert.

The aim of this book is to make good on these admittedly sweeping claims. The aim of this chapter, however, is merely to set the stage for those further arguments. I start by briefly sketching two models of social provision: alms to the needy and social provision. I then outline how, over the course of the eighteenth and nineteenth centuries, Anglo-American criminal law emerged as a field of public law. I suggest that the gradual assertion of public control over most aspects of the criminal

---

6. I follow Robert Goodin in understanding an institution to be, "in its most general characterization, nothing more than a 'stable, valued, recurring pattern of behavior.'" Robert Goodin, "Institutions and Their Design," introduction to *The Theory of Institutional Design*, ed. Goodin (Cambridge University Press 1996), 21. The significance of institutions is that they render expectations about behavior stable and predictable. This is not, as Goodin writes, "an incidental by-product of institutionalization—not merely the consequence of 'coming to value a certain organization or procedure' for some independent reasons. Instead, that very stability and predictability is, to a very large extent, precisely why we value institutionalized patterns and what it is we value in them" (22).

process made it possible to think about crime and punishment as a matter of social provision rather than as akin to alms to the needy. Just as the rise of the welfare state transformed the otherwise private tragedies of unemployment or poor health into publicly shared risks, the emergence of criminal law as public law transformed crime from a series of independent wrongful acts into a collective problem calling for a socially organized response. This proposition sets the stage for my argument, in Chapters 2 and 3, that justifying the criminal law is, first and foremost, a matter of applying principles of political justification to the operation of policies and institutions, and only secondarily a matter of applying conceptions of moral responsibility, desert, or blameworthiness to individual cases.[7]

1.2 Two Models of Social Welfare

Suppose a group of people living together in a shared territory have a problem: to wit, that some of their number suffer from chronic need and malnutrition, and would, if left to their own devices, face a future of disease, deprivation, and premature death. Supposing that their compatriots felt some desire to improve their situation, how might this society go about achieving that aim? One model is "alms to the needy": the poor are provided for, to the extent they are, primarily by private ordering—by families, churches, and other nonstate institutions. These provisions are provided in an ad hoc and partial manner, out of a sense of charity, and are intended to stave off humanitarian disaster. This is presumably how the *DeShaney* majority saw Wisconsin's Department of Social Services: well intentioned and altruistic, but supererogatory. Another model—the "social provision" model—is more demanding. Under a social provision scheme, society, through a range of redistributive social policies such as unemployment insurance, old age security, subsidized healthcare, public education, and

7. Unless otherwise indicated, throughout this book the term "criminal law" refers not merely to statutory and decisional law, but also to the institutions and practices that comprise the criminal justice system in a more general sense. Here, as elsewhere, I am following Lindsay Farmer, who has criticized the familiar distinction between criminal law (an "autonomous philosophical system") and criminal justice ("particular practices or policies or systems of enforcement"). See Farmer, *Criminal Law, Tradition and Legal Order* (Cambridge University Press 1997), 9.

housing, insures all its members against at least some of the major evils associated with poverty.[8]

Social provision is distinct from alms to the needy in at least three important respects. First, the social provision model is statist. Its policies take the form of policies that are enacted in public law rather than in the decisions of private individuals, families, solidaristic communities, or markets.[9] This is not to say that certain aspects of public provision might not be devolved to private actors, only that doing so requires an antecedent public decision.

Second, social provision treats poverty as a problem to be managed collectively, not as a private affliction. Rather than leaving harms to fall where they may, social provision policies spread the burdens of poverty collectively.[10] The justifications for doing so have tended to be essentially egalitarian in orientation, in that the risks insured against are considered to be risks that everyone could face: any of us could fall onto hard times, have been born into disadvantage, or suffer from oppression.

Finally, social provision is provided as a matter of right rather than as a matter of discretion or charity. Public law generates legitimate expectations that people will see their rights and interests protected in certain ways, and on terms that do not leave them open to the intrusive and humiliating judgments of officials, the powerful or other social elites. On the model of social provision, you are not entitled to treatment in an emergency room or to a public education because some official has reviewed your record and deemed you worthy or deserving. You are entitled to those services simply because you are a member of the polity.

While the contrast between alms to the needy and social provision is highly stylized, it tracks in broad terms a slow, and still incomplete, shift over the course of the twentieth century in American political thought

---

8. S. Kuhnle and A. Sander, "The Emergence of the Western Welfare State," in *The Oxford Handbook of the Welfare State*, ed. F. Castles, S. Leibfried, J. Lewis, H. Obinger and C. Pierson. (Oxford University Press 2010): 61–80.

9. Richard Rose and Rei Shiratori, eds., *The Welfare State East and West* (Oxford University Press 1986), 34. Excerpted in Rose, "The State's Contribution to the Welfare Mix," in *Welfare Theory and Development*, ed. Peter C. Alcock and Martin Powell (SAGE 2011), 82.

10. I follow Asa Briggs's definition of a welfare state; see "The Welfare State in Historical Perspective," in *Welfare Theory and Development*, ed. Peter C. Alcock and Martin Powell (SAGE 2011), 1:14. Compare David Garland, *The Welfare State: A Very Short Introduction* (Oxford University Press 2016), ch. 1.

about social welfare, from a matter of charity to a claim of right.[11] More distantly, the origins of the social provision model might be traced back to Bismarck's creation of compulsory schemes of social insurance that protected against sickness, accidents, old age, and invalidity in the waning decades of the nineteenth century. Bismarck's initiatives proved popular, and rapidly spread across Europe, Scandinavia, England, Australia, and New Zealand.[12] Shortly thereafter, Britain became the first country to enact legislation providing for compulsory unemployment insurance.[13] The social provision model reflected a sea-change in attitudes toward government: rather than "a negative political force to be limited," government became "a positive social force to be harnessed and put to productive use."[14]

However, administrative government oriented toward securing the common good predates the creation of large-scale social insurance programs of this kind. In the United States, for instance, the "first real administrative agencies" were emergent already in the early nineteenth century in the form of local health boards. These boards had "vast governmental powers, concerning basic rights of property, economy, and personhood," and were empowered to make and enforce rules (including, in some instances, by issuing search warrants) regarding a broad range of public-health-related concerns.[15] In a similar vein, the American administrative state—comprised of permanent and lay officers charged, typically by statute, with developing policy and applying law in a wide array of contexts—has roots stretching well back into the nineteenth century.[16] In the continental context, the expansion of police powers—that is, of administrative capacity oriented toward public welfare—extends back at least to

11. See Karen M. Tani, *States of Dependency: Welfare, Rights, and American Governance, 1935–1972*. (Cambridge University Press 2016).

12. Briggs, "The Welfare State in Historical Perspective," 28.

13. Briggs, "The Welfare State in Historical Perspective," 33. The classic account is T.H. Marshall, *Citizenship and Social Class* (Cambridge University Press 1950). See also Garland, *Punishment and Welfare*, ch. 5.

14. Garland, *Punishment & Welfare*, 135.

15. William Novak, *The People's Welfare: Law and Regulation in Nineteenth-Century America* (University of North Carolina Press 2002), 201–4.

16. Jerry Mashaw, *Creating the Administrative Constitution* (Yale University Press 2012). See also Darryl Brown, *Free Market Criminal Justice* (Oxford University Press 2016), ch. 7.

the eighteenth century.[17] These accounts belie more familiar narratives of the administrative state as a twentieth century creation. In any case, in a suitably general sense, *every* state is a regulatory state; every state establishes laws or policies oriented at promoting this or that aspect of the public welfare.[18]

Before proceeding further, a note is in order regarding my conception of the "administrative state." This phrase is associated with regulations promulgated and enforced through administrative agencies housed in the executive branch of government. The feature of the administrative state that I wish to most emphasize is the existence of public institutions that seek to promote the common good across an expansive range of social life. For my purposes, how these institutions are classified under the traditional separation of powers is less important than their character as institutions that represent a social effort to achieve a collectively willed end. (Sometimes, when my emphasis is on the end rather than the means, I shall refer to the welfare state.) Of course, administrative states differ in terms of where they draw the line between public and private ordering, as well as in terms of how they conceive of the purpose of public provision.[19]

What is novel about the modern administrative/welfare state is not that it asserts public power to further the public welfare, but that it does so in a manner that spreads the costs of commonly shared social risks across citizens generally (or at least, in the case of social insurance, among those who pay into the system through their wages), rather than allowing the harms to fall where they may. Doing this requires not only a means of providing income support to the aged, healthcare to the sick, and education to the young, but also a means for raising revenue that goes beyond a fee-for-service model. The development of more systematic control over fiscal inputs is, as Richard Rose has pointed out, a necessary condition for the growth in public provision of goods and services.[20] It is in virtue of

17. Mireille Hildebrandt, "Justice and Police: Regulatory Offenses and the Criminal Law," *New Criminal Law Review* 12 (2009): 43–68, 59.

18. Markus Dubber, *The Police Power: Patriarchy and the Foundations of American Government* (Columbia University Press 2005), ch. 1.

19. Gøsta Esping-Andersen, *The Three Worlds of Welfare Capitalism.* (Princeton University Press 1990).

20. Richard Rose, "Common Goals but Different Roles: The State's Contribution to the Welfare Mix," in *The Welfare State East and West*, ed. Richard Rose and Rei Shiratori (Oxford University Press 1986), 13–39, 19.

spreading the costs of social provision broadly that public institutions are able to transform private tragedies into publicly shared risks. Consider, in this context, the fin de siècle debates in the United States surrounding the creation of a progressive income tax. The prevailing "benefits principle" treated taxes as "quite simply the price that individual citizens paid in exchange for the benefits of government protection," and was "based, first and foremost, on the logic of reciprocal exchange."[21] The benefits principle respected pre-politically negative rights in property, but made the proposition that some people should be made to pay more in taxes than they could expect to recoup in benefits extremely problematic. As Mehrotra has documented, the introduction of a progressive income tax in the United States was defended on the basis of a more robust conception of equal citizenship. Under this more demanding conception of "fiscal citizenship," as Mehrotra puts it, equality of sacrifice was required to sustain the civic order; fiscal citizenship required a basic break with the Lockean premise that states exist to better protect an individual's own natural rights, such as the right to property. This more robust conception of equality was defended by progressive American economists who, influenced by intellectual trends in German historicism—where Bismarck's social insurance schemes were beginning to take root—emphasized the interdependence of citizens with each other, an interdependence crystallized in the form of public institutions.[22] The introduction of the progressive income tax thus already went far beyond the "charter of negative rather than positive liberties" that the Seventh Circuit would, a century later, appeal to in *DeShaney*.

In any case, notwithstanding the *DeShaney* court's truculence, social provision schemes are now familiar and ubiquitous. Wisconsin's Department of Social Services is just one out of thousands of public agencies at the municipal, state, and federal levels oriented at promoting the common good in a staggering variety of ways.[23] These are the institutions of the welfare state, and their role is to operationalize systems of social provision,

---

21. Ajay K. Mehrotra, *Making the Modern American Fiscal State: Law, Politics, and the Rise of Progressive Taxation, 1877–1929* (Cambridge University Press 2013), 61.

22. See Mehrotra, *Making the Modern American Fiscal State*, ch. 2.

23. The Census Bureau estimates that there are over 90,000 "local governments" in the United States; see Carma Hogue, "Government Organization Summary Report: 2012," available at: http://www2.census.gov/govs/cog/g12_org.pdf.

from public education to environmental protection to consumer safety to financial regulation to family law.

This is not the place to consider in any detail the historical question of why welfare state institutions arose when they did, or the degree to which the institutions and policies of various countries conform to the model of social provision. My purpose in sketching the social provision model is to provide a model for thinking about the somewhat earlier transformation (roughly from the late eighteenth century through to the early twentieth) of the criminal law from a system of private remedy to one of public administration. As public officials began asserting more systematic, and less ad hoc, control over the criminal process, they gradually began to create institutions that made it possible to view crime as more than an uncontrollable consequence of social life and rather as a collective problem that could be managed by intelligent and informed policy.[24] The criminal law, in other words, became both more statist and more capable of dealing with crime at the level of policy, rather than merely at the level of individual cases. Moreover, because police, prosecutorial, and correctional budgets are drawn from general revenue, rather than collected on a fee-for-service model, they are in effect redistributive. Those who stand to benefit the most from the provision of criminal justice services are not necessarily those who pay the lion's share of its costs.[25] As a result, criminal justice is a matter of collective concern not simply because of the moral concern individual citizens might take in how others are treated, but because the costs of providing criminal justice services are spread collectively rather than privately borne. Finally, the requirement that police, prosecutors, judges, and other criminal justice officials treat people fairly and equally is a basic feature of the political morality of criminal justice. Virtue has nothing to do with it: police, prosecutors, and judges are required to give your interests and claims equal respect whether or not they consider you morally righteous. Consequently, the institutional development of the criminal law has made the model of social provision increasingly more apt, and the model of alms to the needy increasingly less so.

---

24. See Garland, *Punishment and Welfare*, 154; and Garland, *The Culture of Control*, ch. 2, especially 44–51.

25. This is a point, like so many others, on which Bill Stuntz's work has been pioneering. See for example: William J. Stunz, "The Pathological Politics of Criminal Law," *Michigan Law Review* 100 (2001): 505–600.

1.3 The Emergence of Criminal Law as Public Law

Although it is now customary to think of criminal law as public law, for much of its history in the common law world, the criminal law was not a particularly state-centered institution. The distinction between crime and tort was not between a public and a private wrong, but rather a choice open to the private plaintiff: Did he want to pursue vengeance or compensation?[26] One and the same act could be either a crime or a tort not because it might be both a private wrong (enforceable by the victim) and a public wrong (enforceable by the king), but simply because the victim had the option of choosing between seeking his satisfaction in a punitive remedy or a compensatory one. Insofar as criminal law was state-centered, it was not because criminal acts injured a victim in which the king held a benevolent interest; rather, it was an affront to the political authority of the sovereign. In the premodern era, as Garland has noted, "law enforcement" did not connote protecting the public from crime by means of police, prosecutors, and prisons. It was rather "a matter of lordship and political rule . . . through which the King's sovereign will was imposed against that of his enemies and against rebellious or unruly subjects."[27] The idea that the criminal law could be defined by reference to the nature of the wrong done to the victim was first introduced by Blackstone in his *Commentaries*; it is, in that respect, a thoroughly modern idea.[28] Up until the eighteenth century, breaches of the criminal law were largely privately investigated and privately prosecuted. Punishments were, of course, carried out by public officials, but since incarcerating large numbers of people did not become an established feature of criminal justice until the nineteenth century, it did not require constant oversight of sprawling, hard to govern, and resource-intensive institutions.

Consider, first, the history of policing in the common-law world. While the idea that the safety and security of its citizens is in some sense the

---

26. David J. Seipp, "The Distinction between Crime and Tort in the Early Common Law," *Boston University Law Review* 76 (1996): 59–87 at 84.

27. Garland, *The Culture of Control*, 29. That we so intuitively associate "law enforcement" with "crime control," Garland suggests, "reveals the extent to which we have become used to thinking about the state as the standard mechanism for dealing with crime."

28. David Lieberman, "Mapping Criminal Law: Blackstone and the Categories of English Jurisprudence," in *Law, Crime and English Society, 1660–1840*, ed. N. Landau (Cambridge University Press 2002), 139–61; William Blackstone, *Commentaries on the Laws of England*, 4 vols (Oxford 1765–9), 1:122, and 4:5–6.

state's responsibility no doubt has a longer lineage, the idea that it might be the state's role to protect those interests through public policing and prosecution of criminal offenses is relatively novel, at least in the United Kingdom and North America. The history of organized policing as a publicly provided service of any kind did not arise in Britain until the middle of the nineteenth century. The first public police force in Britain—Peel's Metropolitan Police—was only instituted in 1829, with versions in North American cities following in subsequent decades.[29] The institution of professional policing was already well established in continental jurisdictions, but they were staunchly resisted in England on the grounds that the police were a quasi-military surveillance apparatus inconsistent with English liberty.[30]

Prior to the development of professional policing over the middle decades of the nineteenth century, most of what we would now regard as "police" work was carried out by private citizens (the literal nightwatchmen of libertarian political theory), part-time constables, and thief-takers, as well as the victims themselves, and other members of the community in a more or less ad hoc and informal manner. Victims took it upon themselves to track down perpetrators, sometimes by offering rewards, and the government sometimes also offered rewards for information leading to a conviction (an early form of today's qui tam action) or pardons for criminals who betrayed their compatriots (an early form of today's conspiracy law.) This seems to have worked about as well as one might expect, with frequent complaints of abuse, dishonesty, and entrapment.[31]

---

29. See Eric H. Monkkonen, *Police in Urban America* (Cambridge University Press 2004), ch. 1; Samuel Walker, *Popular Justice: A History of American Criminal Justice*, 2nd ed. (Oxford University Press 1998), ch. 2.

30. Clive Emsley, *The Great British Bobby: A History of British Policing from the Eighteenth Century to the Present* (Quercus 2009), 33–36. Emsley writes that "there was concern that a centralized police was something peculiarly foreign, worst of all French"; he also notes that "there was even greater concern about central government encroaching on the rights of local government." "The History of Crime and Crime Control Institutions," in *The Oxford Handbook of Criminology*, ed. M. Maguire, R. Morgan, and R. Reiner (Oxford University Press 2002): 203–30 at 212. Markus Dubber has traced kingly delegations of "police powers"—in the sense of general administrative powers—to municipalities in Europe to the late fourteenth century in France and the mid-fifteenth century in Germany. See Dubber, *The Police Power*, 69–70.

31. John Langbein, Renée Lettow Lerner, and Bruce Smith, *History of the Common Law: The Development of Anglo-American Legal Institutions* (Wolters Kluwer Law & Business 2009). For an account of thief-taking, see Ruth Paley, "Thief-Takers in London in the Age of the McDaniel Gang," in *Policing and Prosecution in Britain 1750–1850*, ed. Douglas Hay and

Hence, it is perhaps unsurprising that the popularity of the idea that policing might be an inherently public function appears to track the growth in the capacity and professionalism of the public police.[32] As compared to the alternative, public policing might well have come to seem attractive.

Not only was the investigation of crime and the apprehension of criminals a largely private matter, so too was the prosecution of criminals once they were caught.[33] As with policing, other systems devoted greater institutional resources to the prosecution of crimes, such as an office of a public prosecutor, rather than relying on victims of crime to initiate and prosecute a criminal case.[34] But, as with policing, in England the idea that the cost of criminal prosecutions should be publicly borne was seen as inconsistent with "that perfect freedom of action and exemption from interference, which are the great privileges and blessings of society," and it was believed that the gains in protecting people from criminal victimization in a more systematic manner were outweighed by the costs to liberty of a system of public policing and prosecutions.[35] For reasons that remain obscure, public prosecution in the common-law world first arose in a systematic way in North America. Private prosecutions remained the norm in England until much later: the office of the Director of Public Prosecutions was not created until 1879, and another century went by before the Crown Prosecution Services was created in 1986.[36] Admittedly, the practice of

Francis Snyder, 301–40; John M. Beattie, *Crime and the Courts in England, 1660–1800* (Clarendon Press 1986), 55–59. Henry Fielding, whose Bow Street Runners were a forerunner to the Peel's Metropolitan police, famously satirized the thief-takers (and the government of the day) in *The Life and Death of Jonathan Wild, the Great.*

32. David Alan Sklansky, "The Private Police," *University of California Los Angeles Law Review* 46 (1999): 1165–287 at 1219.

33. Douglas Hay and Francis Snyder, "Using the Criminal Law, 1750–1850: Policing, Private Prosecution and the State," in *Policing and Prosecution in Britain 1750–1850*, ed. Hay and Snyder (Clarendon Press 1989), especially 16–25; Beattie, *Crime and the Courts in England*, 35–41.

34. David Philips, "Good Men to Associate and Bad Men to Conspire: Associations for the Prosecution of Felons in England, 1760–1860" in *Policing and Prosecution in Britain 1750–1850*, ed. Douglas Hay and Francis Snyder (Clarendon Press 1989), 118.

35. "Report from the Select Committee of the Police of the Metropolis, 1822," 9–11, cited by Mark Koyama, "The Law & Economics of Private Prosecutions in Industrial Revolution England," *Public Choice* 159 (2014): 277–98 at 286, n.28. As Koyama notes, given the level of corruption and patronage in English institutions at this time, "these fears were neither irrational nor necessarily driven by ideology."

36. Jack M. Cress, "Progress and Prosecution," *Annals of American Academy of Politics and Social Science* 423 (1976): 99; Crown Prosecution Services: https://www.cps.gov.uk/

private prosecution persisted in the United States well after the introduction of public prosecutors, "because some wealthy crime victims did not trust the low-paid, often inexperienced, and understaffed public prosecutors."[37] However, although private prosecutions remain possible today, that power is typically thoroughly circumscribed by official discretion.[38]

Strikingly, Nozick's famous parable of voluntary protective associations—the philosophical anarchist's riposte to the Lockean argument for a state—has a historical precedent in the emergence of private prosecution associations in eighteenth century England.[39] These associations were designed to provide their dues-paying members with what we would now think of as public prosecutorial services. "All associations," Philips notes, "offered their members at least two basic forms of assistance: in the detection and apprehension of suspected offenders, and in the prosecution of those arrested people."[40] However, the significance of these private prosecution clubs declined as the century wore on and professional police forces became more established and expert in investigating and prosecuting crime; over time, public law enforcement substituted for private.[41]

Notably, Crown responsibility for prosecuting regulatory crimes has a longer and more established history than Crown responsibility for prosecuting ordinary felonies. This probably had to do with the growth in specialized institutions—the Mint, the Treasury, the Bank of England, the Post Office—that sought to enforce the laws that lay within their

---

basic-page/history (accessed May 8, 2018). While prosecutions in some Scottish courts were directed by government officials by the early nineteenth century, the formal expansion of centralized, government-controlled prosecution had to wait until 1975. See Farmer, *Criminal Law, Tradition and Legal Order,* 85. For an account of the history of public prosecutions in the colonies, see Carolyn B. Ramsey, "The Discretionary Power of 'Public' Prosecutors in Historical Perspective," *American Criminal Law Review* 39 (2002): 1309–93.

37. Walker, *Popular Justice,* 71.

38. As by statute in Canada: see *Criminal Code,* RSC 1985, c C-46, s.504.

39. Robert Nozick, *Anarchy, State and Utopia* (Basic Books 1974), ch. 2.

40. Philips, "Good Men to Associate and Bad Men to Conspire," 137–38; see also Beattie, *Crime and the Courts in England,* 48–50.

41. See Koyama, "The Law and Economics of Private Prosecutions in Industrial Revolution England," 288, fig. 2. As Koyama notes, Scotland Yard ("the first modern detective agency") was established in 1842, and provided a level of expertise that the amateur policing efforts of the private prosecution clubs could not hope to match. See also Philips, "Good Men to Associate and Bad Men to Conspire," 123, 150–51.

particular mandates.[42] The immediate point, however, is that once criminal prosecution comes under centralized public control, public officials acquire a new means for setting criminal justice policy. Public officials, whether line prosecutors or attorneys general, decide which crimes will be taken seriously, how they will be charged, what sorts of pleas will be accepted, and so forth.[43]

The growth of public institutions for sharing risk affected the substantive law in other ways as well. If one of the motivations for having the criminal law is to deter antisocial conduct, then it must surely matter how likely it is that someone who engages in such conduct will be caught and prosecuted.[44] In the era of the nightwatchman state, this probability could not have been very high. Criminal prosecutions were rare occurrences relative to the rate at which crimes were committed. Peter King has reviewed evidence of prosecutorial activity in Essex in the middle of the eighteenth century, and concluded that the vast majority of property crime went unreported and unprosecuted.[45] Indictments, King concludes, "cut a pitiful figure when compared to the huge number of indictable but unprosecuted acts of appropriation" that occurred during that period.[46] Hence, it should not be surprising that the criminal law in eighteenth and nineteenth century England—which had no public police, and no public prosecution service—was notoriously severe. This was a system of crime and

42. See Langbein, Lerner, and Smith, *History of the Common Law*, 686–87.

43. On the prosecutors' role in setting criminal justice policy, see William Stuntz, "Plea Bargaining and the Criminal Law's Disappearing Shadow," *Harvard Law Review* 117 (2004): 2548–69.

44. For evidence (from Germany) that policies regarding investigation, prosecution, and diversion affect crime rates to a greater degree than incarceration rates, see Horst Entorf, "Crime, Prosecutors, and the Certainty of Conviction," IZA Discussion Paper No. 5670 (April 2011).

45. Peter King, *Crime, Justice and Discretion in England 1740–1820* (Oxford University Press 2003), 11–12, 132–34. King's evidence suggests that the ratio of indicted to indictable offenses was in the range of 1–10 percent. It must be said, though, that the rate at which property crimes are prosecuted today remains similarly low. For a very rough comparison (arrest rates for offenses known to police, rather than prosecutions relative to crime overall) to contemporary figures in the United States, see *Sourcebook of Criminal Justice Statistics Online*, table 4.1.2007, available at: http://www.albany.edu/sourcebook/pdf/t4212007.pdf (accessed May 8, 2018). See also Nicola Lacey, *In Search of Criminal Responsibility: Ideas, Interests, and Institutions* (Oxford University Press 2016), 112–13.

46. King, *Crime Justice and Discretion in England*, 134.

punishments that depended on inflicting exemplary punishments on a relatively small number of people.

To replace a system of harsh, exemplary punishments with a system of moderate penalties uniformly imposed required a much more developed set of public institutions than was available at the time. At a minimum, it would require a more organized effort to apprehend criminals. Indeed, Clive Emsley has suggested that an important motivation behind the establishment of the Metropolitan Police was meliorating the harshness of Britain's "Bloody Code" by raising the likelihood of conviction and punishment through an organized effort at policing.[47] Consider that in 1820, English criminal law contained "well over" two hundred capital offenses, whereas by 1841—barely a decade after the establishment of London's Metropolitan Police in 1829—only two capital offenses remained, murder and treason.[48] Eric Monkkonen makes a similar observation:

> The creators of the new police introduced a new concept in social control: the prevention of crime. . . . Taking an argument of the Italian criminal law reformer, Beccaria, they claimed that regular patrolling, predictable detection of offenses, and rational punishment would deter potential offenders. They even extended Beccaria's argument, claiming that the sight of the police uniform itself would deter potential offenders.[49]

This same period also witnessed the gradual transformation of modes of punishment, from localized, private, and exemplary to national, publicly supported, and uniform. This period, the late nineteenth to early twentieth century, witnessed the rise of prisons as standard forms of punishment.[50] Although workhouses for poor and vagrant individuals trace back to the

---

47. Clive Emsley, *Policing in Its Context, 1750–1870* (Macmillan 1983), 59. Emsley cites a contemporary reformer's observation that while Britain had 223 capital offenses, France—which had a public police force—had only 6. However, Walker has suggested that American police forces, which were as a rule less professional, and more corrupt, than their English counterparts, were unlikely to have had much of an impact on crime. See Walker, *Popular Justice*, ch. 2.

48. Lacey, *In Search of Criminal Responsibility*, 127.

49. Monkkonen, *The Police in Urban America*, 40–41; Douglas Hay, "Property, Authority and the Criminal Law," in *Albion's Fatal Tree*, ed. Douglas Hay, Peter Linebaugh, John Rule, EP Thompson and Cal Winslow (Pantheon 1976), 17–63, 18.

50. For an overview of this history in the United States, see Walker, *Popular Justice*, ch. 3.

latter half of the sixteenth century, it took another three centuries before imprisonment (at hard labor) became systematically used as a response to crime.[51] During the eighteenth century, not only were prisons also used to house debtors—that is, to enforce private obligations rather than public wrongs—but they were themselves largely private enterprises. They were "self-financing operations," in which "the jailer was supposed to derive his income from the fees owed by prisoners for various legal services," including the provision of "commercial opportunities" such as the sale of bedding materials or beer.[52] Although punishment was a matter of ongoing controversy throughout the 1700s, it was not until the early part of the 1800s that reform efforts took on a national cast.[53] Nineteenth-century reformers claimed that because ease of travel on the railways made crime into a national rather than local problem, so too should punishment be administered on a national level. Local prisons began to be supported, in part, out of central government revenues, culminating ultimately in the nationalization of local prisons under Disraeli.[54]

Moreover, although punishment remained harsh, it became subject to greater demands for uniformity across cases, with correspondingly less tolerance for obviously exemplary forms of punishment. Reformers came to oppose capital punishment because of its spectacle, and because it "emphasized the discretionary element of justice."[55] Punishment, they claimed, should be carried out in solitude, and it should be focused on reform of the offender's soul-perhaps by means of tormenting his body, but not carried out for that reason. Facing the problem of a steady increase in the number of people being committed for trial, and the removal of transportation to the colonies as an option, reformers opted instead to turn to imprisonment. Although initially imprisonment took the form of prison ships moored in the Thames (the "hulks"), eventually reform efforts

---

51. John Langbein, "The Historical Origin of the Sanction of Imprisonment for Serious Crime," *Journal of Legal Studies* 5(1) (1976): 35–60 at 53.

52. Randall McGowen, "The Well-Ordered Prison: England, 1780–1865," in *The Oxford History of the Prison*, ed. Norval Morris and David J. Rothman (Oxford University Press 1995), 79–110 at 82.

53. McGowen, "The Well-Ordered Prison," 80.

54. Sean McConville, "The Victorian Prison: England, 1865–1965," in *The Oxford History of the Prison*, ed. Norval Morris and David J. Rothman (Oxford University Press 1995), 131–68 at 139–44.

55. McGowen, "The Well-Ordered Prison," 93.

settled on the construction of permanent prisons.[56] By means of the prison, criminals became separated from the social world and were subject to strict and all-encompassing forms of discipline and labor; those who returned from prison were no longer simply people who had been punished, but had become "criminals."[57]

Although I have so far been focusing on institutions, the substantive law was changing as well. Particularly with rapid industrialization of the economy in the nineteenth century, the laws that public officials were called upon to enforce also began to shift. Peter Ramsay observes that during this period,

> the criminal law was developed to perform a quite different function from the adjudication of right and wrong implied by the Enlightenment theories . . . [t]hat function was the regulation of otherwise lawful everyday behaviour, such as productive and commercial activity or the use of public space, by means of statutory offences, prosecuted under summary procedure and often containing no fault element at all.[58]

In a similar vein, Lindsay Farmer notes that these decades saw a proliferation of new statutes regulating and licensing public trade, safety, pollution, revenue, and so on. While this type of offense was not completely new, as is often assumed, there was a drastic change in the scale and quality of governmental intervention and a transformation of criminal liability. From the factory legislation of the 1830s onward, central government became increasingly involved in legislating to prevent accidents, license certain types of activity, and set standards of quality, as well as the criminalization of socially harmful activities.[59]

Ramsay and Farmer both argue that this same period saw courts first attempt to use the framework of homicide prosecutions as a regulatory device to ensure minimum levels of care in carrying out risky activities,

---

56. For discussion of the significance of the hulks in Victorian penal policy, see Beattie, *Crime and the Courts in England*, 565–66.

57. McGowen, "The Well-Ordered Prison," 99–108.

58. Peter Ramsay, "The Responsible Subject as Citizen: Criminal Law, Democracy and the Welfare State," *Modern Law Review* 69 (2006): 29–58 at 32.

59. Farmer, *Criminal Law, Tradition and Legal Order* at 122.

a role that was ultimately assumed by a body of statutory law that created new safety-related offenses articulating uniform standards of conduct calculated to maintain acceptable levels of risk. By creating less serious, conduct-based offenses as substitutes for more serious, intent-based ones, the law in effect spread the social costs of preventing accidents among a wider class of defendants. Rather than relying purely on a case-by-case ex post approach that held a hapless defendant liable for the full social harm caused by his negligence, the law spread liability more broadly, but more thinly, through the mechanism of relatively more minor regulatory offenses. Ramsay puts the point well: "Regulatory law is less concerned with punishing wilful wrongdoing than it is with distributing the burden of avoiding the risk of harm. It tends to socialize responsibility, rather than focusing on individual moral agency."[60]

Not only was the content of substantive criminal law changing to meet the needs of more centralized and more powerful regulatory states: its form was changing as well. Lacey and Farmer have recently emphasized that this same period saw sustained efforts to codify the criminal law, rather than leaving it to ad hoc pronouncements by local courts.[61] Although efforts to codify the criminal law of England failed, it succeeded elsewhere—notably, Canada, where resistance to common-law criminalization has been a basic principle of criminal law since *Frey v Fedoruk* rejected "breach of the King's peace" as a legitimate catch-all authorization for criminalizing antisocial conduct.[62] The rejection of a common law of crimes represents, as Lacey puts it, an impulse to "systematize" the criminal law, ideally by "reconstruct[ing] it as a coherent body of doctrine capable of being applied in an even-handed and impersonal way." This impulse, Lacey suggests, is "closely related to the developing project of modern governance."[63]

Similar patterns of criminalization could be observed in the American colonies. As Novak has documented, state and municipalities engaged in extensive amounts of regulation related to a sundry list of common social

60. Ramsay, "Responsible Subject as Citizen," 32. See also Farmer, *Criminal Law, Tradition and Legal Order*, 125.

61. Farmer, *Criminal Law, Tradition and Legal Order*, 161–71; Lindsay Farmer, *Making the Modern Criminal Law* (Oxford University Press 2016), ch. 5.

62. *Frey v Fedoruk*, [1950] SCR 517.

63. Lacey, *In Search of Criminal Responsibility* at 118.

problems, from liquor regulation to control of fires.[64] By the 1830s, for instance, Michigan had created criminal provisions pertaining to "obstructing highways, dueling, defrauding or cheating at common law, unlawfully assembling or rioting, the importing or selling of obscene books or prints, exciting disturbance at public meetings or elections, and selling corrupt or unwholesome provisions."[65] What these offenses suggest is that the criminal law was not simply a matter of the state providing a forum for resolving disputes about pre-politically rights that people would have had in the state of nature. Rather, the criminal law served a wide range of governmental and regulatory aims, a role that is perhaps unsurprising given the comparative paucity of actual regulatory institutions at this time. After all, the New Deal and the creation of the modern American administrative state was nearly a century away. In its absence, the criminal law was being pressed into service as a primitive form of regulation, as a means of providing increasingly broad forms of security and social provision.[66]

In short, the century from the mid-1700s to the late-1800s witnessed a thoroughgoing transformation in the institutions of the criminal law. The functions of preventive patrolling and investigating crime were taken over by organized public police forces. The functions of deciding whether and how to prosecute a crime—especially in North America—were similarly taken out of the hands of private parties and consolidated in the hands of public officials. In addition, punishment became less exemplary and more uniform, less a matter of private, local control and increasingly a matter of national (or at least regional) legislation and policy. Substantive law incorporated regulatory offenses, with new offenses aimed at preventing harms rather than simply responding to willful and malicious attacks. The result was a criminal law, and criminal justice system, that lost its local and private character and became "bureaucratic, largely impersonal, and increasingly centralized."[67]

Lest this narrative give the impression of a just-so story, it is important to note that not only is there no historical necessity to these changes (there is no hidden hand behind them), but the esmergence of a

64. Novak, *The People's Welfare*.

65. Novak, *The People's Welfare* at 15–16.

66. Brown, *Free Market Criminal Justice*, ch. 7.

67. Emsley, "The History of Crime and Crime Control Institutions," 226; Garland, *Punishment and Welfare*, 225.

centralized set of institutions and policies for responding to crime is also, at best, very much an incomplete and contested development. As many have observed, the criminal justice system—most evidently in the United States—is not really a system, in the sense of a coherently and efficiently designed set of roles and functions.[68] Although public officials make all the important decisions about crime and punishment, their decision-making is largely uncoordinated, and scattered among an incredibly large and diverse array of different offices and agencies. There are, for instance, nearly 18,000 distinct state and local law enforcement agencies in the United States, ranging from a great many tiny offices employing fewer than ten full-time officers all the way through to large law enforcement bureaucracies employing over 1,000 full-time officers.[69] The diversity of offices and agencies is further complicated by the overlap among municipal, state, and federal levels of jurisdiction. These decision-makers often have incompatible incentives, different policy agendas, and only very partial control over ultimate outcomes, given the power of other parties to effectively undermine or otherwise respond to decisions made elsewhere in the system. The diversity of offices and agencies, and the inevitable division of powers and functions among them, might be all for the best. Or it might not. In any case, it seems mostly to have developed by accident, and to be subject to no meaningful centralized oversight.

In addition, some areas of the criminal law have resisted modernization. The most notable is the law of sentencing. In Canada, for instance, sentencing remains resolutely discretionary, on the theory that each case calls for a nuanced moral judgment of such fineness that it would be spoiled by imposing so much as a "starting point" for this or that general type of offense.[70] The lack of meaningful oversight is perhaps why the Supreme Court of Canada's efforts to lessen the overrepresentation

---

68. This is a theme in the work of John F. Pfaff; see his *Locked In: The True Causes of Mass Incarceration—And How to Achieve Real Reform* (Basic Books 2017), and *Sentencing Law and Policy* (Foundation Press 2016), 81–84.

69. "Census of State and Local Law Enforcement Agencies, 2008," Bureau of Justice Statistics, tbl. 1 & tbl. 2, available at https://www.bjs.gov/content/pub/pdf/csllea08.pdf.

70. *R v McDonnell*, [1997] 1 SCR 948 (per Sopinka J); See also *R v M (CA)*, [1996] 1 SCR 500; *R v Shropshire*, [1995] 4 SCR 227. For background, see Julian Roberts, "Structuring Sentencing in Canada, England and Wales: A Tale of Two Jurisdictions," *Criminal Law Forum* 23 (2012): 319–45.

of Indigenous offenders in Canadian prisons have borne so little fruit.[71] Without some form of systematic oversight of sentencing decisions, it is difficult to devise sentencing policy in any meaningful sense. Despite the disproportionate scholarly attention given to the Federal Sentencing Guidelines, sentencing in many American states also remains highly discretionary, with an overlay of ad hoc mandatory minima.[72] More generally, recent decades have witnessed a partial rolling back of public institutions, with private ordering and notions of individual responsibility increasingly filling the void left by diminished public institutions and weakened commitments to social equality.[73]

Finally, new modes of governance have opened up new avenues of domination and oppression. Radical and conservative critics of penal welfarism were not wrong to detect condescension, oppression and, discrimination in an allegedly rehabilitative criminal process.[74] While the development of professional police forces probably greatly eased the burden on victims of crime to track down and apprehend those who injured them, it also paved the way for new risks of authoritarian domination, invasions of privacy, and outright abuse and domination. Eighteenth century prisons were undoubtedly chaotic places, but it was the nineteenth century that saw the full flowering of bureaucratic interest in bending and reforming the criminal's soul, whether through long periods of enforced solitude, physically grueling labor, or submission to the will of the warden. These efforts could be brutal, but they could also operate more subtly, through humiliation and subordination rather than outright violence. Consider,

---

71. *R v Gladue*, [1999] 1 SCR 688 (exhorting courts to take an offender's Indigenous status into consideration at sentencing); *R v Ipeelee*, 2012 SCC 13, [2012] 1 SCR 433 (noting that in the thirteen years following *Gladue*, representation of Indigenous persons in custody not only failed to decrease, but actually increased).

72. Kevin Reitz, "The Disassembly and Reassembly of US Sentencing Practices," in *Sentencing and Sanctions in Western Countries*, ed. Michael Tonry and Richard Frase (Oxford University Press 2001), 222–58 at 231. For a comparative discussion of guideline sentencing, see Sarah Krasnostein and Arie Freiberg, "Sentencing Guideline Schemes across the United States and Beyond" (October 9, 2014). Oxford Handbooks Online; Criminology & Criminal Justice; available at: http://www.oxfordhandbooks.com/view/10.1093/oxfordhb/9780199935383.001.0001/oxfordhb-9780199935383-e-001.

73. See Garland, *The Culture of Control*, especially ch. 7.

74. For an account, see Garland, *The Culture of Control*, ch. 3. The oppressive use of state power is a prominent and longstanding theme in scholarship on the administrative state. See e.g., Charles Reich, "Individual Rights and Social Welfare: Emerging Legal Issues," *Yale Law Journal* 74 (1965): 1245–57; and, more recently, Tani, *States of Dependence*.

for instance, Elizabeth Hinton's description (drawn from a Virginia prison in the 1970s) of how prison officials "rewarded" good behavior:

> Seven days a week, a white college graduate with a degree in psychology visited [the prison] armed with a clipboard and a checklist. The inspector was to ascertain whether the mostly black inmates in the unit had tidied their five-foot-by-nine-foot cells, if they had made their beds, and if they were willing to engage in "polite" conversation. For each bit of approved behavior, the incarcerated person would be awarded a point, which was punched into a wallet-sized green credit card to be cashed in later for commissary items or Polaroid snapshots with family members during visitation. A prisoner who scored well and otherwise behaved well could advance to the next stage and move to a lower-security field camp. Many recognized the [system] for what it was. "It's a subtle coercion," one of the participants . . . remarked.[75]

McConville offers a similar account of an accelerated release program in use a century earlier in England. This program was not "coercive," in the sense of threatening a prisoner with an evil; rather it offered the prisoner an inducement, namely early release conditioned upon demonstrated good behavior. According to McConville, this system allowed officials to exercise a kind of petty tyranny over prisoners, punishing any deviation in behavior—even "indifferent behavior"—with a revocation of progress toward early release: "energy, commitment, and complete submission were the supposed prerequisites of early release." Even after being released, a convict was still not free. "Those who won early release knew that they were being watched and could be recalled even if their misbehavior was not criminal."[76]

Although incomplete, partial, and still quite controversial in various ways, the transformation of criminal law into public law has made it possible for political institutions to take a more systematic, preventive, and

75. Elizabeth Hinton, *From the War on Poverty to the War on Crime: The Making of Mass Incarceration in America* (Harvard University Press 2016), 171. This is in addition, of course, to old-fashioned abuse and domination; see *id.* at 191–202 (documenting a brutal and violent campaign of policing in Detroit in the early 1970s).

76. McConville, "The Victorian Prison," 138. For yet another account, see Walker, *Popular Justice*, 96–99.

law-governed approach to crime. "The expansion and elaboration of penal-welfare institutions," as Garland has written, "paralleled that of the welfare state as a whole."[77] The emergence of criminal law as public law suggests that the state's relation to crime and punishment more closely resembles social provision than alms to the needy. Criminal law, and criminal justice policy more generally, can no longer be interpreted as simply a venue in which private parties vindicate their natural rights against wrongdoers, at their discretion and at their own initiative. By seizing control over the criminal process, public institutions provide a systematic approach to crime and punishment as a shared social burden. Crime becomes a problem for society, rather than a series of private tragedies to be dealt with on a case-by-case basis. Public officials determine which neighborhoods will be patrolled, which crimes will be investigated and which types of victim will be prioritized, and they have the institutional and legal wherewithal to control the conditions in which punishment is meted out. These institutions are public in that they are funded by, and operated in the name of, the sovereign. They thus represent efforts to redistribute the costs of protecting oneself from victimization more broadly, instead of simply leaving them to fall where they may. Under these conditions, it seems reasonable to hold public institutions accountable for the policies and practices they end up adopting. By asserting control over the criminal process, the state takes center stage as the main agent responsible for, as Rachel Barkow puts it, "administering crime."[78] It would seem morally shortsighted to focus on the merits of individual transactions to the exclusion of the responsibility of public institutions for dealing with crime in a way that is fair to all, potential victims and potential wrongdoers alike.[79]

Such an expectation would have been fantastical in earlier eras. Without either an organized police force for apprehending criminals and investigating crimes, or a bureaucracy devoted to their prosecution, criminal punishment was an inevitably ad hoc affair, depending largely on a miscreant having the misfortune of selecting a victim who had

77. Garland, *The Culture of Control*, 48; see also Garland, *Punishment and Welfare*, 225–26.

78. "Administering Crime," *UCLA Law Review* 52 (2005): 715–814; see also Gerard Lynch, "Our Administrative System of Criminal Justice," *Fordham Law Review* 66 (1998): 2117–51.

79. See Christian List and Philip Pettit, *Group Agency* (Oxford University Press 2011), ch. 3 (arguing that focusing exclusively on individual responsibility ignores the distinctive responsibilities of group agents).

the opportunity, means, and initiative to prosecute. However, the establishment of publicly administered policing and prosecution services in England and North America represent major steps toward creating the institutional capacity required to treat crime systematically, as a problem of social policy whose costs are to a large extent borne publicly. Although the criminal law remains in many respects decentralized, uncoordinated, and privatized, over the course of the eighteenth and nineteenth centuries, the criminal law gradually emerged as a body of public law, overseeing the operation of a wide range of officials and institutions, oriented to a diverse and frequently conflicting set of objectives.

Modern criminal justice systems are substantially larger and more powerful than their eighteenth-century forbears. The growth of the regulatory state occasioned controversy between different conceptions of the rule of law and, in particular, the role of courts in overseeing the actions of administrative agencies.[80] How best to regulate that power, and ensure that it is used appropriately, remains extremely unclear. Some, such as Darryl Brown, have argued that the American commitment to popular control over government by amateurs rather than professional bureaucrats—most characteristically, perhaps, through the regular election of judges and prosecutors—represents a fundamental challenge to the rule of law.[81] Others, such as Bill Stuntz and Stephanos Bibas, have argued that American criminal justice institutions require more localism and popular control, not less.[82] These disputes about the proper balance of democratic and expert input are but the latest iteration of a debate that is as old as the American regulatory state itself. The growth of the regulatory state in the early decades of the twentieth century occasioned disputation concerning different conceptions of the rule of law, from a version of the continental *Rechtstaat* to Dicey-inspired visions of the supremacy of the common law to, as Daniel Ernst has suggested, compromise positions granting both broad discretion to expert agencies as well as some measure of oversight by the courts, with deference conditioned upon the quality of

80. For an accounting of this history, see Daniel M. Ernst, *Tocqueville's Nightmare: The Administrative State Emerges in America, 1900–1940* (Oxford University Press 2014).

81. This is the overarching theme of Brown's recent book, *Free Market Criminal Justice*.

82. William J. Stuntz, *The Collapse of American Criminal Justice* (Harvard University Press 2011); Stephanos Bibas, *The Machinery of Criminal Justice* (Oxford University Press 2015), ch. 6.

deliberation and process observed by the agencies.[83] However, whether one regards the administrative state as a retreat from the rule of law or its fullest flowering, still it seems reasonably clear that "[t]he rise of the modern administrative state is based largely on a perception that aggressive governmental action, repudiating the common law, [had] become necessary."[84]

That the criminal law and its associated institutions are in some sense "public" now strikes us as obvious and beyond question; indeed, some philosophers have argued that the distinction between crime and tort rests on the idea that the former is "public" whereas the latter is "private."[85] But that idea has a history, and that history is one of a gradual and piecemeal assertion of public control over the criminal process, from the investigation of crime, to its prosecution and the execution of a sentence. By this telling, the institutional history of the criminal law in the English-speaking world is bound up with eventual acceptance of the idea that crime is not just a problem of case-by-case adjudication of independent rights violations, but rather a problem of social policy whose resolution required the development of controversial and powerful new institutions.

1.4 Criminal Law as the Vindication of Private Right

I have juxtaposed two ideas: the rise of the welfare state and the gradual emergence of criminal law as public law. I have suggested that the gradual assertion of centralized, public control over most aspects of the criminal process, as well as the creation of a range of new institutions and offices, transforms criminal law from a matter of ad hoc private dispute resolution into a matter of public policy. The rest of this book seeks to motivate the thought that the time has come for the philosophy of criminal law to catch up.

For too long, the philosophy of criminal law has been dominated by a conception of criminal law as the vindication of private rights—the rights people would have in the state of nature. Consequently, philosophers have treated the morality of the criminal law as derived from, or otherwise

83. Ernst, *Tocqueville's Nightmare.*

84. Cass Sunstein, "Lochner's Legacy," *Columbia Law Review* 87(5) (1987): 873–919, 902.

85. R.A. Duff, *Answering for Crime: Responsibility and Liability in the Criminal Law* (Hart Publishing 2007), 217.

closely related to, the morality of punishment in private life, ignoring the institutional and political character of the criminal law.[86] In the theory of criminalization, this has taken the form of the so-called "wrongfulness" constraint, allegedly limiting the criminal law to those types of harmful acts that also amount to pre-political moral wrongs. In the theory of punishment, this has taken the form of theories that attempt to justify practices of legal punishment solely in terms of pre-political rights against victimization and punishment, while ignoring the significance of the public institutions that have been created to manage the shared risks of crime. A conception of the criminal law as the vindication of the private rights of individuals may, at best, have been appropriate in the context of a privatized, uncoordinated, and victim-driven system of criminal law—although, given how difficult it was for victims to use the criminal law to vindicate their rights in the early common law, it is doubtful that system really fits a rights vindication model either. Be that as it may, as Farmer has noted, the relentlessly individualistic focus of modern criminal law theory is "especially strange" as it arises "at precisely the moment that the practice of the law and the means of attributing liability are expanding."[87] Such a conception is beyond anachronistic today, when the modern administrative state is a mature and stable political reality, not just a nascent form of bureaucratic governance.

A conception of criminal law as the vindication of private right obscures what I take to be the central moral concern with modern criminal law: its legitimation as a *political* institution. From the point of view of vindication of private right, the question of legitimacy boils down to the question of whether those who punish are accurately tracking the moral deserts (or pre-politically rights) of those who are being punished. When a private right theorist considers the role of the state in punishment, it is from a curiously apolitical point of view: as simply enforcing, for instance, the moral entitlements and obligations that were there anyway.[88] According to John Gardner, for instance, "[g]overnmental agents answer to all valid reasons for action, just like you and me . . . [p]olitical morality . . . is just ordinary morality as it bears on the circumstances in which certain agents

---

86. For an early statement, see Herbert Morris, "A Paternalistic Theory of Punishment," *American Philosophical Quarterly* 18(4) (1981): 263–71.

87. Farmer, *Criminal Law, Tradition and Legal Order*, 141.

88. Victor Tadros, *The Ends of Harm: The Moral Foundations of Criminal Law* (Oxford University Press 2011), 12–13, 309–11.

(certain officials and institutions) find themselves." The differences between private morality and public policy, according to Gardner, is simply one of scale: the latter are "but large-stakes examples of the same kind of responsibilities that we all have as friends, employers, teachers, neighbours, and so on."[89] Similarly, Doug Husak has argued that the authority the state claims in punishing is "no more in need of explication than the authority to punish in other kinds of case in which wrongs are committed against whoever inflicts a punitive sanction."[90] Andreas von Hirsch insists that the censure in criminal punishment "involves everyday normative judgements, that are used in a wide variety of social contexts, of which punishment is merely one."[91]

These are astonishing claims, as they suggest a conception of coercive state power as simply larger-scale manifestation of private moral relationships, a conception dramatically at odds with most forms of political liberalism. No political liberal, I take it, could concede that we need not worry about the legitimacy of public law so long as public institutions treat you in just the ways that friends and family members are wont to do. For liberals, public institutions would lose their legitimacy if they were to treat you in those ways, for they would then be in the business of making remarkably intrusive, potentially demeaning, and in any case highly contentious judgments about a person's actions, character, and personality, and backing those judgments with overpowering force. As Corey Brettschneider has astutely observed, retributivists have prioritized "the question of what is deserved by the criminal *qua* person rather than the question of what punishment the state can rightfully mete out." [92]

It is worth reflecting on this remarkable state of affairs. Excepting the power to make war, the criminal law is perhaps the most dramatic instance of coercive state power familiar to us today. Yet, by and large, neither philosophers of criminal law, nor their counterparts in political

89. John Gardner, "The Negligence Standard: Political Not Metaphysical," *Modern Law Review* 80(1) (2017): 1–21 at 2.

90. Doug Husak, "State Authority to Punish Crime," *The New Philosophy of Criminal Law*, ed. Chad Flanders and Zach Hoskins (Rowman and Littlefield 2015),] 104.

91. Andreas von Hirsch, *Deserved Criminal Sentences* (Bloomsbury 2017), 19.

92. Corey Brettschneider, "The Rights of the Guilty: Punishment and Political Legitimacy," *Political Theory* 35(2) (2007): 175–99 at 183. Though I would add: not just retributivists. Some non-retributive theorists, such as Victor Tadros, defend accounts of punishment that are similarly based upon pre-politically individual rights.

philosophy, have spent much time considering whether there is good reason to exempt the criminal law from the usual principles of political justification, principles that seem so crucial in other areas of public law and public policy.[93] This book represents an attempt to think through what it would mean to treat the criminal law, and its associated institutions, as fully subject to those more familiar principles of political justification.

Here, one might object that I have been too single-minded in my criticism of criminal law as the vindication of private right. Surely, one might suggest, public institutions ought to *both* vindicate private right *and* secure the conditions for civic flourishing. As states became institutionally denser, they acquired further powers and responsibilities. Among those responsibilities, one might argue, is the responsibility to take over from individuals the moral task of calling wrongdoers to account and meting out upon them the punishment they deserve. Surely, in other words, the development of the modern administrative and welfare state empowers public institutions to include retributive justice in their growing panoply of legitimate public functions.[94]

Could it be the case that a legitimate function of the modern administrative and welfare state is to ensure that wrongdoers receive the censure and punishment they deserve? Perhaps; at least, I do not argue in this book that such an account of political legitimacy is somehow impossible or indefensible. However, what is striking about standard forms of political liberalism is just how little room they leave for pre-politically desert in settling controverted questions of justice.[95] This does not mean, of course, that giving people what they pre-politically deserve could not be reconciled with other basic political values or defended in other ways. We might come to reject liberalism, for instance. Whatever the explanation, I do not challenge the possibility of a political philosophy that is more open to the claims of retribution and desert. That is not the political

93. Samuel Scheffler, "Justice and Desert in Liberal Political Theory," *California Law Review* 88 (2000): 965–90, remains, to my knowledge, the most sensitive account of this issue. I consider Scheffler's argument further in Chapter 2. See also Scheffler, "Distributive Justice, the Basic Structure and the Place of Private Law," *Oxford Journal of Legal Studies* 35(2) (2015): 213–35.

94. I owe this objection to Leora Dahan-Katz.

95. See Samuel Scheffler, "Responsibility, Reactive Attitudes and Liberalism in Philosophy and Politics," *Philosophy & Public Affairs* 21(4) (1992): 299–323; Chad Flanders, "Criminals behind the Veil: Political Philosophy and Punishment," *Brigham Young University Journal of Public Law* 31 (2016): 83–109.

morality that I sketch (in Chapter 3 and following) in this book. But I do not suggest it is per se impossible or unreasonable for political institutions to consider the moral value of retribution in designing social policy.

What I am at pains to reject, however, is the thought that a political morality of this kind could be sufficiently motivated simply by attending to the moral value of retribution. There are lots of ways of responding to wrongdoing, and the choice among those responses is, or so I shall argue, a substantive political decision for the citizens and officials of a given polity. I deny that how a polity should respond to wrongdoing is dictated by conceptual analysis of "wrongdoing," "punishment," "authority," or other such traditional categories.[96] The argument that securing retributive justice could be a legitimate function of the welfare state should be defended on the field of substantive political morality: Why, when the pursuit of retribution conflicts with other political values that we have reason to care about, should preference be given to retribution? Answering that question would require retributivists to turn from reflections on interpersonal morality to assessing the morality of large public institutions operating over diverse populations under conditions of both significant scarcity and substantial uncertainty.

A further remark is in order at this point. When we think of the criminal justice system today, we think not just of the criminal law and punishment, but also of policing and prevention. Those who defend conceptions of the criminal law as the vindication of private rights tend to focus all but exclusively on the former, leaving the latter to be explicated by appeal to other values or principles. Perhaps this is only to be expected, as a purely ex post conception of criminal law has a difficult time explaining how punishing crime after it happens is morally related to preventing it from happening in the first place. Yet "there is," as Tapio Lappi-Seppälä puts it, "an inverse relation between commitment to welfare (the generosity of welfare provisions) and the scale of imprisonment."[97] Looking specifically at the United States, Katherine Beckett and Bruce Western have similarly concluded that state-level expenditure on welfare is negatively correlated with incarceration rates. "States with less generous welfare programs,"

---

96. Contrast Malcolm Thorburn's account of "robust authority" in "Punishment and Public Authority," in *Criminal Law and the Authority of the State*, ed. Antje du Bois-Pedain, Magnus Ulväng, and Petter Asp (Hart 2017), 7–32.

97. Tapio Lappi-Seppälä, "Trust, Welfare and Political Culture: Explaining Differences in National Penal Policies," *Crime and Justice* 37(1) (2008): 313–87 at 356.

they write, "feature significantly higher incarceration rates, while those with more generous programs incarcerate a smaller share of their residents."[98] Beckett and Western conclude that "the contraction of welfare programs aimed at the poor and the expansion of penal institutions in the 1980s and 1990s reflects the emergence of an alternative mode of governance that is replacing, to varying degrees, the modernist strategy based on rehabilitation and welfarism."[99] What this suggests is that ex post punishment and ex ante investment in social welfare are *substitute* goods. Yet a focus on the criminal law as the vindication of private right obscures this relationship between prevention and punishment.

For egalitarian reasons canvased in Chapters 3 and 7, I believe that we generally have reason to prefer ex ante to ex post methods, and that we should regard the retreat of the "modernist" strategy of rehabilitation and reform with dismay. In contrast, from the point of view of the vindication of private right, how much we should invest in social welfare programs is simply not part of retributive justice. It is a question that is extrinsic to the morality of the criminal law. But once we acknowledge that public institutions are fully in the business of collectively managing the risk of crime, then the choice between ex ante and ex post methods is not some *further* question to be decided by different principles of political morality, as if we could decide how much it is appropriate to invest in punishing people for their transgressions without deciding how much it is appropriate to invest in creating just and equitable social institutions. It is the function of public institutions, including criminal justice institutions, to connect our fates by spreading the costs and benefits of social cooperation broadly and fairly. In trying to decide how to do this, we ought not pretend that ex ante social welfare and ex post punishment are morally unrelated phenomena, answering to completely independent standards of fairness, such as those suggested under the traditional headings of "distributive" versus "retributive" justice.

By insisting on the criminal law as an institution devoted to blaming and punishing individuals for their wrongful acts, while ignoring the significance of other public institutions in responding to crime as a collective problem for the polity, a private right conception finds common

98. Katherine Beckett and Bruce Western, "Governing Social Marginality," *Punishment & Society* 3(1) (2001): 43–59 at 55.

99. Beckett and Western, "Governing Social Marginality," 55.

ground with the *DeShaney* court. That court, after all, was concerned with Wisconsin's obligation to protect private rights to the exclusion of any obligation to serve even the most primal needs of its constituents.[100] This concern mirrors the retributivist preoccupation with what an *individual* is responsible for, rather than what *public institutions* are responsible for.[101] But if it is reasonable to expect more from public institutions than simply respect for pre-politically negative rights, it is not just *DeShaney* that we should leave behind. We should also leave behind a conception of the criminal law as essentially a matter of vindicating the private rights of individuals.

1.5 Conclusion

In this chapter, I have contrasted two ideal types: a model of alms to the needy and a model of social provision. Where alms to the needy relies on private actors and discretionary judgments of moral worth, social provision relies on public institutions to collectively manage shared social risks, and to do so as a matter of basic political entitlement rather than as a matter of moral grace. I have further sketched the gradual emergence of criminal law as a body of public law, and suggested that in virtue of becoming public law, crime is gradually transformed from a private tragedy for which the state merely provides a remedy into a shared social problem generating duties on the part of public institutions for protection and prevention. Finally, I have suggested that prevailing approaches to criminalization and punishment—largely, though not exclusively, retributive in orientation—obscure the questions of fair distribution and political legitimacy that are so central to the modern criminal law.

The general objective of this book is to convince you that, in the age of the administrative state, the criminal law is no longer—if ever it was—primarily a matter of publicly vindicating pre-politically negative rights. The criminal law and its associated institutions have become more statist

100. As it happens, the United States Supreme Court has repeatedly emphasized its view that the criminal law is distinctively retributive, an issue that arises in cases where people are asserting procedural rights that the United States Constitution has reserved for "criminal" defendants. See my discussion in Chapter 6.

101. Malcolm Thorburn, "The Radical Orthodoxy of Hart's *Punishment and Responsibility*," in *Foundational Texts in Modern Criminal Law*, ed. Markus Dubber (Oxford University Press 2014), 290–92.

and more redistributive than ever before. It should also become more egalitarian than it is, or so I shall suggest. For this to happen, we must move beyond our preoccupation with what people deserve for their assorted transgressions. We should be more concerned than we are with determining when a criminal law intervention is most likely, out of the range of possible interventions, to optimally promote everyone's basic rights and interests; by the same token, we should be more concerned than we are with ensuring that the criminal law does not itself undermine this very ideal of social equality. These are questions about institutions, discretion, and democracy; they are, by and large, not questions about individual transactions, pre-politically rights, or the conditions of moral blameworthiness.

The next chapter begins the task of developing a normative theory of criminal law as public law. Although that account is meant to be self-standing, what motivates it is the thought that in the age of the administrative state, the legitimacy of the criminal law rests in its ability to fairly and effectively protect each person's basic needs, interests, and rights, whether that person is a potential victim, potential offender, or both. By, on the one hand, drawing upon a broad base of public support and cooperation, and, on the other, exerting comprehensive jurisdiction over the social environment, public institutions have now come to embody, in Rawls's evocative phrase, the variety of ways in which we share in one another's fate.[102] The account developed over the remaining chapters is intended to consider what this might mean for the criminal law.

102. John Rawls, *A Theory of Justice* (Harvard University Press 1971), 102.

2

Criminal Law as Public Law II

STRUCTURE

2.1 Introduction

Perhaps it goes without saying that the criminal law and its associated institutions—law enforcement, prosecutors, courts, prisons, parole agencies, sentencing commissions, and so forth—are institutions that we have set up to punish people. And perhaps it similarly goes without saying that the people we have set them up to punish are, in the usual case, guilty not just of a legal infraction but also some form of moral transgression. This seems, after all, to simply fall out of our understanding of the sort of practice *punishment* is—not just hard treatment, but hard treatment motivated by, and expressive of, resentment directed at morally wrongful conduct. By its very nature, punishment—and hence the criminal law—serves to expressively vindicate rights and condemn wrongs. To justify the criminal law, therefore, is to explain when criminal punishment is, and when it is not, a morally appropriate means for making manifest a shared reactive attitude of resentment at moral wrongdoing.[1]

In this chapter, I sketch an alternative view of what the criminal law is for, and show how rethinking the place of the criminal law in the modern administrative state recalibrates our understanding of what is required to justify it. In condemning wrongs and vindicating rights, the criminal law arguably fulfills a wide variety of functions. It probably, at least sometimes, deters people from engaging in wrongdoing, gives people the

1. Doug Husak describes this account of the criminal law as the "orthodox view." "Retribution in Criminal Theory," *San Diego Law Review* 37 (2000): 959–86 at 960.

punishment they deserve, incapacitates the dangerous, and reforms their characters. Perhaps it would be legitimate for the criminal law to pursue any or all of these purposes. There is, however, one important function that the criminal law serves that enjoys a qualified priority over any other functions it may additionally serve. The criminal law promotes social cooperation under stable public institutions. It does this by stabilizing shared attitudes of reciprocity, a function it carries out by making it rational to expect that those who cooperate will not be victimized or exploited by those who might be tempted to defect.[2] Stable public institutions rely on the voluntary cooperation of their constituents to function. But since the realization of whatever other goals the criminal law may have—retribution, incapacitation, deterrence, and so forth—plausibly depends upon stable public institutions, there is a functional priority to the criminal law's role in fostering social cooperation.

From this point of view, the criminal law is first and foremost an institution that contributes to making social cooperation possible, regardless of whether it is or is not also an institution devoted to the pursuit of retributive justice. In other words, the criminal law is an integral component of society's basic structure—"society's main political, social, and economic institutions, and how they fit together into one unified system of social cooperation from one generation to the next"—and should be understood and justified in those terms, regardless of whether it does or does not additionally punish moral wrongdoing as such.[3]

That is the argument in a nutshell. In what follows, I elaborate the argument in three steps. First, I contend that the criminal law, particularly in the context of modern administrative/welfare states, is what I call a generically coercive rule-enforcing institution. Second, I argue for the functional priority of generically coercive rule-enforcement over retributive punishment. In the third stage of the argument, I consider how this account reorients the philosophical enterprise of justifying the criminal

---

2. This is, of course, a central Hobbesian insight. For further discussion of this point, see Alice Ristroph, "Hobbes on 'Diffidence' and the Criminal Law," *Foundational Texts in Modern Criminal Law*, ed. Markus D. Dubber, (Oxford University Press University Press 2014), 31.

3. John Rawls, *Political Liberalism* (Columbia University Press 1993), 11. I am not the first to notice punishment's salience for social cooperation. See, for instance, Matt Matravers, "Political Theory and the Criminal Law," in *Philosophical Foundations of Criminal Law*, ed. R.A. Duff and Stuart Green (Oxford University Press 2011), 67–82; Richard Dagger, *Playing Fair* (Oxford University Press 2018); E. Melissaris, "Toward a Political Theory of Criminal Law," *New Criminal Law Review* 15(1) (2012): 122–55.

law, and defend what I refer to as a "fully political" standard of evaluation. These three ideas jointly define a public law conception of criminal law. Finally, I consider and respond to a range of objections.

2.2 Negative Reciprocity and Cooperation

The criminal law stabilizes a public sense of justice by providing assurance that cooperation with legal rules will not leave one open to victimization or exploitation. This claim can be illustrated by considering the kind of cooperative problem presented by an indefinitely iterated prisoner's dilemma. Recall that a prisoner's dilemma is a strategic game in which two players seek to coordinate their conduct in order to obtain individually beneficial outcomes, while facing a set of costs that push them toward acting in an uncooperative manner ("defecting").[4] In a prisoner's dilemma, the unique Nash equilibrium is for the parties to defect, even though they would be better off cooperating with each other. Importantly, a prisoner's dilemma is not an epistemic problem, as both players may understand the structure of the cooperative landscape. It is rather a problem of assurance. The temptation to defect is such that each party cannot be sure that the other will not defect regardless of what he or she chooses; but since that reasoning is symmetrical, both players are liable to find themselves locked into a suboptimal strategy of mutual defection.

Prisoner's dilemmas are not intractable, nor do they necessarily require anything like a state to resolve. Indeed, when they occur in the context of ongoing social relationships, a robust and stable strategy is simple reciprocity: a willingness to cooperate ab initio, with subsequent moves simply mirroring those of the other player. "Tit-for-tat," as this strategy is known, embodies both a willingness to cooperate and a readiness to retaliate. Notably, tit-for-tat has been shown to be robust against more complex, and more opportunistic, strategies, at least in cases where the players face

4. More fulsomely, a prisoner's dilemma is a cooperative game in which the payoffs are structured as follows: $T > R > P > S$, and $R > (T+S)/2$, where T is the payoff for unilateral defection, R the payoff for mutual cooperation, P the payoff for mutual defection, and S the payoff for unilateral cooperation. The first condition ensures that unilateral defection is tempting to the players, and the second condition ensures that, in the context of an iterated prisoner's dilemma, the socially optimal outcome is for the players to cooperate rather than take turns exploiting each other. See Robert M. Axelrod, *The Evolution of Cooperation* (Basic Books 2006), 9–10.

repeated opportunities to cooperate.[5] Even from a purely self-serving point of view, the players do better by adopting a tit-for-tat strategy over a more opportunistic one. Moreover, tit-for-tat is robust in that once it gains a foothold in a population, it can eventually displace more selfish strategies. Conversely, once it becomes a society's dominant strategy, it is difficult for more selfish strategies to displace it. Tit-for-tat it is, therefore, an evolutionarily stable strategy.[6]

Two features of tit-for-tat bear emphasizing. The first is simply that it requires a willingness to impose costs on defection. Participants begin by cooperating, but must not hesitate to punish when others seek to take advantage of their willingness to do so. However, tit-for-tat also does not *over*punish. The memory of tit-for-tat is short, and it forgives defection after one round.[7] More generally, in contexts in which people use their partner's reputation as a basis for deciding whether to cooperate or defect—that is, in contexts where there is a social norm based on reputation—both punishment and forgiveness play a central role. Social norms that seek to maintain a high level of cooperation must be sensitive to prior defection, punishing it with a refusal to cooperate in the current round; but they will also allow defectors to regain good standing after they demonstrate a willingness to cooperate.[8] In short: high levels of sustained cooperation appear to depend, in part, upon a willingness to punish defection from a shared norm or rule as well as a readiness, under certain conditions, to forgive defection.

The second point is that punishment in tit-for-tat is not valuable simply as a way of vindicating rights or condemning wrongs, even though it may achieve those objectives as well. Punishment is instrumental *as a cooperative strategy*: it enables high levels of social cooperation among a group of people who are stuck with each other for the foreseeable future. The prospect of losing the benefits of cooperation in the future changes the

---

5. For an early and influential discussion, see Axelrod, *The Evolution of Cooperation* at 27–72.

6. Axelrod, *The Evolution of Cooperation* at 27–54, 64–69; Robert Sugden, *The Economics of Rights, Co-operation and Welfare* (Palgrave Macmillan 2005), ch. 6.

7. In order to prevent endless cycles of retribution, tit-for-tat can be configured to probabilistically engage in spontaneous "forgiveness," that is, to cooperate even in the face of defection in the previous round.

8. Hisashi Ohtsuki and Yoh Iwasa, "The Leading Eight: Social Norms That Can Maintain Cooperation by Indirect Reciprocity," *Journal of Theoretical Biology* 239 (2006): 435–44, especially 438–39; Axelrod, *The Evolution of Cooperation*.

payoff structure in iterated prisoner's dilemmas such that—provided the discount rate for future gains is not too high, or the end of cooperation is not immediately foreseeable—ongoing cooperation becomes individually rational.[9] This is true regardless of whether defection from a shared rule constitutes a moral wrong.

These two features of tit-for-tat can be summarized in terms of *negative reciprocity*:

(1) Negative reciprocity, that is, the use of sanctions conditional on defection from a shared rule, is instrumental to ongoing cooperation.

As Sugden has noted, negative reciprocity "may be more important in stabilizing co-operative practices than are the more attractive motivations of positive reciprocity."[10] The reason is straightforward: even when attitudes of benevolent reciprocity are broadly shared, "co-operation is liable to unravel in the presence of a small minority of determined free-riders." A readiness to respond to free-riding with punishment and revenge can consequently stabilize cooperative practices.

Experimental research supports this conclusion. In studies of repeated public goods games, for instance, those games in which players have the ability, at some personal cost to themselves, to sanction those who they perceive to have contributed too little in previous rounds tend to exhibit far greater levels of cooperation, both in amount and in duration, than public goods games without the option of sanctioning free-riders. This might seem surprising given that the cost of sanctioning a free-rider is greater than the loss directly caused by that person's defection. Yet in the long run, iterated games in which individuals personally expend resources to punish those who they perceive to have defected generally result in greater levels of cooperation than games in which people act in a purely self-regarding manner.[11] As Ernst Fehr and Simon Gächter put the point,

9. It is important that cooperation be extended into the future. Not only do the cooperative gains of punishment take time to emerge, but they drop precipitously once it becomes evident that there will be no more cooperation in the future. See S. Gächter, E. Renner, and M, Sefton, "The Long-Run Benefits of Punishment," *Science* 332 (5907) (December 5, 2008): 1510.

10. Sugden, *The Economics of Rights, Co-operation and Welfare*, 218.

11. See Ernst Fehr and Simon Gächter, "Cooperation and Punishment in Public Goods Experiments," *American Economic Review* 90(4) (2000): 980–94. These findings hold both in the context of games where the players are scrambled randomly to prevent the

> The apparent willingness to punish constitutes a credible threat for potential free riders and causes a large increase in cooperation levels: very high or even *full cooperation* can be achieved and maintained in the punishment condition, whereas the same subjects converge toward *full defection* in the no-punishment condition. [12]

In a similar vein, van Prooijen has recently surveyed some of the experimental literature on punishment and cooperation, including experiments involving the public goods game, and concluded that punishment fosters prosocial cooperation "in situations where people face a dilemma of choosing between self-interest and contributing to the group's interest."[13] Moreover, a prosocial cooperative attitude can become evolutionarily stable—resistant to displacement once it has become rooted in a population—when there are sufficient numbers of people who are willing to absorb some costs by punishing noncooperators.[14] Fehr and Gächter thus suggest that "altruistic punishment is a key force in the establishment of human cooperation."[15]

The connection between punishment and cooperation also appears robust across cultures. Henrich et al, for instance, report field studies involving nearly 1800 people spread across fifteen cultures and five

---

development of individual reputations, as well as in the final round of games, where mass defection would be expected. Mass defection does in fact occur in the final round when there is no sanctioning option, and cooperation during other rounds is also substantially lower under such conditions. However, as Fehr and Gächter note in another paper, this does not mean that the explicit threat to sanction defection will elicit relatively high levels of cooperation; it is possible that, under some circumstances, explicit incentives "crowd out" spontaneous reciprocity. See Fehr and Gächter, "Fairness and Retaliation: The Economics of Reciprocity," *Journal of Economic Perspectives* 14(3) (2000): 159–81, especially 170–72. For a more formal discussion of the role of punishment in promoting high levels of cooperation, and the importance of "conditionally cooperative enforcers," who are willing to cooperate provided others do, and who are also willing to absorb costs in order to sanction free-riders, see Ernst Fehr and Klaus M, Schmidt, "A Theory of Fairness, Competition and Cooperation," *Quarterly Journal of Economics* 114(3) (1999): 817–68, especially 836–42. For a general overview of the experimental literature, see Samuel Bowles and Herbert Gintis, *A Cooperative Species* (Princeton University Press 2011), 19–45.

12. Fehr and Gächter, "Cooperation and Punishment," 993.

13. Willem van Prooijen, *The Moral Punishment Instinct* (Oxford University Press 2018), 134.

14. Robert Boyd and Peter J. Richerson, "Punishment Allows the Evolution of Cooperation (or Anything Else) in Sizable Groups," *Ethology and Sociobiology* 13 (1992): 171–95.

15. Ernst Fehr and Simon Gächter, "Altruistic Punishment in Humans," *Nature* 415 (6868) (2002): 136–40.

different continents, each of whom participated in an ultimatum game as well as a third-party punishment game.[16] A willingness to absorb some costs in order to punish other players who were perceived as unfair is widely spread across many societies. In every case, those who offered their partners less than equal shares were punished more than more generous players. Although the researchers found substantial variation in the degree to which people from different societies are inclined to punish, they noted that a willingness to punish is positively correlated with altruism, as measured by offers made in a dictator game.[17]

Hence, although negative reciprocity may come across as vindictive, or advancing a cynical view of human nature, I do not think we should understand it in these terms. Negative reciprocity does not suggest that the only reason people comply with the law is out of a fear of sanctions. To the contrary, the theory presupposes that people are willing to cooperate with each other, but that they are anxious to ensure that doing so will not leave them open to adventitious defection.[18] Punishing rule-violators is, in this respect, a "signal of trustworthiness"; where rule violations go unpunished, social attitudes of trust are harder to sustain.[19] Hence, the willingness to punish defectors enables what Rawls referred to as citizens' "sense of justice"—the capacity of citizens to formulate and abide by fair

---

16. In an ultimatum game, one player is given a sum of money and asked to choose some portion to offer to another player. That player then decides whether to accept or reject the offer; in the latter case, the entire sum is forfeit. A third-party punishment game resembles the ultimatum game, except that a third party is given the option, at some personal cost, to impose punishment on the offering party if the third party deems the offer unfair.

17. J. Henrich et al., "Costly Punishment across Human Societies," *Science* 312 (5781) (2006): 1767–70. At an intra-social level, it is possible that differential valuation of victims could partially explain variations in punitiveness. See, for instance, Eyal Aharoni and Alan Fridlund, "Moralistic Punishment as a Crude Social Insurance Plan," in *The Future of Punishment*, ed. Thomas Nadelhoffer (Oxford University Press 2013): 213–29; Simon Gächter and Benedikt Herrmann, "Reciprocity, Culture and Human Cooperation: Previous Insights and a New Cross-Cultural Experiment," *Philosophical Transactions of the Royal Society B* 364 (2009): 791–806.

18. The relation between "trust" and "power" in generating prosocial attitudes is complex; for a model in the context of tax compliance see Erich Kirchler, Erik Hoelz, and Ingrid Wahl, "Enforced versus Voluntary Tax Compliance: The 'Slippery Slope' Framework," *Journal of Economic Psychology* 29 (2008): 210–25.

19. J. Jordan et al., "Third-Party Punishment as a Costly Signal of Trustworthiness," *Nature* 530 (2016): 473–76. Significantly, however, third-party punishment is not the only, or even necessarily the best, signal of trustworthiness. An offer of help to someone in need is, it turns out, a stronger signal of trustworthiness than willingness to incur costs by punishing wrongdoers. I consider the relevance of this latter point in Chapters 3 and 7.

terms of social cooperation—to become stable and effective.[20] So while it would be fair to describe negative reciprocity as a form of deterrence—deterring defection from shared cooperative norms—negative reciprocity does not start from the same point as traditional deterrence theories of punishment. It does not start by assuming that people are uncooperative, suggesting that sanctions be used as a way of terrorizing people into compliance. Rather, it starts by assuming that people are willing cooperators who share a sense of justice. Punishment contributes to making it the case that acting upon that sense of justice is not just reasonable, but rational as well, at least when there is the prospect of cooperation in the future.[21]

As I have noted, negative reciprocity does not necessarily imply statism. It is possible for tit-for-tat to emerge spontaneously, even in chaotic and competitive environments. The state of nature need not inevitably be quite as anarchical as Hobbes portrayed it.[22] But without a centralized state of some kind, it is probably still fairly chaotic and dangerous. Tit-for-tat is subject to cycles of cooperation and defection. In part, this is because tit-for-tat is subject to "drift," as non-punishers free-ride on punishers, leading in turn to defection rather than cooperation, leading to increased levels of punishment. In part, this is because of random errors in operationalizing a cooperative strategy, which can lead to cycles of retribution.[23] Hence, there is a role for a centralized means of controlling punishment—possibly, but not necessarily, something like a state.

Socially coordinated sanctions become particularly attractive when the risk of indefinite cycles of retribution is high—when, for instance, the

---

20. Rawls, *Political Liberalism*, 19.

21. See Rawls, *Political Liberalism*, 42; Richard Dagger, "Citizenship as Fairness: John Rawls's Conception of Civic Virtue," in *A Companion to Rawls*, ed. Jon Mandle and David A. Reidy (Wiley 2014), 302; H.L.A. Hart, *The Concept of Law* (Oxford University Press 1994), 198.

22. During World War I, some of the soldiers in the trenches worked out a system whereby each side refrained from attacking the other so long as that restraint was reciprocated. Trench warfare must surely approximate a state of nature, but even here spontaneous cooperation in the absence of an overarching sovereign seems to have been possible, at least so long as the same groups of soldiers faced off against each other on an ongoing basis. See Axelrod, *The Evolution of Cooperation*, 73–87. For further discussion of the extent to which coordinated social action requires coercive public authority, see Elinor Ostrom, *Governing the Commons: The Evolution of Institutions for Collective Action* (Cambridge University Press 1990), 1–28; Elinor Ostrom, James Walker, and Roy Gardner, "Covenants with and without a Sword: Self-Governance Is Possible," *American Political Science Review* 86(2) (1992): 404–17; and Robert C Ellickson, *Order without Law: How Neighbors Settle Disputes* (Harvard University Press 1991).

23. Martin Nowak, "Evolving Cooperation," *Journal of Theoretical Biology* 299 (2012): 1–8, at 2.

parties disagree as to what type of conduct constitutes defection, either because they disagree as to the nature of the cooperative enterprise or because they disagree about how it is to be implemented.[24] As populations sharing a territory become more heterogeneous and hold increasingly divergent conceptions of the good, these kinds of interpretative conflicts are likely to become ever more pervasive. Moreover, the advantages of a coordinated institution for promulgating and enforcing public rules gain in significance as the range of activities in which mutually accepted norms of conduct are required for the activity to be viable—from fencing livestock to use of the roads to protecting shared environmental resources—expand. The costs of privately negotiating terms of cooperation on an individual basis become prohibitive under such conditions. Perhaps unsurprisingly, the transition from nonstate to state-based forms of social organization appears to also be correlated with a dramatic decrease in the rate of violent death.[25]

In the previous chapter, I emphasized the emergence of criminal law as public law over the course of the eighteenth and nineteenth centuries. One could understand this positively, as the expansion of the rule of law, and increasingly coordinated and centralized control over an important, but destructive, means for ensuring social cooperation. One might speculate that the transformation of criminal law into public law presaged the subsequent growth of the modern administrative/welfare state, which seeks to provide highly complex forms of cooperation over vast areas of social, economic, and political life. That is largely the perspective I adopt in this book. But one might be more skeptical, and view the transformation of criminal law into public law as self-serving aggrandizement on the part of bureaucrats and public officials of all kinds.[26] One might believe that the policing, prosecution, and punishment functions would have been adequately provided for by the market or other informal social organizations.

---

24. A concern with the instability of private judgment, and the consequent demand to enter into political society, is a theme familiar in Locke; see *The Second Treatise on Government*, §§ 87–91. For a more recent discussion, see Mark Reiff, *Punishment, Compensation and Law* (Cambridge University Press 2005), 73–74.

25. According to Steven Pinker's estimates, an average of 14–15 percent of all deaths were violent in nonstate societies, which compares to a rate of about 3 percent averaging over all state societies throughout history, and to about 0.008 percent in the contemporary United States. See Pinker, *The Better Angels of Our Nature* (Penguin Books 2011), 47–56.

26. See, e.g., Nils Christie, "Conflicts as Property," *British Journal of Criminology* 17(1) (1977): 1–15.

Perhaps informal reputational sanctions or other forms of spontaneously arising ordering would be sufficient to do much of what the criminal law now does. One might doubt that criminal justice constitutes a public good in that sense.[27]

I take no particular view here as to the conditions under which public ordering becomes desirable and/or legitimate. While my sympathies lie on the statist end of the spectrum, I am inclined to agree with Simmons's claim that "whether political membership best discharges our duties and respects others' rights" is a question that might be answered differently on different occasions.[28] Similarly, I have no quarrel with Sugden's observation that it is all too easy to overemphasize the importance of planned, formal ordering while overlooking "the possibility that social order might be spontaneous."[29] I shall, however, assume that there are at least *some* cases in which "political membership" and public ordering is the best way of discharging our duties and respecting other peoples' rights. I am assuming, that is, that there is an important range of cases in which there is a need for centralized, law-governed institutions to facilitate valuable social cooperation. The argument thus far is that the criminal law, in the bare sense of sanctions imposed for deliberate rule violation, plays a crucial role in facilitating social cooperation.[30]

I avoid the term "punishment" in this context because its moralistic connotations can be misleading, notably its connotation that punishment necessarily involves the aim of imposing punishment on someone in virtue of that person's real or perceived transgression. These connotations have an unfortunate tendency to prejudge the question of what the criminal law is for, by suggesting that insofar as the criminal law centrally involves punishment, it is inevitably a matter of responding to moral

---

27. See Mark Koyama, "The Law & Economics of Private Prosecutions in Industrial Revolution England," *Public Choice* 159 (2014): 277–98 at 278–79, for a discussion of this literature and relevant citations.

28. Simmons, "Justification and Legitimacy," *Ethics* 109 (1999): 739–71 at 768.

29. Sugden, *The Economics of Rights, Co-operation and Welfare*, 57.

30. In filling this role, the criminal law is a form of "meta-cooperation": cooperation that facilitates other forms of cooperation. Richard Dagger, "Republicanism and the Foundations of the Criminal Law," in *Philosophical Foundations of the Criminal Law*, ed. Duff and Green (Oxford University Press 2011), 44–66.

wrongdoing.[31] Instead, I shall describe a public institution that imposes sanctions for deliberate failure to comply with a rule as a "generically coercive rule-enforcing institution."[32]

Summing up, then, the argument so far can be put thus:

(2) Whatever it is that makes them legitimate, public institutions that engage in generically coercive rule-enforcement are engaged in a practice of negative reciprocity, that is, a practice of sustaining social cooperation.

What does this mean for the criminal law? Since, whatever else they are, criminal justice institutions are plainly institutions that sanction deliberate failure to comply with a rule, criminal justice institutions are generically coercive rule-enforcing institutions. And because generically coercive rule-enforcing institutions rely on negative reciprocity to sustain cooperation with public institutions, it follows that

(3) Whatever else they are, criminal justice institutions are institutions that stabilize ongoing social cooperation, paradigmatically cooperation with legal norms established by public institutions.

To be clear, while sanctioning noncompliance is *a* means for promoting cooperative attitudes, it is not the *only* way. Other means of encouraging cooperation include increasing the salience of the future to participants, for instance by extending the expected duration of cooperative interaction, or by reducing the rate at which the gains from future cooperation are discounted. Cooperation can also be promoted by integrating people into society's major institutions, not just by threatening them if they engage in antisocial conduct. What is distinctive about coercive rule-enforcement is the relative simplicity of the means utilized, requiring little more than an ability to apprehend criminals and a more or less effective monopoly on the use of violence.

---

31. An approach long endorsed by the United States Supreme Court; see, e.g., Smith v. Doe, 538 U.S. 84 (2003). I discuss the Supreme Court's understanding of "punishment" in Chapter 6.

32. On the normative gap between punishment and general state coercion, see Nathan Hanna, "Liberalism and the General Justifiability of Punishment," *Philosophical Studies* 145(3) (2009): 325–49; and Hanna, "Facing the Consequences," *Criminal Law & Philosophy* 8(3) (2014): 589–604.

Within the context of developed administrative states, it is at least possible that the criminal law may become increasingly less salient than would be expected in contexts with lesser institutional capacity. This is a familiar Durkheimian point: societies characterized by an advanced division of labor do not rely as heavily on exemplary rituals of punishment to sustain cooperative attitudes as societies bonded by kinship, clan membership, or religious or ethnic affiliation. Punishment is less central in societies with a developed division of labor because in such a context, the importance of cooperation is manifest in virtually every aspect of social life and does not need to be constantly reaffirmed through social ritual.[33] Or, to put a more overtly normative gloss on the same basic point, insofar as we have a choice in the matter, we have reason to prefer a scheme of social cooperation that is "made stable by an effective public sense of justice" where that sense of justice is sustained by means that minimize the need for "a severe and costly apparatus of penal sanctions, particularly when this apparatus is dangerous to the basic liberties."[34]

2.3 The Priority of Cooperation

In this section, I defend what I call the "functional priority" claim. This is the claim that:

(4) Stabilizing cooperation with public institutions is the most basic function of criminal justice institutions.

In defending the functional priority claim, I do not maintain that criminal justice institutions could not also legitimately secure retributive justice (or deterrence, denunciation, incapacitation, etc.) Nor am I asserting anything about the intentions of people who set up criminal justice institutions. Rather, the claim is that the rule-enforcing function of criminal justice institutions is, in one important respect, more fundamental than whatever other functions they may fulfill.

Imagine a hypothetical constitutional convention at which citizens undertake to agree upon the fundamental principles governing society's basic structure. Suppose that, cognizant that partiality and error will be

33. See Emile Durkheim, *The Division of Labor in Society* (Free Press 2014).

34. Rawls, *Political Liberalism*, 316–17.

unavoidable and will sometimes lead to punishment of the innocent and overpunishment of the guilty, a result they may reasonably consider to be intolerable, our constitutional framers decide not to set up retributive institutions. Giving wrongdoers the punishment they morally deserve is, after all, a tricky business; who can say whether they would not fall into grave moral error in attempting to do so? Hence, in setting up their society's major institutions, our framers direct those institutions to ignore moral deservingness as a reason for punishing people.[35] Some philosophers (and, coincidentally, the United States Supreme Court) have thought that it is essential to punishment that it is motivated, at least in part, by a belief in wrongdoing on the part of the person ostensibly being punished.[36] On this account of punishment, the institutions set up by our hypothetical framers will never, strictly speaking, *punish* anyone. The question now is: Would the lack of genuinely punitive institutions also rule out generically coercive rule-enforcement?

Clearly not. For regardless of what our constitutional framers decide with respect to punishment, they would undoubtedly still want to ensure that the institutions they *do* set up are effective and stable over the long run. There are a variety of ways of doing this, but attaching threats of coercive sanctions conditioned on noncompliance is likely to be prominent among them, particularly if the other means of promoting cooperation presuppose a developed institutional capacity that our fledgling society lacks. After all, threatening to punish people for breaking the rules, and occasionally making good on that threat when they do, seems to require rather less by way of elaborate forms of social cooperation (institutions, agencies, regulations, schools, police, etc.) than other ways in which we might encourage people to develop and act upon cooperative attitudes. Hence, even if a society forswears retributive aims, it may well still find itself in need of institutions that stabilize cooperation by imposing sanctions on deliberate rule violations.

To the degree that this is the case, generically coercive rule-enforcement enjoys a functional priority to retributive punishment: by contributing to the possibility of long-term social cooperation, coercive rule-enforcement contributes to the very possibility of organized social institutions, and this

35. I am focusing here on "positive" retributivism; I discuss "negative" retributivism in Chapter 5.

36. For further elaboration on this claim, see Chapter 6, Section 6.1.

is true even if those institutions do not, strictly speaking, ever "punish" anyone. Generically coercive rule-enforcing institutions might come to resemble the criminal law and its associated institutions, including imposing sanctions on people who violate basic rights. This is because even if they do not accept punishment as a means of retributive blame, still our constitutional framers will want to protect people's basic rights from being violated. Establishing rules prohibiting the deliberate violation of rights, and following up on those rules with sanctions, is one way in which they can ensure that people's rights are protected. This process will also ensure, among other things, that people who believe that someone has deliberately violated their rights do not seek to resolve those claims through self-help, but rely instead on the dispute resolution mechanisms that our framers have set up.[37]

However, the opposite implication does not hold. Our imagined constitutional framers could not reasonably choose to pursue retribution, in the sense of giving people the punishment they have come to deserve on account of their moral wrongdoing, while foregoing stable and effective public institutions. After all, for the state to organize itself around the pursuit of retributive justice requires an extraordinary degree of social coordination. It requires that people come to a stable agreement on, among other things, how to define the conduct rules for which retribution is deemed appropriate, as well as the range of relevant justifications and excuses. It also requires people to acknowledge the authority of courts in resolving disputes about these terms and in applying general retributive norms to concrete facts, and to ensure that aggrieved parties do not seek self-help in the face of decisions with which they disagree. It calls for consensus on the responsibilities of a range of offices—prosecutors, judges, police, and so forth—and it demands a way of resolving disputes about those offices and whether someone holding such an office adequately discharged his or her duties.[38] Setting up public institutions devoted to retribution is very likely to entail, in other words, defining a range of rules and shared expectations, and attaching sanctions of one kind or another for failure to abide by those rules and expectations.

---

37. It is surely important in this context that a significant amount of crime is motivated by a desire to get even for some prior wrong, rather than as simple self-dealing: see Donald Black, "Crime as Social Control," *American Sociological Review* 48(1) (1983): 34–45.

38. My thanks to Veenu Goswami for discussion of this point.

In short, the organized pursuit of retributive justice will likely require the existence of generically coercive rule-enforcement in one form or another, whereas generically coercive rule-enforcement does not require the existence of retributive institutions.[39] Hence, generically coercive rule-enforcement is a more fundamental social function than the organized pursuit of retributive justice. To be clear, this does not mean that our constitutional framers could not endorse retribution as a basic principle of their society's political morality. Rather, it means that they cannot endorse retribution without *also* endorsing non-retributive means of stabilizing cooperation, including under that heading institutions set up to provide generically coercive rule-enforcement.

A few points of clarification may be in order. First, am I claiming that retributive punishment *in general* requires organized legal rules backed up by coercive sanctions? No. A group of people who do not seek to organize themselves into a stable political society can of course spontaneously pursue retribution against some wrongdoer without any regard to the possibility of further cooperation. But this possibility does not bear on the question facing our hypothetical constitutional framers, who are seeking to establish the state's basic institutions rather than informal practices of punishing moral wrongdoing. For them, retribution as an ongoing end of social cooperation presupposes a functioning system of generically coercive rule-enforcement.

Second, is it not the case that a hypothetically non-retributive state slides back into retribution when it sanctions those who violate the legal rules it does establish? If so, that would vitiate the priority I have claimed for generically coercive rule-enforcement. However, our framers do not implicitly renege on their abstemiousness about retributive punishment when they establish generically coercive rule-enforcing institutions. The actions of public officials in this society need not be motivated by any sort of condemnatory intentions, and therefore do not necessarily qualify as "punishment" in the retributive sense. Public officials could potentially view the sanctions simply as costs that are calculated to make defection sufficiently unattractive. True, given the nature of our moral sentiments, over time,

---

39. It appears that the actual framers of the American Constitution did rely rather extensively on the threat of coercive sanctions, including criminal penalties, to keep federal officials from shirking their duties. See Jerry Mashaw, "Recovering American Administrative Law: Federalist Foundations, 1787–1801," *Yale Law Journal* 115 (2006): 1256–344 at 1316–18 and 1321–22.

generically coercive rule-enforcement is likely to become understood *as* retribution for wrongdoing. And, given the importance of cooperation, it might be all for the best that we have evolved to adopt retributive moral sentiments when faced with antisocial behavior. But how punishment feels from the inside does not determine the question of which purposes, if any, it serves.[40]

Third, I am not claiming that public law implies coercive sanctions as a purely conceptual matter. My claim is practical, not conceptual: setting up a public institution is likely to require some form of coercive rule-enforcement if the institution is to prove viable over the long run, given the inevitable temptations toward free-riding and defection. Whether law is necessarily coercive is controversial. I hope to avoid that question here.

Finally, it is worth emphasizing that I am only claiming a *functional* priority for generically coercive rule-enforcement. The priority of generically coercive rule-enforcement rests upon its contribution to stabilizing cooperation. I am not claiming that cooperation is in some ultimate sense more important or morally more urgent than other goals, such as vindicating moral rights. A libertarian could agree, for instance, that sustained cooperation requires some means for sanctioning deliberate noncompliance with a legal rule, while also believing that the only justification for mandating such cooperation is to secure protection of a small set of negative liberties. Or, one might believe that we are morally compelled to create a politically ordered society precisely *so that* we can better vindicate people's moral rights with retributive punishment. One might in that way subordinate the moral significance of cooperation to the retributive aim of ensuring that people get what they deserve, even while accepting that one would not be able to secure that retributive

40. The possibility that the retributive moral emotions might—despite how they appear "from the inside"—serve some broader social purpose is, of course, not a new thought. For instance, on Adam Smith's view, human sociability requires punishment to restrain "unmerited and unprovoked malice," but although people are "naturally endowed with a desire of the welfare and preservation of society, yet the Author of nature has not entrusted it to this reason to find out that a certain application of punishments is the proper means of attaining this end; but has endowed him with an immediate and instinctive approbation of that very application which is most proper to attain it." Knud Haakonsen ed., *The Theory of Moral Sentiments* (Cambridge University Press 2002), 89–90, n.10. For a more contemporary version of this point, see Adam Bear and David Rand, "Intuition, Deliberation, and the Evolution of Cooperation," *Proceedings of the National Academy of Sciences* 113(4) (2016): 936–41 (comparing, in contexts where repeated transactions are likely, development of cooperation based on intuition rather than deliberation).

aim without also ensuring that those who deliberately break the law are sanctioned in a non-retributive sense. However, although nothing I have argued rules out that we might *also* wish to set up specifically retributive institutions, so long as it is the case that negative reciprocity is instrumental to social cooperation, that retributive function will always be additional to the more basic cooperative function of generically coercive rule-enforcement.[41]

2.4 A Fully Political Standard of Justification

I have thus far presented an account of what the criminal law is for: stabilizing social cooperation with public institutions by providing assurance that those who cooperate will not be met with defection and exploitation. But what does this have to do with the task of *justifying* the criminal law? In other words, what is the relation between how we answer the question, "what is the criminal law for?" and how we answer the question, "when, if ever, is it appropriate to rely on the criminal law?" The answer I shall defend is, roughly, this: if the primary function of the criminal law is to support social cooperation with public institutions, then a moral evaluation of the criminal law should be drawn from an account of our reasons for supporting public institutions in the first place, rather than directly from the norms of interpersonal morality.

As a first approximation, it is not enough that criminal justice institutions promote cooperation with public institutions; we want to know whether those institutions are themselves just. There would, evidently, be little value in effectively supporting an oppressive regime. Promoting cooperation is, after all, not an end unto itself. As Matt Matravers puts it, we cannot separate "the question of the moral permissibility of attaching

41. Kit Wellman has defended a similar claim, with respect to protecting rights: Wellman argues that, of the traditional rationales, protecting rights alone is necessary and sufficient to justify exclusive state punishment. If exclusive state punishment is required to protect rights, then it is justified even if it does not further any of punishment's other aims. Conversely, if exclusive state punishment is not necessary or sufficient for protecting rights, then it could not be justified even if it advanced punishment's other aims. See Wellman, *Rights Forfeiture and Punishment* (Oxford University Press 2017), 48. My account of functional priority parallels Wellman's claim, although in terms of stabilizing social cooperation rather than protecting rights, since, on my view, secure social cooperation is required to stably protect rights.

threats to rules" from "questions concerning the rules themselves."[42] This suggests the following principle:

(5) The criminal law is worth supporting only if the institutions whose rules it enforces are worth supporting.

This principle should not be interpreted overly strictly. In particular, it should not be interpreted to require that public institutions be perfectly, or even substantially, just. The criminal law may be worth supporting even when the institutions it supports are corrupt or unjust in various respects. Enforcing the criminal law may potentially be an important stepping stone on the way to more fully just public institutions. However, perhaps just as often, enforcing the criminal law vigorously can be corrosive of political legitimacy when that legitimacy has come to be suspect. Perhaps the most that can be said is that institutions are "worth supporting" in the relevant sense when failing to support them would lead to even more (or more serious) injustice over the long run. Under those conditions, we might well have all-things-considered reason to support even flawed and imperfect institutions.[43]

Note, that (5) states a necessary condition, not a sufficient one. It does not claim that the criminal law is worth supporting just so long as the institutions it supports are worth supporting. Just institutions, after all, might be sustained by unjust means. Suppose one endorses a principle, P, that explains why we should have public institutions. If the fact that public institutions comply with P were sufficient to license just *any* means of coercive enforcement of those institutions, then one is likely to wind up endorsing means of enforcement that themselves violate P. For example, suppose that unregulated access to drugs has a significant impact on public health and safety. Suppose further that a state would act justly in seeking to limit access to these drugs. Nevertheless, it might be unjust for a state to try to achieve this policy goal by relying on extremely harsh criminal sanctions. This would be the case if a highly punitive "war on drugs" approach would *itself* have a significant impact on public health and safety, for instance by making drug markets criminogenic and deterring users

42. Matt Matravers, *Justice and Punishment: The Rationale of Coercion* (Oxford University Press 2000), 7.

43. My thanks to David Enoch, Talia Fisher, and Veenu Goswami for discussion of the points raised in this paragraph.

from more easily regulated forms of drug use. In this case, the values that explain why the state has a legitimate interest in restricting access to drugs would also explain why it should not rely on the criminal law as its primary means of doing so.

Hence, we can identify a second principle:

(6) The criminal law is worth supporting only if its use in a particular context would be consistent with the principles that make the institutions whose rules it enforces worth supporting in the first place.

Taken on its own, (5) is consistent with standard forms of fair play theory, which similarly emphasize the role of criminal punishment in securing a just social distribution of benefits and burdens. However, the public law account sketched here departs from fair play theory in insisting that the morality of punishment cannot be detached from the principles that makes that distribution just. Rather, as (6) makes clear, the *same* principles of justice that explain why a pre-violation status quo is worth preserving are also relevant in explaining why preserving that status quo by means of criminal punishment is itself appropriate. Consequently, the morality of punishment cannot be detached—treated as a purely remedial question—from the broader question of why public institutions are worth supporting in the first place. This distinguishes criminal law as public law from standard forms of fair play theory.[44]

Taken together, (5) and (6) yield a *fully political standard of justification*. A fully political standard states that:

(7) The criminal law is worth supporting if and only if:
  a. the institutions whose rules it enforces are worth supporting, and
  b. its use in a particular context would be consistent with the principles that make those institutions worth supporting in the first place.

A fully political standard of justification requires that the criminal law be justified on terms that are consistent with how public institutions generally are justified. This is reflected in the fact that the same normative standard applies in both (a) and (b). Our reasons for deeming a public

44. See Matravers, *Justice and Punishment*, ch. 2, especially 52–57.

institution as worthy of support in (a) apply, in (b), to determining whether such an institution would itself support the use of the criminal law as a means of rule-enforcement. In other words, the use of the criminal law is subject to the same principles of public justification that apply to public institutions generally. It is in this sense that (7) articulates a *fully* political standard.[45]

While the idea that a normative theory of the criminal law is in some sense part of an overarching political theory is one that many theorists would endorse, the idea that the standard of evaluation should be fully political in this way is more contentious. What (7) entails is that notions of blame, culpability, and moral responsibility do not have a special significance in the justification of the criminal law. They have the *same* significance for the justification of the criminal law as they do in, for instance, the justification of public healthcare, public education, a system of property law, tax policy, and other basic public institutions. Many philosophers reject the relevance of desert in distributive justice, while nevertheless resolutely holding onto traditional notions of desert and responsibility in the arena of retributive justice. This strategy would appear to be inconsistent with a fully political standard of justification for the criminal law.

The fully political standard of justification flows from (1–4). To see this, suppose that one were to accept (1–4) but deny (7). Suppose, that is, that one were to accept that criminal justice institutions are properly devoted to securing social cooperation, but nevertheless doubt that the standard by which those institutions should be evaluated flows from a general standard of public justification. One might insist that the criminal law is properly centered on questions of pre-politically desert: the question whether A should be criminally punished depends upon whether A deserves to be punished in light of his moral wrongdoing. But because how other public institutions should treat A need not depend on individual desert, it could be the case (as per (1)) that negative reciprocity would be required to shore up cooperation with those institutions in ways that do not map onto individual deservingness. Yet shoring up cooperation with public institutions is

45. My account of a fully political conception of criminal law parallels Liam Murphy and Thomas Nagel's defense of a "conventionalist" view about property rights, according to which the justification of a system of property "cannot appeal, at the fundamental level, to property rights." *The Myth of Ownership: Taxes and Justice* (Oxford University Press 2002): 75. Similarly, on the view sketched here, the justification of a system of criminal law cannot appeal, at the fundamental level, to the natural rights of persons.

one of the functions of criminal justice institutions (as per (3).) Hence, we are faced with a contradiction, in that individual moral desert would yield a set of recommendations about what should be criminalized, and who should be punished, that is at odds with what we would deem legitimate when we consider the criminal justice system as a system of generically coercive rule-enforcement. Under (4), we cannot resolve the contradiction by jettisoning punishment as a means of stabilizing social cooperation; that function is presupposed by any other function we may care to assign to a system of punishment. The only alternative is to jettison pre-politically desert as a freestanding principle of justification for the criminal law. Individual moral desert should matter to the criminal law only insofar as it is consistent with more general principles of political justification.

Consider a concrete example. Suppose a society sets up a public institution to ensure stable and fair access to clean drinking water. The municipal water authority might institute a variety of rules that govern who is entitled to draw water, how much, at what frequency, under what conditions, and so forth. It may be the case that the municipal water authority would in some cases rely upon the threat of criminal punishment to ensure compliance with those rules: for instance, someone who refuses, after some number of warnings, to stop siphoning more than his fair share of water from the town's water supply will be punished by a criminal fine. Now along comes Walter, who just won't listen to the municipal water authority and keeps siphoning water after being told to knock it off—one times, two times . . . *n* times. (Walter says to himself: What do they know? There is plenty here for me, and others besides.) Would it be unjust to punish Walter?

On the one hand, if it emerges that people can simply ignore the rule against siphoning water, we may expect that people will worry that the others will start siphoning away all the water, leaving *them* high and dry, and so will be motivated to siphon water themselves. They may reason this way even if they would prefer to cooperate rather than defect. Since this reasoning is perfectly symmetrical, we may expect that many people will soon begin to siphon water on the basis of their own private judgment. So, the rule ought to be enforced, and Walter made to pay the fine.

On the other hand: this is criminal punishment! And criminal punishment is, or so we assumed, only to be imposed on those who are morally deserving it—those whose wickedness is so plain that no institution that held itself out to be just could fail to acknowledge that such a person ought really to be punished. Is that true of Walter? It's not that Walter *himself* drained the reservoir; what other people may choose to do cannot be laid at his doorstep, morally speaking. After all, he didn't force them to do anything; they siphoned on the basis of their own judgment. All *he* did was ignore some bureaucrat's warnings and rely on his own private judgment about how much water was appropriate for him to take. For all we know, his private judgment may have been perfectly reasonable for his own case. This suggests that we may not punish Walter.[46]

What should be done? Cooperation with the municipal water authority's policies is likely to require being ready to sanction people who deliberately violate its rules, especially when cooperation imposes an obvious cost. This requires being ready to sanction people who deliberately violate the rules, regardless of whether their conduct in doing so would qualify as a pre-politically wrong. Since, by hypothesis, the municipal water authority is not constrained to allocate water on the basis of pre-politically, moral desert, and since the basic function of criminal justice institutions is to stabilize cooperation with public institutions, it would, I submit, be permissible to punish Walter for substituting his private judgment for that of the municipal water authority. At least, it would be permissible to do so if we have good reason to endorse having a municipal water authority in the first place, and if the enforcement policy in question does not itself tend to undermine those reasons (for instance, by being so harsh as to encourage outrage and resistance to its policies).

I stress that I have not sought to rule out the possibility that the criminal law might *also* pursue more specific aims, such as retribution. Hence, it is always possible that in evaluating the criminal law, our conception of what is required by way of retributive justice might come into conflict with this or that account of why we should support public institutions. However, for the reasons just given, I conclude that when there is conflict, the pursuit of purely retributive aims should give way to more general principles of political justification.

Of course, to say that the *same* evaluative standard should apply in the criminal law as applies elsewhere is not yet to say *what* that standard is. So retributively minded philosophers might well respond to the argument of this chapter by, in essence, scaling up their retributivism, and defending retributivism as a *general* principle of political justification. (What are public institutions for? To give people what they morally deserve.) That

46. I discuss the issue of punishment for so-called *mala prohibita* offenses in greater detail in Chapter 5.

would not, I think, be a very attractive political philosophy. But it is a possible one, which is all that concerns me at the moment. My aim in this chapter is to defend a fully political standard of justification for the criminal law. I leave for the next chapter the task of considering how one might give normative substance to this abstract standard. That said, I can now explain more precisely what I mean by a public law conception of the criminal law. A public law conception is a conception that endorses (1–4) and (7). It is a conception of the criminal law as a means of facilitating cooperation with shared public institutions; and, consequently, one that insists the criminal law meet the same standard of political justification that applies to public institutions more generally.

Perhaps it is worth stepping back and asking why a fully political standard is a plausible standard to apply here. For my purposes, the basic reason is that a fully political standard coheres with a sense of the criminal law as a central part of the regulatory and legal apparatus of the modern welfare state. As Garland has put it, the same set of social, economic, and political problems that engendered the rise of the welfare state also gave rise to a form of penal welfarism that looked beyond the narrow bounds of individual moral desert to the broader objectives of social institutions.[47] A fully political standard gives philosophical expression to the thought that ideals of justice do not stop at the prison gates, but apply equally to everyone living under the rule of shared public institutions.

2.5 Justice: Retributive and Distributive

One might object here that I have simply been assuming that generically coercive rule-enforcement will be required to sustain an adequate level of social cooperation. But perhaps it may turn out (say, in institutionally dense welfare states) that we are able to secure adequate social cooperation *without* relying on sanctioning people who break the law. Does that free up the criminal law to pursue other, perhaps more overtly retributive, aims? Perhaps the transformation of criminal law into public law then enables the state to take on board, as a collective social aim, the objective of giving wrongdoers the punishment they deserve.

A full answer to this objection must wait for Chapter 3, where I sketch how one might give substantive moral content to the fully political standard

47. David Garland, *The Culture of Control* (University of Chicago Press 2001), ch. 2.

of justification. However, what can be said here is that under a fully political standard, the question is whether our reason for supporting social cooperation with public institutions extends to punishing wrongdoers because they are wrongdoers—and not, for instance, because doing so protects important rights from violation, secures a fair distribution of benefits and burdens, or contributes in some other way to the maintenance of a civil order.

Of course, retributivists will deny that punishment must serve some purpose; in the usual case, it is permissible, they will claim, so long as it is true that those punished deserve it (that is, so long as punishment is a morally appropriate way of responding to a wrongdoer). The point I am insisting upon here is that regardless as to whether this is plausible as an account of everyday interpersonal morality, from the point of view of a fully political standard of justification, retributivists owe us an explanation of why our reasons for supporting public institutions extend to ensuring that those institution give people the punishment they pre-politically deserve. It will not suffice to observe that, as a matter of interpersonal morality, we tend not to object to punishing people when they deserve it. We would still be owed some further account to establish that (for instance) the value of public institutions is derived from their ability to vindicate private, interpersonal morality on a much larger scale.

To see how illiberal such a view would be, suppose that it were the case that the value of public institutions arose in some large measure out of their ability to treat people according to their pre-political moral deserts. From the point of view of a fully political standard, this suggests that the basic principle of the modern welfare state is to ensure that people get what they deserve, whether in the form of punishment or in the form of health care, education, housing and so forth. Giving desert this kind of central role conflicts with the thought that certain entitlements are universal, in that you are entitled to health care or education regardless of whether you are deemed deserving. Could one try to reconcile a retributive political morality with a universalist approach to social welfare? It is hard to see how. Simply insisting that those other functions are not part of "criminal law," whereas "punishment" is, clearly will not do. For that begs the very question at issue, which is whether the criminal law should be evaluated according to principles of justification that apply to public institutions *generally*. Obviously, if one defines the criminal law to be essentially retributive, then no non-retributive theory will do. The question is whether we have reason to define the criminal law in that way.

Samuel Scheffler has provided the most thoughtful and sophisticated attempt to provide a principled philosophical basis for the traditional legal distinction between criminal law and non-criminal (private, regulatory, etc.) law. Scheffler's argument might be drawn upon here to support the idea that the morality of the criminal law cannot be assimilated to the political morality of other public institutions. Let us consider that argument.

"The problem of retributive justice," Scheffler has claimed, "is not the problem of how to allocate a limited supply of benefits among equally worthy citizens but rather the problem of how society can ever be justified in imposing the special burden of punishment on a particular human being."[48] Adopting Scheffler's terminology, we may say that desert functions pre-justicially in cases where desert is "prior to and independent of the principles of distributive justice themselves, and by reference to which the justice of institutional arrangements is to be assessed."[49] On a pre-justicial conception, a judgment of the form "A deserves X" provides a basis for evaluating institutions and policies: they become more just insofar as they tend to provide someone like A with something like X. In contrast, a legitimate-expectations view of desert holds that "[p]eople are entitled to the economic benefits that just institutions lead them to expect"; judgments of the form "A deserves X" may be "perfectly legitimate" insofar as they express "nothing more than claims of institutional entitlement," meaning that the expectations are evaluated by reference to just institutions, not vice versa.[50]

---

48. Samuel Scheffler, "Justice and Desert in Liberal Theory," *California Law Review* 88 (2000): 965–90 at 986. Scheffler presents his proposal as a way of making sense of Rawls's ambiguous comments about punishment rather than in his own voice. Nevertheless, because Scheffler's distinction underpins the widely-shared assumption that the criminal law is normatively special, it is worth probing the argument in some detail, regardless of whether it tracks Scheffler's (or Rawls's) views on the merits.

49. Scheffler, "Justice and Desert in Liberal Theory," 978.

50. Scheffler, "Justice and Desert in Liberal Theory," 978. Scheffler's defense of the "asymmetry of desert" has spawned a minor literature. See Eugene Mills, "Scheffler on Rawls, Justice and Desert," *Law and Philosophy* 23(3) (2004): 261–72; Jeffrey Moriarty, "Against the Asymmetry of Desert," *Noûs* 37(3) (2003): 518–36; Saul Smilansky, "Control, Desert and the Difference between Distributive and Retributive Justice," *Philosophical Studies* 131(3) (2006): 511–24; Douglas Husak, "Holistic Retributivism," *California Law Review* 88 (2000): 991–1000; Thomas Hurka, "Desert: Individualistic and Holistic," in *Desert and Justice*, ed. S. Olsaretti (Oxford University Press 2003), 45–58; Matt Matravers, "Mad, Bad or Faulty? Desert in Distributive and Retributive Justice," in *Responsibility and Distributive Justice*, ed. C. Knight and Z. Stemplowski (Oxford University Press 2011), 136–51; and Melissaris, "Toward a Political Theory of Criminal Law," 150–53.

It is plausible, Scheffler suggests, to give pre-justicial desert a much greater role in the context of the criminal law than in other areas of law. This is because desert in the retributive context is *individualistic*: what a person deserves by way of punishment can be ascertained on the basis of facts about her—for instance, that she voluntarily and knowingly caused a particular type of injury to another. In contrast, it is not possible to specify what a person deserves by way of, say, income, without appeal to a broad range of facts concerning the institutions, social practices, and preferences that determine the market value of a particular talent or skill. "[C]itizens' material prospects," as Scheffler puts the point, "are profoundly interconnected through their shared and effectively unavoidable participation in a set of fundamental practices and institutions—the economy, the legal system, the political framework—that establish and enforce the ground rules of social cooperation."[51] In contrast, "those whom the criminal justice system legitimately punishes have normally done something that would be wrong even in the absence of a law prohibiting it."[52] The individualistic way in which we assess desert in certain kinds of transactions—murder, rape, or assault, for instance—provides a pre-justicial basis for allocating punishment. But when it comes to income, healthcare, educational opportunities, or share of the tax burden, our inability to reliably draw individualistic judgments means that desert must take the form of legitimate expectations: what a person deserves under any of those headings is simply a matter of what just institutions would legitimately lead him to expect.

Scheffler's account suggests that the *philosophical* distinction between "retributive" and "distributive" justice maps onto the *legal* distinction between "criminal" and non-criminal branches of law. The fully political standard of justification that I have proposed resists this mapping of retributive justice onto the criminal law. The emphasis I have placed on the criminal law as a way of stabilizing cooperation with public institutions more generally suggests that the criminal law is as much a matter of fair distribution as it is a matter of individual moral desert. As such, I have suggested that the principles of political evaluation that apply to how public institutions create and allocate advantage should take precedence over principles drawn from interpersonal

51. Scheffler, "Justice and Desert in Liberal Theory," 985.

52. Scheffler, "Justice and Desert in Liberal Theory," 978.

morality.[53] But Scheffler's claim that there is an asymmetry in how desert operates in those two contexts—individualistic and pre-justicial in the one, holistic and institutional in the other—would seem like an attractive way of vindicating deeply held intuitions about the meaning of punishment and the criminal law.

Many, perhaps most, of the people convicted of crimes are responsible for doing so, in the sense that they voluntarily chose to do the act or bring about the outcome that the law prohibits. And in a substantial number of cases, what the law prohibits is conduct that would have been wrong anyway. Yet to conclude that the criminal law is therefore the manifestation of retributive rather than distributive justice ignores the fact that the criminal law *also* plays a substantial role in creating and allocating scarce and valuable social goods. The importance of this latter dimension of the criminal law has, I suggest, increased as the criminal law has gradually become the domain of public institutions that are staffed by large bureaucracies, that possess comprehensive powers over nearly all aspects of criminal procedure, and that exercise jurisdiction over hundreds of thousands, or indeed millions, of transactions.

How does the criminal law facilitate the creation and distribution of social advantage? I have argued that it does so by stabilizing cooperation with public institutions, institutions that Scheffler concedes are properly evaluated from the point of view of distributive justice. The criminal law can perform this function either directly or indirectly. The criminal law directly creates and allocates social advantage when its operation—through policing, prosecution, and corrections—comprises a society's primary institutional means of enforcing some legal rule. For instance, the rule against assault is not just a matter of vindicating a right to bodily integrity ex post. It is also a way of protecting people from being assaulted ex ante. The criminal law is, of course, not the *only* social institution that protects the bodily integrity of its members. Other institutions contribute to that aim, for instance by providing services (education, healthcare) that are negatively correlated with violent criminal offending. Insofar as the criminal law, however, is the primary means of protecting people from being assaulted, then it is the direct

53. See Jonathan Wolff and Avner de-Shalit, *Disadvantage* (Oxford University Press 2007), 79 (arguing that, in the context of distributive justice, the question of what people are morally responsible for should be treated separately from the question of what burdens it is reasonable to impose on them).

institutional provider of that social good. In other contexts, the criminal law's role is more indirect, in that it serves as a backup line of enforcement to another primary means of providing a good or service, in the way that, for instance, using the criminal law to enforce Medicare fraud helps support the institution of Medicare. In cases of this sort, the criminal law creates and allocates a social good indirectly, by stabilizing cooperation with a public institution that is more directly involved in the creation and allocation of that good.

Whether directly or indirectly, the criminal law creates social advantage insofar as it is causally connected to a state of affairs in which more people enjoy some good (e.g., sexual autonomy) or enjoy it more intensely (e.g., as against everyone, not just strangers) than would otherwise be the case. It distributes social advantage through its impact on patterns of victimization and offending (e.g., if aggressive policing in one suburb shifts crime to a neighboring one.) In some cases, the impact of the criminal law in creating and allocating advantage is obvious, as in the case of most violent crime, sexual offenses, and drug policy. In other cases, it is subtler, operating primarily as a backup means of enforcement for a diverse range of regulations; for instance, tax evasion or environmental regulations. But, just as with any other socially provided good, the goods created and allocated with the help of the criminal law can be allocated more or less fairly. The common law, for instance, long resisted the idea that married women could be sexually assaulted by their husbands. Abolishing the common law's marital rape exception made the common law fairer than it had been before because it allocated a valuable social good—protection from sexual assault—more fairly than had previously been the case. Conversely, just as the benefits of the criminal law can be unfairly distributed, so too can the burdens. In the United States, the criminal law has forced African Americans and Latinos to bear a disproportionately large share of the costs of criminal justice even as they also enjoy a disproportionately small share of its benefits. The criminal law in Canada has imposed a similarly inequitable allocation on Indigenous persons.

But perhaps most tellingly, Scheffler's own account suggests that the criminal law is subject to the norms of distributive justice. Distributive justice, Scheffler argues, has three defining features. First, it "is concerned with the proper division of social advantages—that is, with the allocation of things that people are presumed to want." Second, it arises "primarily for societies that find themselves in conditions of moderate scarcity that make it impossible for them to fully satisfy the demand for such advantages." Finally, "because goods are scarce and their allocation is heavily dependent on social institutions, any provision of advantages to some may affect the supply available for others," which means that "the problem of distributive justice is seen as the problem of how to allocate scarce goods among moral equals."[54]

Each of these features applies in a straightforward way in the context of criminal justice. The criminal law stabilizes legal rules that allocate social advantage across a population. Consider again the criminalization of marital rape: by closing the common law exception, legislatures allocated an important benefit that had been unjustly denied to women, namely the ability to be free of sexual violence from their spouses. This is a form of social advantage that is of undeniable importance, and that continues to be the object of significant social struggle. Second, criminal justice is plainly scarce, in the sense of consuming limited resources. In 2006, American federal and state governments are estimated to have spent over $214 billion on criminal justice.[55] That was $214 billion that could have been spent on many valuable social goals other than punishing people who broke the law.[56] Finally, there is no reason to think that those to whom the criminal law applies—those to whom it is allocating social advantage under conditions of scarcity—are anything but moral equals. Hence, by Scheffler's own lights, the criminal law would appear to be a matter of distributive justice, rather than purely a matter of individualistic, pre-justicial desert.[57]

---

54. Scheffler, "Justice and Desert in Liberal Theory," 986.

55. Bureau of Justice Statistics, *Sourcebook of Criminal Justice Statistics Online*, Table 1.1.2006, http://www.albany.edu/sourcebook/pdf/t112006.pdf.

56. Bureau of Justice Statistics, *Sourcebook of Criminal Justice Statistics Online*, Table 4.21.2007, http://www.albany.edu/sourcebook/pdf/t4212007.pdf; Bureau of Justice Statistics, *Sourcebook of Criminal Justice Statistics Online*, Table 5.0002.2004, http://www.albany.edu/sourcebook/pdf/t500022004.pdf.

57. Although I have focused on Scheffler's account, other theorists have provided different reasons for treating the civil-criminal distinction as philosophically fundamental. Newhouse, for instance, argues that the Kantian distinction between material and formal wrongdoing—wrongdoing based in a property of one's "physical action" as opposed to wrongdoing based on the maxim on which one acts—underlies the traditional distinction between civil wrongs and crimes. Marie Newhouse, "Two Types of Legal Wrongdoing," *Legal Theory* 22 (2016): 59–75, 68. Even if we accept the Kantian distinction, however, contrary to Newhouse's suggestion, it does not follow that the state "must" respond to those wrongs in fundamentally different ways. It seems plausible enough that states often *do*, but rather less plausible that they necessarily *must*, respond differentially in the way that Kant (and Newhouse) suggest.

2.6 Wrongdoing, Fair Play, and Guilt

I conclude by considering three objections. First, one might object that people who commit murder or rape are not punished because they broke the rules; they are punished because what they did was *wrong*. Even if much or most of what criminal justice institutions actually do is not punishment of pre-politically wrongful conduct, one might reason that it is nevertheless a serious failing of a public law conception if it cannot get this aspect of criminal punishment squarely in view.[58]

Naturally, I would not want to deny that crimes such as assault and murder are wrong, and wrong independently of what public institutions happen to say about them. However, it is important to distinguish between our reasons for regarding certain types of conduct as wrongful, and our reasons for setting up public institutions and policies for responding to conduct of that kind. Crimes such as assault and murder are seriously harmful and wrongfully invade the rights of others. But that they are serious interpersonal wrongs is neither necessary nor sufficient to establish that we ought to use public institutions to punish them. Resolving that question requires showing that punishment in those instances would be in conformity with an accepted standard of political justification.

Since ensuring that citizens can lead their lives reasonably secure from physical assault is central to any plausible account of just social arrangements, it is hardly surprising that states would be eager to protect their citizens from such conduct, and justified in doing so. But to acknowledge that *punishment's* legitimacy, even in so-called *mala in se* cases, depends on an underlying account of *political* legitimacy is not to be committed to the view that such crimes are only conventionally wrong. It is, rather, to be committed to the view that what public institutions should do in response to interpersonal wrongs is determined by political, rather than interpersonal, morality—that is, by moral principles designed to evaluate the operation of complex and law-governed institutions that claim authority over large and diverse populations, rather than face-to-face interactions between private individuals acting on their own consciences. From a public law point of view, the decision to use criminal sanctions to

58. See George Sher, *Desert* (Princeton University Press 1987), 80–82; R.A. Duff, *Punishment, Communication, and Community* (Oxford University Press 2001), 56–59. This has typically been the main objection to fair play theories of punishment. See, e.g., David Dolinko, "Some Thoughts on Retributivism," *Ethics* 101(3) (1991): 537–59, especially 546–49; R.A. Duff, *Trials and Punishments* (Cambridge University Press 1986), 213.

do so is at bottom a political decision for collective determination, not the conscience—however morally refined—of private citizens.[59]

Second, it might be thought that the kind of public law approach I have been defending ultimately reduces to a form of "fair play" theory of punishment, according to which the point of punishment is to ensure that criminals who take advantage of the cooperation of others are punished as a way of cancelling out that advantage. Criminal law as public law is clearly closely related to this idea of fair play. But there are important differences as well.[60]

A public law account shares with fair play theory the view that the criminal law helps secure a just distribution of benefits and burdens. It also shares fair play theory's emphasis on the importance of punishment in securing cooperation with public institutions. The principal difference with fair play theory is that my account does not view punishment as intrinsically remedial, for instance as restoring a balance that has been upset, or re-establishing the status quo ante. On a public law account, the morality of punishment is not simply a matter of punishing people to restore a fair distribution, but is rather assessed in terms of the contributions a system of punishment makes to ensuring fair terms of social cooperation in the first place. Hence, from a public law point of view, justifying punishment requires showing that fair terms of social cooperation would

59. Since Orestes did in fact violate a sacred norm by murdering his mother, Clytemnestra, he can hardly complain when the Erinyes in turn seek his destruction: they are only seeking the same as he was, namely to avenge a wrongful murder. The same could be said for Clytemnestra, who murdered her husband, and the father of her child; though of course the same could be said of Agamemnon for his murder of the innocent Iphigenia. True, he acted under divine command; but then by what right did the gods require such a sacrifice from Agamemnon? A public law conception offers a different interpretation of the *Oresteia*. It is not that Orestes, or Clytemnestra, or Agamemnon—or even the Erinyes—*misunderstood* what their morality required of them. It is not as if Orestes was acting to secure a private advantage for himself when he kills Clytemnestra, for he acts out of a sense of a moral duty owed to his father. Whether this duty is enough to cleanse him of guilt for murdering his mother—of *deserving* punishment in the pre-justicial sense—is precisely what is at issue between the Erinyes and Apollo. ("What spur can rightly goad to matricide?") Yet the resolution of *this* dispute—the retributive logic of tit-for-tat—is beyond even Athena's power; what resolves the dispute is not divine moral insight but rather the transformation of a conflict of private right into a question of public law, a matter for the citizens of Athens to decide. The *Oresteia* is, in this respect, a story about the triumph of public institutions—of the rule of law—over private right.

60. For sympathetic accounts of fair play theory, see Sher, *Desert*, and Richard Dagger, "Playing Fair with Punishment," *Ethics* 103(3) (1993): 473–88; Dagger, *Playing Fair*, ch. 7. My account of criminal law as public law is closer to Dagger's version than to Sher's, given Dagger's emphasis on the rule of law as a cooperative practice.

include relying on criminal sanctions to stabilize expectations of cooperation with public institutions. Because it is not centrally focused on punishment as a backward-facing effort to restore the status quo, the public law account is less retributive than standard forms of fair play theory.[61]

For example, suppose someone commits an armed robbery. Fair play theory suggests that the criminal has taken for himself an advantage (the proceeds of the robbery, and the thrill of having committed it) that others have sworn off for the sake of the common good, and that punishment is warranted to annul that advantage. In contrast, the public law account suggests that insofar as public institutions are justified in punishing that person, it is because (1) fair terms of social cooperation do not include being deprived of one's property at the whim of another, and (2) empowering public institutions to protect people from that type of conduct by threatening to punish individuals who engage in armed robbery would itself be consistent with those fair terms of cooperation. From a public law point of view, the fairness of the rule prohibiting armed robbery is not alone sufficient to justify punishment. The system of punishment must also be consistent with the norms that explain why that rule is a fair one.

Third, one might worry that the public law conception fails to appreciate that punishment is a distinctive type of good, one whose distribution does not hinge upon the considerations of fairness and efficiency that characterize the distribution of other goods. This line of thought draws sustenance from the observation that it would make no moral sense to let a murderer go free if she turns out to be very badly off, or to punish an innocent person if that turns out to promote the optimal distribution of welfare in society. Punishment, and with it the criminal law, must respond to wrongdoing. That is something altogether different from ensuring a fair distribution of resources, opportunities, welfare, and so forth.

Naturally, it makes little sense to treat the criminal law as a means for fairly allocating a fixed stock among a group of people without regard to guilt or innocence. The criminal law is not a free-floating Ministry for the Rectification of Maldistribution, handing out punishments whenever doing so would seem to rectify unfair distribution elsewhere in the system. But that is not what it means to treat the criminal law as subject to a fully political standard of justification. What is meant is that the criminal law stabilizes cooperation with public institutions, institutions

---

61. This line of critique draws from Matravers, *Justice and Punishment*, especially at 61–62.

whose rules and policies—ranging from "don't murder other people" to "pay your taxes" to "if you are a resident, you are entitled to healthcare"—are frequently matters of creating and allocating social goods. It does this by attaching costs to willful defection from a legal rule. Sometimes the criminal law stabilizes that allocation indirectly, by serving as a backup sanction once other modes of generating cooperation have failed, and sometimes the criminal law is itself the primary means of allocating social advantage. A fully political standard applies to the overall allocation of benefits and burdens that flow from a legal regime that relies on criminal sanctions, directly or indirectly, to stabilize cooperation.

It is worth remembering (if a reminder is needed) that the criminal law can be a more or less fair way of enforcing a society's laws. Consider complaints about the failure to criminalize marital rape, or about trial procedures that turn a sexual assault proceeding into a referendum on the complainant's reputation, or about the disproportionate targeting of young minority men for humiliating searches, or complaints about neighborhoods where the police are simply absent, leaving residents to fend for themselves. These are most naturally understood as complaints about how the benefits and burdens of social cooperation are allocated. They are not complaints about the need to punish some people more in order to compensate for an unfair advantage they have arrogated to themselves; nor are they complaints about morally innocent people being punished; nor are they complaints about people being punished more than they deserve. They are complaints about public institutions showing less-than-equal respect and concern for their constituents, either through the degree of protection they provide, or through the humiliating and discriminatory ways in which they choose to provide it.[62]

It is true that the public law conception I have articulated breaks dramatically with traditional understandings of the criminal law. Many philosophers of the criminal law are inclined to view the criminal law as structured by an internal logic of its own, rather than as a broader political enterprise.[63] Others, while insisting that the morality of the criminal law is part of a broader political morality, nevertheless insist upon a traditional

---

62. For a parallel argument in the context of hate crimes, see Alon Harel and Gideon Parchomovsky, "On Hate and Equality," *Yale Law Journal* 109(3) (1999): 507–39. See also Sharon Dolovich, "Legitimate Punishment in Liberal Democracy," *Buffalo Criminal Law Review* 7(2) (2004): 307–442 at 352–56.

63. See Michael Davis, "The Relative Independence of Punishment Theory," *Law and Philosophy* 7 (1989): 321–50 at 329–30. Portions of Davis's account have turned out to be

understanding of the criminal law as occupying a morally distinctive role within that broader political morality. Antony Duff, for instance, suggests that conceptual analysis can reveal the essential features of any system of criminal law—features that jointly describe the criminal law as "a distinctive kind of institution" playing a special role in the life of a political community.[64] For Duff, that role is to serve as a civic code of ethics—as roughly analogous to a professional code of ethics, only for citizens rather than members of a regulated profession.[65] This is consistent with Duff's earlier claim thatthe criminal law is distinctive in that it "purports to define, and provide for the condemnation of, certain kinds of moral wrong," and that "to justify the criminal law's content we must therefore show that what it defines as crimes are indeed wrongs of the appropriate kind."[66] In contrast, the public law conception emphasizes the continuities between criminal law and regulatory law, as well as the discontinuity between the criminal law and interpersonal morality. Because I start with a social function rather than a traditional legal category, the resulting account is one of revision rather than rational reconstruction.

There are many ways that public institutions can foster the conditions of social trust; on a public law conception, the criminal law is distinctive largely in virtue of (1) its reliance on sanctions that tend to be on the harsher end of the spectrum, and that (2) are applied ex post, that is after a rule has been violated. While these features, (1) in particular, do carve out the criminal law as an institution of special moral concern, this is not because of the criminal law's allegedly special connection to moral wrongdoing. It is simply because the criminal law is one of the most coercive forms of state power familiar to us today.

2.7 Conclusion

In this chapter, I have defended a conception of criminal law as public law. This conception rests on the claim that sanctioning deliberate

---

rather more controversial than he anticipated: see Malcolm Thorburn, "Justifications, Power, and Authority," *Yale Law Journal* 117(6) (2008): 1070–130.

64. Antony Duff, *The Realm of Criminal Law* (Oxford University Press 2018), 13.

65. *The Realm of Criminal Law*, 80–91.

66. Antony Duff, *Answering for Crime: Responsibility and Liability in the Criminal Law* (Hart Publishing 2007), 81.

violation from a shared rule or norm serves to foster deeper and more sustained levels of social cooperation. Generically coercive rule-enforcing institutions provide assurance that those who are willing to cooperate with public law will not be taken advantage of or exploited by those who are tempted to defect. Whether cooperation in a particular context is worthwhile, and whether criminal sanction is a legitimate means of securing it, are questions to be resolved by appeal to more general principles of political justification, rather than by appeal to interpersonal morality. From a public law point of view, the criminal law is oriented at securing cooperation with public institutions whether or not it is also oriented at securing retributive justice. Hence, the terms in which we justify the criminal law ought to be continuous with the terms in which we evaluate society's basic structure generally, whether or not they are also continuous with the interpersonal morality of blame, resentment, and punishment.

Criminal law as public law emphasizes the connections between a society's criminal justice institutions—as generically coercive rule-enforcing institutions—and the justice, or injustice, of its basic structure more generally. In doing so, the public law conception adopts a distinctive account of what it is to justify the criminal law. From a public law point of view, we cannot cleanly distinguish what an individual deserves for his crimes from his overall place in a broad skein of public institutions and the private relations those institutions structure and make possible. While the criminal law surely does punish people for their pre-justicial wrongs, that is not all it does. Indeed, that is not even primarily what it does, either in principle or in practice.[67] The criminal law is a rule-enforcing institution before it is a punishment-imposing institution. By enforcing a set of legal rules, the criminal law serves to stabilize a pattern of social advantage across a population. Assessing the criminal law's contribution in securing the justice of social arrangements generally requires a fully political standard of justification, one that does not treat the criminal law as sealed off from the more general principles and values of a society's political morality.

That said, a public law conception is consistent with a wide range of commitments in normative political theory, whether libertarian or egalitarian, rights-based or welfarist, perfectionist or democratic.

67. See Chapter 5, Section 5.2.

Demonstrating the viability of a public law conception requires showing not just that basic political principles apply to the criminal justice system; it requires working through what this might mean in the context of a particular conception of justice. I begin to take up that task in the next chapter.

3

Criminal Law as Public Law III

CONTENT

"It is perfectly true that given a just system of cooperation as a scheme of public rules and the expectations set up by it, those who, with the prospect of improving their condition, have done what the system announces that it will reward are entitled to their advantages. In this sense the more fortunate have a claim to their better situation; their claims are legitimate expectations established by social institutions, and the community is obligated to meet them. But this sense of desert presupposes the existence of the cooperative scheme; it is irrelevant to the question . . . [of how] in the first place the scheme is to be designed."[1]

"Even prisoners are supposed to be the beneficiaries of welfare state policies; even the prisons are run according to the logic of a universal right to welfare . . . [w]elfare aid is yours if and when you need it, regardless of whether you have deserved it in a moral sense."[2]

3.1 Introduction

In the previous chapter, I argued that a central function of the criminal law is to promote cooperation with public institutions, and thereby to promote the values, whatever they may be, that arise out of a shared life under public institutions. I also argued that the goal of securing the conditions of ongoing social cooperation enjoys a functional priority over other ends that we might plausibly want the criminal law to pursue, such as systematically

1. John Rawls, *A Theory of Justice* (Harvard University Press 1971), 103.

2. Thomas Ugelvik, "Prisons as Welfare Institutions? Punishment and the Nordic Model," in *Handbook on Prisons*, ed. Y. Jewkes, B. Crewe, and J. Bennett (Routledge 2016), 394; see also John Pratt, "Scandinavian Exceptionalism in an Era of Penal Excess, Part I: The Roots of Scandinavian Exceptionalism," *British Journal of Criminology* 48 (2008): 119–37.

and publicly condemning wrongdoing. I argued that this account of what the criminal law is for yields, in turn, an account of the standard that a justification of the criminal law should meet. A justification of the criminal law should provide an account of (1) when the institutions whose rules it enforces are worth supporting, as well as (2) whether its use in a particular context would be consistent with the principles that make those institutions worth supporting in the first place. I referred to this as a "fully political" standard of justification, and described the resulting view as a "public law" conception of criminal law.

In this chapter, I turn from describing the structure of a public law conception to sketching one possible account of its normative content. A public law conception is consistent with a wide range of commitments in normative political philosophy, whether liberal, libertarian, utilitarian, or otherwise. This chapter presents one such set of commitments—a view I shall refer to as the political ideal of anti-deference. Drawing upon the work of Elizabeth Anderson, Phillip Pettit, and Niko Kolodny, the political ideal of anti-deference describes a society of peers in which every person can, in Pettit's evocative phrase, look every other person in the eye without fear or deference.[3] From the point of view of anti-deference, public institutions should strive to ensure that each person is able to live as a peer among peers. They do this by ensuring that each person has an equal opportunity for influence over the laws and policies that they are subject to; and, subject to that democratic principle, effective access to the capabilities that count, in that society, as constitutive of basic equality.

Of course, any account of the reasons we have to value public institutions will be controversial. The particular interpretation I favor is democratic, egalitarian but not equalizing, and focused on a form of freedom—central capability—as its basic evaluative currency. Perhaps you favor an account that is more rights-based or more utilitarian than the account I sketch. Or perhaps you favor an account that is more populist, or more elitist, than the version I favor. Or perhaps you favor a resource or preference-based metric of evaluation. I shall not engage such high-level philosophical issues here, much less try to resolve them. The appeal of the account sketched here rests largely on its ability to stake out attractive

---

3. See Phillip Pettit, *On the People's Terms: A Republican Theory and Model of Democracy* (Cambridge University Press 2013).

positions on the criminal law, a task I take up in greater detail in subsequent chapters. Without foreclosing the possibility of other accounts, my aim is to suggest how one approach to egalitarian political thought might be carried through to the context of criminal justice.

The chapter proceeds as follows. First, I quickly sketch the basic parameters of the political ideal of anti-deference in a general way. I then outline a set of principles based on the ideal of anti-deference that provide a framework for evaluating the criminal law and its associated institutions. I focus on four: equal opportunity for influence, anti-subordination, optimality, and inclusive aggregation. I consider objections in Sections 3.3 and 3.4.

3.2 The Political Ideal of Anti-deference

The political ideal of anti-deference holds that public institutions should strive to promote effective access to central capability for all. It is meant to be an ideal of "anti-deference" because it embodies an ideal of status equality. People enjoy equality in this sense when they are able to live on terms that do not require them to show deference before others, or to accept demeaning or humiliating judgments about their worth, as a condition of accessing the basic goods and services that are constitutive of equal status in their society. In a society of this kind, as Philip Pettit has vividly put it, each person can "look others in the eye without reason for the fear or deference that a power of interference might inspire; they can walk tall and assume the public status, objective and subjective, of being equal in this regard with the best."[4] Public institutions contribute to the construction of an egalitarian society of this kind by securing for each person effective access to the capabilities that articulate, in a given social context, equal social status.

Democratic equality is, obviously, a complex idea. Two dimensions stand out as especially salient. The first is political equality, in the sense of having a voice in a range of collective decision-making procedures. The second is substantive equality, in the sense of sharing equally in the benefits and burdens generated by those procedures. Anti-deference, as I propose to understand the term, offers an interpretation of both of these dimensions of equality.

4. Pettit, *On the People's Terms*, 84.

Niko Kolodny has recently argued that the question of justifying democracy is in large part a question of social equality.[5] A society of equals is one in which no one is "above" any other, and hence no one is "below" any other either. According to Kolodny, a society of equals would be threatened if some people exercised non-reciprocal power and authority over the lives of others, even if that power and authority is only ever used for their good. Kolodny argues that "it is a particularly important component of relations of social equality among individuals that they enjoy equal opportunity for influence over the political decisions to which they are subject."[6] The reason equal opportunity for influence is so important is because when it comes to decisions that have a final authority on how one's life goes, particularly decisions that are backed up coercively, the failure to provide equal opportunity for influence over those decisions suggests that, in one respect or another, those subject to the decisions are social inferiors. It suggests that others speak *for* them rather than *with* them. Even if well intentioned and wise, a condition under which some are subject to the rule of others is a condition of paternalistic supervision rather than one of equal freedom. Unequal influence might be less of a concern when jurisdiction is contingent upon consent, or where compliance is voluntary rather than mandatory. However, public institutions typically insist upon compliance, even from those who never explicitly consented. Under such conditions, political equality requires more than simply ensuring good outcomes. Plausibly, it also requires ensuring that those who are subject to the law have an equal say in determining its content.[7]

Political equality is consistent with a wide range of policies. Substantively, which ones should we prefer? It would be foolhardy to attempt a general answer to this question. For my purposes, a partial answer is sufficient. Anti-deference suggests that, all else being equal, we should prefer policies that maximally protect each person's freedom to engage in the activities, or achieve the outcomes, that are generally understood as

---

5. "Rule over None I: What Justifies Democracy?," *Philosophy & Public Affairs* 42(3) (2014): 195–229, and "Rule over None II: Equality and the Justification of Democracy," *Philosophy & Public Affairs* 42(4) (2014): 287–336.

6. "Rule over None II," 308.

7. To be sure, representatives and public officials have greater opportunities for influence than private citizens. But insofar as the former are the latter's agents, exercising only the powers delegated to them by the people, and insofar as the delegation itself is suitably democratic, then representative democracy does not per se undermine equality opportunity for influence. See Kolodny, "Rule over None II," 317–20.

required in that society to lead a decent and independent life. From this point of view, what impairs equal status is not that some have more than others per se, but rather that some do not have enough to live a decent life on their own, and consequently depend upon the beneficence of others.

For reasons that I explore more fully in Chapter 6, I adopt a capability-based account of the activities and outcomes that are constitutive of democratic equality. I shall describe a capability as a central capability if it is required for a person to live in that society as a peer. One of the attractive (if also complicating) features of a capability-based approach is its pluralism. Leading a decent and independent life requires, for instance, that one be able to access public space—streets, sidewalks, malls, and so forth—on terms befitting an equal. It is not just about objective resources, or happiness, or any other single-valued metric. The underlying concern is to ensure that a person's entitlement to the material basis associated with equal status is not conditioned on intrusive and humiliating judgments of moral worth. You should not have to prove to a landlord, employer, doctor, bureaucrat, or teacher that you are a worthy person, or otherwise morally deserving, in order to be entitled to housing, healthcare, income, or a seat in a university classroom—or indeed to any of the other goods that are central to a life led as a peer among peers. That kind of requirement fosters relations of social subservience and deference to authority that are inconsistent with the ideal of a society of equals.[8]

How are political and substantive equality related? The fairness of a procedure should not insulate an outcome from criticism, but neither should the substantive justice of an outcome make it irrelevant as to how that outcome was reached. I follow Pettit in prioritizing political over substantive equality.[9] Public institutions should ensure that those under their jurisdiction have equal opportunity for influence over the laws and policies that apply to them. Subject to that condition, policies and institutions should be evaluated in terms of the degree to which they secure the material basis of social equality, namely the capabilities associated, in a given society, with equal basic status. The rationale for prioritizing political equality is that imposing social policy by diktat is inconsistent with the underlying ideal of status equality. Under conditions of reasonable disagreement, it might be thought condescending for one group to rely on their private

---

8. Here, I follow Elizabeth Anderson's lead; see "What Is the Point of Equality?," *Ethics* 109 (1999): 287–337, especially at 325–26.

9. See Pettit, *On the People's Terms*, 24–25; see also Kolodny, "Rule over None II."

conviction that they are right to exclude dissenters from weighing in. At worst, it appears to be rule by some (the wise) over others (the benighted).[10] For this reason, political and substantive equality should not be simply weighed against each other: that model would suggest that the more confident you are in the righteousness of your cause, the more entitled you should feel to prevent others from challenging you. Instead, democratic equality should take priority over substantive equality. This priority is qualified, however. When the effect of a decision is to subordinate and exclude some from political participation, democratic values themselves speak in favor of overriding an ostensibly democratic decision.[11]

The general picture is this: peers should have equal voices in determining the terms of cooperation that structure their relations to each other. In many cases, respecting this constraint will not uniquely determine an outcome. All else being equal, we should prefer outcomes that maximally protect universal access to central capability. However, the democratic process should generally be respected even when it yields outcomes that we might regard as suboptimal from one or another philosophical point of view. After all, equal voice is a constituent part of democratic equality, and tends to be of particular value under the conditions of reasonable disagreement that characterize most developed democracies.

3.3 Anti-deference and the Criminal Law

Recall that a fully political standard of justification imposes two conditions on a normative theory of the criminal law. It states that:

(7) The criminal law is worth supporting if and only if:
  a. the institutions whose rules it enforces are worth supporting, and
  b. its use in a particular context would be consistent with the principles that make those institutions worth supporting in the first place.

The primary aim of this chapter is to consider how anti-deference as a political ideal can be extended to the evaluation of the criminal law; it is, in other words, to provide an interpretation of (7)(b). Taking anti-deference

---

10. See generally Jeremy Waldron, *Law and Disagreement* (Oxford University Press 1999).

11. In the context of judicial review, this view is most closely associated with John Hart Ely; see *Democracy and Distrust: A Theory of Judicial Review* (Harvard University Press 1980).

as my starting point, I shall sketch four desiderata for the criminal law. First, criminal justice institutions should afford their constituents *equal opportunity for influence*, by offering those whose lives they affect an equal opportunity to weigh in on its basic policies and values. Second, the criminal law should not be used in ways that reflect humiliating judgments about those subject to the law: it should be consistent with a norm of *anti-subordination*. Third, because the criminal law foreseeably impairs effective access to central capability among those it sanctions, it should be called upon only if no other reasonably available, and democratically accessible, policy would do better in terms of protecting such access for all. It should, in other words, *optimally* protect effective access to central capability. Finally, criminal justice institutions should adopt a principle of *inclusive aggregation*: the interests of those who have committed crimes should not be discounted relative to those who have not.[12]

Equal opportunity for influence. Often, the people over whom public institutions have jurisdiction did not consent to live under those institutions, and lack meaningful options for exit. These facts can make public institutions look like bullies—well-intentioned ones, but bullies nonetheless. The anxiety that our institutions might amount to little more than gussied-up bullying has a tendency to become a full-blown panic attack when we turn our attention to the criminal law. Here, the bullying looks to be at its most evident: do X—*or else*. Indeed, the source of the anxiety goes further than this. It is not just the threat that seems bullying. Criminal justice institutions go beyond threatening punishment if we do not comply with the law. Notably, they also include permanent and armed police forces who are engaged, in part, in preventing people from failing to comply with the law, often by intrusive and forcible means. Historically, common law countries were slow to create such forces out of a suspicion that the presence of a quasi-military occupying police force was inconsistent with a condition of civilized liberty. Reports of humiliating and violent interactions between citizens and the police may suggest that such fears were not entirely unwarranted.[13]

---

12. Melissaris has articulated a set of conditions that parallel, in some respects, the account developed here. "Toward a Political Theory of Criminal Law," *New Criminal Law Review* 15(1) (2012): 122–55 at 142.

13. The juxtaposition of extreme violence, and a highly doubtful claim to legitimacy, is a theme in the work of Alice Ristroph. For a recent statement, see "Conditions of Justified Punishment," in *The New Philosophy of Criminal Law*, ed. Chad Flanders and Zachary Hoskins (Rowman & Littlefield International 2015).

In a society of peers, it is important that each person subject to the criminal law have an equal opportunity for influencing its content, from the formal definition of the law to on-the-ground policies about policing and prosecution. A concern with democratic equality explains why a criminal law devised and operated by an entirely unaccountable panel of experts would be objectionable even if otherwise just. The criminal law purports to have the authority to tell us what to do, and to use coercion to ensure we do it. For some to have the unilateral power to call the shots when it comes to making criminal justice policy—what kind of conduct to criminalize, which neighborhoods to police, whom to search, whom to prosecute, and what counts as an appropriate punishment for a crime—is to grant those people power and authority over others. This power and authority gives them a status that others lack: citizens in such a society are merely subject to the law that the officials make. Perhaps this might be less problematic in areas of public policy that are less overtly coercive, or where the possibilities of opting out are more realistic. But the criminal law is both mandatory and highly coercive. By allowing for equal opportunity for influence over the criminal law—both formally and as it exists in practice—criminal justice institutions meliorate the concern that they boil down to gussied-up bullying, however fair and effective the criminal law may otherwise be. For even if you have no say as to whether you are under the jurisdiction of the criminal law, and even if the criminal law's rules are coercively enforced against you, there is a sense in which you are not treated as someone of lesser worth if you have the same opportunity for influence over the content and operation of the criminal law as anyone else.[14]

One way of ensuring that no one lords it over anyone else is to make decisions through a random process, for instance by running a lottery over every proposed policy change. In that case, no one's views have any more weight than anyone else's: everyone has a right to propose a policy, and the decision among them is made in an entirely impartial way. Whatever other objections one might have to setting criminal justice policy by lottery, one presumably could not object that it treats people unfairly. However, there just doesn't seem to be any reason to think that the outcomes reached by a

---

14. Perhaps we might thus understand Pratt's observation that, high levels of trust in expertise notwithstanding, Scandinavian prisons vest prisoners with a substantial voice in penal policy: "prisoners . . . have direct input into prison governance." Pratt, "Scandinavian Exceptionalism in an Era of Penal Excess," 120.

series of lotteries merit our respect, no matter how fair the process behind them.[15] (Although choosing *policies* by lottery should perhaps be distinguished from selecting *representatives* by lottery.[16])

Hence, the relevant question becomes whether there might be some way of ensuring equal opportunity for influence over the criminal justice system while also ensuring that the outcomes of criminal justice policy better satisfy substantive equality than a purely random procedure. In other words, one might understand the structure of anti-deference like this: *first*, consider whether a particular means of democratic decision-making provides an equal opportunity for influence; *second*, rank those that do by the likelihood that the policies they produce will tend to be substantively acceptable, recognizing that in the rivalry between competing conceptions of justice characteristic of a pluralistic and democratic politics, sincerity of conviction is not a substitute for support of the governed.[17]

Ensuring that each person has real, substantively equal opportunity for weighing in on the laws and policies that affect him or her clearly does not uniquely specify any single approach to democratic decision-making. It does not require direct electoral input on every major policy decision in criminal justice.[18] In principle, this principle could be consistent with both popular and bureaucratic models of oversight over criminal justice. The equal opportunity for influence principle would appear to be satisfied so long as the powers officials exercise are delegated to them by the people, subject to suitably robust democratic conditions. (Specifying those conditions, either

---

15. Though a reversion to the baseline fairness of a lottery might be defensible as a second-best where substantive decision-making by the relevant officials results in a racially discriminatory pattern of outcomes, as appears to be the case with both traffic stops and stop-and-frisk encounters with the police. I explore this idea in "*Ex Ante* Fairness in Criminal Law and Procedure," *New Criminal Law Review* 15(2) (2011): 277–332.

16. See Alexander Guerrero, "Against Elections: The Lottocratic Alternative," *Philosophy & Public Affairs* 42(2) (2014): 135–78, especially 167, 168–69.

17. Kolodny, "Rule over None II," 313–14.

18. Darryl Brown observes that American criminal law is "perhaps unique in the degree to which it is a product of democratic political process, or put differently, the degree to which it is unmediated in its creation by specialists or expert agencies outside of legislatures." As Brown notes, criminal law is in this respect distinct from other areas of law, such as evidence, commercial law, and procedural law, which are largely the product of specialized commissions operating with modest legislative oversight. See "History's Challenge to Criminal Law Theory," *Criminal Law and Philosophy* 3 (2009): 271–87 at 283.

in general, or with respect to a certain type of delegated power, is a challenge I leave for another occasion.) There seems to be no more reason to insist that judges and prosecutors be made directly accountable through elections than to insist that, for instance, we should directly elect the chairperson of the Federal Reserve, the attorney general, or the director of the Environmental Protection Agency. Arguably, the equal-opportunity-for-influence principle could also be satisfied by a suitably robust procedure for consulting with affected communities. This could take the form of a civilian board of commissioners, or, as some have suggested, through a period of notice and comment rule-making. Or perhaps a novel institutional mechanism would be appropriate.[19]

However, it is important to stress that what is at issue here is not mere formal opportunity to be heard, but equal *actual* opportunity for influence.[20] In this respect, a consultative, participatory model may possibly be superior to an electoral model. Unlike an election, which collapses multiple dimensions of concern into a single up or down vote, discursive consultation allows for the disaggregated airing of views with respect to multiple different areas of concern. Consultative and participatory democracy might be more egalitarian if the selection of representatives for consultation is fairer than access to the ballot, which might be impeded by lack of access to relevant information, as well as more prosaic concerns relating to participation in local elections. Perhaps minority positions, as well as those of the communities that are most likely to be burdened by criminal law enforcement activity, are more likely to be heard in consultation than in electoral politics. For instance, Stuntz has argued that in electoral systems suburban voters tend to have a disproportionate influence on criminal justice priorities, even when they are relatively less affected by them.[21] Finally, consultative and participatory democracy might also do better at avoiding the kinds of demagogic excess that seems to plague

19. See Barry Friedman and Maria Ponomarenko, "Democratic Policing," *New York University Law Review* 90 (2015): 101–83 (defending proposals for greater democratic input and transparency in policing decisions, and noting that the Los Angeles and Seattle police departments operate under civilian oversight commissions); Richard A Bierschbach and Stephanos Bibas, "Notice and Comment Sentencing," *Minnesota Law Review* 97(1) (2012): 1–71 (mounting a similar line of argument with respect to sentencing policy); Bibas, *The Machinery of Criminal Justice* (Oxford University Press 2015), chs. 4–6.

20. Kolodny, "Rule over None II," 334–36.

21. Bill Stuntz, *The Collapse of American Criminal Justice* (Harvard University Press 2011), ch. 1.

direct electoral control over criminal justice officials.[22] Of course, even highly consultative and participatory forms of democracy will, at some point, have to come down to aggregating opinions through some form of voting procedure. The point is only that democratic input need not be interpreted to mean that every significant decision has to be made electorally: democratic criminal law is not necessarily criminal law by referenda.[23]

Practically, the equal opportunity principle is inconsistent with the practice of disenfranchising current or former felons, as is commonly done in the United States.[24] Although criminal disenfranchisement is a widespread practice with a long history, "no other contemporary democracy disenfranchises felons to the same extent, or in the same manner, as the United States."[25] Voting restrictions for criminals have a long history in American law. Such restrictions were pressed into the service of white supremacy during the Reconstruction era, when many Southern states amended their constitutions to use felon disenfranchisement as a functional replacement for categorical disenfranchisement of African Americans.[26] (In a cruel irony, the legal basis for felon disenfranchisement today is found in the text of the Fourteenth Amendment.[27]) Manza

22. Vannessa Barker has argued that a participatory democracy approach tends toward a more moderate sentencing policy. See *Politics of Imprisonment: How the Democratic Process Shapes the Way America Punishes Offenders* (Oxford University Press 2009), 11–13, 85–125.

23. One might in any case wonder about the democratic credentials of elections; for a recent discussion, see Christopher Achen and Larry M. Bartels, *Democracy for Realists: Why Elections Do Not Produce Responsive Government* (Princeton University Press 2016).

24. My account draws from John Kleinig and Kevin Murtagh, "Disenfranchising Felons," *Journal of Applied Philosophy* 22, no 3 (2005): 217–39, Michael Cholbi, "A Felon's Right to Vote," *Law and Philosophy* 21 (2002): 543–65, and Jeffrey Reiman, "Liberal and Republican Arguments against Disenfranchisement of Felons," *Criminal Justice Ethics* (Winter/Spring 2005): 3–18. However, my account is broader than Reiman's, in that Reiman limits his claim to ex-felons who have served out their sentences.

25. Angela Behrens, Christopher Uggen, and Jeff Manza, "Ballot Manipulation and the 'Menace of Negro Domination': Racial Threat and Felon Disenfranchisement in the United States, 1850–2002," *American Journal of Sociology* 109(3) (2003): 559–605 at 562.

26. Behrens, Uggen, and Manza, "Ballot Manipulation and the 'Menace of Negro Domination,'" 596–98 (finding that "the racial composition of state prisons is firmly associated with the adoption of state felon disenfranchisement laws"); Jason Schall, "The Consistency of Felon Disenfranchisement with Citizenship Theory," *Harvard Black Letter Law Journal* 22 (2006): 53–93 at 58–59; Reuven Ziegler, "Legal Outlier, Again? U.S. Felon Suffrage: Comparative and International Human Rights Perspectives," *Boston University International Law Journal* 29 (2011): 197–266 at 217–18.

27. The relevant text reads: "[W]hen the right to vote at any election . . . is denied to any of the male inhabitants of such State, being twenty-one years of age, and citizens of the United

and Uggen have estimated that over 5 million individuals were formally disenfranchised during the 2004 elections in the United States, rising to nearly 6 million if jail and pretrial custody populations are included.[28] In Florida, nearly one in ten people of voting age—or about 827,000—are disenfranchised, a number likely to have been sufficient, under plausible assumptions about turnout rates and political preferences, to have changed the outcome of the 2000 presidential election.[29] Just as troubling, there is evidence that simply having contact with the criminal justice system exerts a strongly negative effect on voting, civic participation, and trust in government. This includes even relatively minor contact, such as having been arrested or questioned by the police.[30]

Felon disenfranchisement raises obvious and serious questions about the democratic legitimacy of criminal justice institutions. As I see it, the equal opportunity principle has a broad scope: it includes not just those who have completed their sentences, but also those currently serving out a sentence.[31] The equal opportunity principle holds that democratic law is distinguished from the mere exercise of power in that those subject to the law to have an equal voice in shaping it. Those serving out criminal sentences are paradigmatically people subject to the law. They are not exempted from the law's jurisdiction; they are not exiles, or put into a state of lawlessness, even temporarily. To the contrary, people serving out a criminal sentence are subjected to much more aggressive regulation and supervision than almost anyone else. In being stripped of equal

---

States, or in any way abridged, *except for participation in rebellion, or other crime*, the basis of representation therein shall be reduced in the proportion which the number of such male citizens shall bear to the whole number of male citizens twenty-one years of age in such State." The constitutionality of felon disenfranchisement was affirmed by the United States Supreme Court in *Richardson v Ramirez*, 418 U.S. 24 (1974).

28. Jeff Manza and Christopher Uggen, *Locked Out: Felon Disenfranchisement and American Democracy* (Oxford University Press 2006), 76.

29. Manza and Uggen, *Locked Out*, 78, 191–92.

30. Vesla M. Weaver and Amy E. Lerman, "Political Consequences of the Carceral State," *American Political Science Review* 104(4) (2010): 1–17; Lerman and Weaver, *Arresting Citizenship*, (University of Chicago Press 2014), ch. 6.

31. I follow Kleinig and Murtagh on this point: "Disenfranchising Felons," 227–32. Only Maine and Vermont permit currently incarcerated people to vote. Internationally, Canada, the Czech Republic, Denmark, Israel, Japan, and South Africa do so as well. See Marc Mauer, "Mass Incarceration and the Disappearing Voters," in *Invisible Punishment: The Collateral Consequences of Mass Imprisonment*, ed. Marc Mauer and Meda Chesney-Lind (The New Press 2002), 50–58.

opportunity for influence, one is in effect told: you are subject to the law, but are in no way its author. For such a person, the rule of law boils down to rule by others.

What would it take for the assertion of authority of this kind to be more than simply the exercise of power of some against others? At a minimum, it would require that those subject to it have an equal opportunity to be heard in public deliberations about how that power is exercised. Hence, laws restricting the ability of people convicted of crimes to participate in the political process erode the law's claim to legitimate authority.[32]

In contrast, Christopher Bennett has recently defended a limited form of felon disenfranchisement—applicable only to those guilty of the most serious offenses—on the ground that the state has a duty to dissociate itself from wrongful acts that violate the law.[33] On Bennett's view, it is at least permissible for the state to discharge its duty to dissociate from those who commit serious crimes by removing their voting rights. Bennett's argument for this claim is telling: he asserts that we have "no better grasp" on how the state can dissociate from criminals "than the grasp we have on the same question in the interpersonal case," which he interprets to require symbols of "distancing or withdrawal," for instance when someone refuses to shake another person's hand or to be in the same room with her.[34] In the context of the state, Bennett suggests that the parallel is to withdraw "partially or temporarily, the kind of special treatment that

---

32. For these reasons, in contrast to Sigler, I doubt that the value of condemning crime as a breach of civic trust can justify disenfranchisement, even while someone is being punished. See Sigler, "Defensible Disenfranchisement," *Iowa Law Review* 99 (2014): 1725–44. By the same token, I do not share Altman's judgment that it is "morally preposterous" to deny that a state may permissibly disenfranchise a genocidaire. The question is not whether someone may deserve to be excluded. The question is whether a democratic state may legitimately do so. See Andrew Altman, "Democratic Self-Determination and the Disenfranchisement of Felons," *Journal of Applied Philosophy* 22 (3) (2005): 263–73 at 268. The need to legitimate coercive state power also weighs against a democratic state's desire to impose a "normative standard of citizenship" by disenfranchising people who have wrongly attacked others. See William Bülow, "Felon Disenfranchisement and the Argument from Democratic Self-Determination," *Philosophia* 44 (2016): 759–74 at 772.

33. Christopher Bennett, "Penal Disenfranchisement," *Criminal Law & Philosophy* 10 (2016): 411–25.

34. Bennett, "Penal Disenfranchisement," 421. The example of refusing to shake hands or share a room occurs at page 420.

those in a political relationship can usually expect as members of that relationship."[35]

Does interpersonal morality require dissociating oneself from people who are guilty of quite serious crimes? I am doubtful. In many cases, it is just as, if not more, appropriate to respond to wrongdoing with engagement and dialogue rather than withdrawal and dissociation. Withdrawal and dissociation would seem to be most appropriate in cases where the future of the relationship is itself in question. Moreover, even if it would be appropriate for a private individual to withdraw and dissociate from someone who had committed a serious wrong, it is not obvious why we should regard the state as similarly situated. Short of those whom it puts to death, the state retains an ongoing relationship with all its members, including those guilty of quite serious crimes.[36] Finally, the state's standing to exclude, even temporarily, people from the democratic process on the supposition that their crimes reveal them to be hostile to democratic governance is rather dubious under conditions of serious background injustice. As Lippke notes, under such conditions, the more plausible inference may be that criminals are hostile to a system of governance that has routinely ignored their interests, rather than that they are hostile to democratic governance as such.[37]

Jean Hampton once defended a limited form of felon disenfranchisement on the ground that it contributes to an "expressive retributive response" that "negates [the] significance" of certain types of crime. She gave as examples violence against women, a racially motivated murder, and treason: crimes that are "destructive of the values and functioning of a democratic society."[38] Allowing such people to vote would be "no way to stand up for" democratic and egalitarian values; denying such people

---

35. Bennett, "Penal Disenfranchisement," 421. In a similar vein, Cholbi construes felon disenfranchisement as a form of symbolic banishment, although Cholbi is more critical of the practice than Bennett; see Cholbi, "A Felon's Right to Vote," 564. See also Gabriel Chin, "The New Civil Death: Rethinking Punishment in the Era of Mass Conviction," *University of Pennsylvania Law Review* 160 (2012): 1789–833.

36. See Martha Nussbaum, *Anger and Forgiveness: Resentment, Generosity, Justice* (Oxford University Press 2016), ch. 6; Erin Kelly, *Limits of Blame: Rethinking Punishment and Responsibility* (Harvard University Press, forthcoming); Corey Brettschneider, "The Rights of the Guilty: Punishment and Political Legitimacy," *Political Theory* 35(2) (2007): 175–99.

37. Richard Lippke, "The Disenfranchisement of Felons," *Law & Philosophy* 20 (2001): 553–80 at 578.

38. Hampton, "Punishment, Feminism, and Political Identity," 41–42.

the right to vote for some period of time would be an appropriate way, Hampton claimed, to vindicate those very values from attack. Unlike Bennett's account, Hampton's account has the virtue of being couched in expressly political values, and indeed egalitarian ones. But it is doubtful that Hampton is any more successful than Bennett in rationalizing the political exclusion of prisoners. After all, even if we accept her premise that we should engage in an "expressive retributive response" to crime, it is far from clear why we don't adequately discharge that duty by prosecuting, convicting, and incarcerating people. Why do we also have to take away their right to vote? Hampton claims that we must do so to "stand up for" democratic and egalitarian values, but that just appears to be so much ipse dixit; one might just as well think that we adequately stand up for those values through the trial process and imposition of punishment. Indeed, one might think that the very same value democratic and egalitarian values that Hampton appeals to show why no one, including criminals, may legitimately be stripped of the right to participate as an equal in the democratic process.[39]

Because criminal punishment represents such an intense use of state power over an individual, disenfranchisement is arguably *least* appropriate for those the state seeks to punish. In the previous chapter (Section 2.3), I argued that in cases of conflict, the criminal law should prioritize basic political values over norms of interpersonal morality. If anything, this point would seem to have special force in the context of political rights, which have a central place in our conception of basic social equality. Hence, I do not think that whatever reasons we may have to dissociate from wrongdoers in the interpersonal context should override our commitment to protecting universal rights of democratic participation as a matter of political morality.

Anti-subordination. The basic function of a system of punishment is to stabilize a broadly shared willingness to cooperate and play by the rules, not to terrorize people into compliance. From the point of view of anti-deference, those rules should promote the conditions of democratic equality, in which people are sufficiently protected in their basic rights and interests such that they can reasonably be expected to relate to each other as equals, rather than as superiors and subordinates. To ensure this kind of equality, it is not enough that one is not actively interfered

39. As the Supreme Court has held, with respect to the right to citizenship: *Trop v Dulles*, 356 U.S. 86 (1958).

with by others. As Pettit has emphasized, a choice is not fully free if it is made in the shadow of a threat, explicit or implicit, of interference should one's choices not align with someone else's preferences. Under such circumstances, they will not need to actually interfere in order to ensure that your choices reflect their preferences. Hence, one's choices must also be sufficiently, if not endlessly, robust, in the sense of protected against the most salient threats of interference with its exercise.

This line of reasoning suggests the following principle: the criminal law should seek to stabilize patterns of cooperation in a manner that is consistent with the equal status of each person relative to every other person. Institutions committed to the ideal of anti-deference could not approve the use of the criminal law, even to secure otherwise valuable aims, when doing so serves to further entrench objectionable patterns of status hierarchy. The effect of entrenched status hierarchy is that those on top will exercise undue power—sometimes veiled, sometimes explicit—over how others lead their lives along a range of important dimensions. Criminal justice in the United States has, to put it mildly, not always been very successful on this score.[40] From the common law's marital rape exception to the ongoing controversies surrounding abusive and discriminatory policing, American criminal justice has a long history of denying equal respect and concern to entire groups of people. Those who are subordinated are, in effect, told that they must show deference to others—masters, husbands, police—if they are to ensure the continued protection of their basic rights and interests.

The rise of retributivism in the waning decades of the twentieth-century was fueled, in part, by a critique of the condescending and discriminatory methods of rehabilitative justice. The anti-subordination principle preserves the core of this critique, while rejecting its retributivist trappings.[41] Indeterminate sentencing, in particular, vested extraordinary powers in public officials in the name of "rehabilitation," and critics were right to call attention to its abuses.[42] In my view, however, rather than appeal to pre-politically notions of desert and wrongdoing in punishment, the

---

40. See James Q Whitman, *Harsh Justice: Criminal Punishment and the Widening Divide between America and Europe* (Oxford University Press 2003).

41. See Garland, *The Culture of Control* (University of Chicago Press 2001), ch. 3.

42. Most famously, Marvin Frankel, *Criminal Sentences: Law without Order* (Hill & Wang 1973).

better response is to ensure that the exercise of that discretion conforms to principles of basic social equality.

Consider the aggressive use of stop-and-frisk policing, as practiced in many cities across North America.[43] This type of policy should be especially troubling to egalitarians. The free use of public space is a crucially important capability, and it should be hard to justify conduct that has the effect of terrorizing people in their use of it. It is particularly hard to justify, given that the brunt of the impact is concentrated on African-American and Hispanic men.[44] This is not simply a matter of being stopped; there is evidence that African Americans who are stopped and frisked are more likely to be met with "non-lethal force," such as slapping, grabbing, or being pushed into a wall or the ground, than similarly situated whites.[45] Consider in this context Forman's description of routine police raids of a high school in Washington, DC:

> [w]hen the police rushed onto our corner, our students were forced to "assume the position," with their legs spread, faces against the wall or squad car, and hands behind their heads. Then they were searched, with the officers feeling every inch of their bodies, turning backpacks and pockets inside out, leaving the sidewalks strewn with notebooks, broken pencils, lipstick, and combs. Not

43. I have in mind here the conjunction of two practices: police detaining individuals on a relatively low level of suspicion for questioning and/or a cursory search, as well as the use of a potential detainee's race as a non-individualized factor in deciding whether to effectuate such a stop. The practice of stop-and-frisk policing was validated in *Terry v Ohio*, 392 U.S. 1 (1968). Justice Douglas, dissenting in *Terry*, raised republican themes in warning of the dangers of granting the police an effectively unreviewable discretion to stop someone "whenever they do not like the cut of his jib." *Terry* at 39. In the Canadian context, see *R v Mann*, [2004] 3 S.C.R. 59; *R v Grant*, [2009] 2 S.C.R. 353.

44. Fagan et al., "Street Stops and Broken Windows Revisited: The Demography and Logic of Proactive Policing in a Safe and Changing City," in *Race, Ethnicity and Policing: New and Essential Readings*, ed. Stephen K. Rice and Michael D. White (NYU Press 2009); Ian Ayres and Jonathan Borowsky, "A Study of Racially Disparate Outcomes in the Los Angeles Police Department" (Report prepared for the ACLU of Southern California, October 2008, available at: https://www.aclusocal.org/en/racial-profiling-lapd-study-racially-disparate-outcomes-los-angeles-police-department) at 5–6. Arrest data tells a similar story; see Robert Brame et al., "Demographic Patterns of Cumulative Arrest Prevalence by Ages 18 and 23," *Crime & Delinquency* 60 (2014): 471–86 at 478 (finding that 49 percent of African-American men and 44 percent of Latino men will have been arrested at least once by age twenty-three).

45. Roland G. Fryer, "An Empirical Analysis of Racial Differences in Police Use of Force" (National Bureau of Economic Research: Working Paper 22399), 3–4.

> once, over the course of about ten searches, did the police recover anything illegal.[46]

From the point of view of anti-deference, the wide use of stop-and-frisk policies makes it reasonable for those targeted by such policies to infer that they are only free to use public space on terms set by others. Given the authoritarian and implicitly threatening context of many police interactions, the message is clear enough: you are not our equals, and you pass through here at our sufferance. It is hardly surprising, then, that studies have found a corrosive effect of aggressive stop-and-frisk policies on cooperation with and trust in police.[47]

There are unresolved empirical questions about whether aggressive stop-and-frisk policing of minorities contributes to lowering the crime rate.[48] Clearly, if aggressive stop-and-frisk does not reduce crime it would be hard to explain what would speak in favor of such a policy. Similarly, even if stop-and-frisk policing does reduce crime, the abusive and humiliating means by which such stops are often carried out are independently objectionable. So suppose that stop-and-frisk policing could be carried out in a respectful and nonabusive manner, and that doing so would lower crime rates. Moreover, suppose that it would lower crime rates in the very communities where access to central capability is deeply insecure, communities that in the United States tend to be predominantly African-American or Hispanic. Surely if that were established, that should weigh in favor of permitting the aggressive use of stop-and-frisk.

---

46. James Forman, *Locking Up Our Own: Crime and Punishment in Black America* (Farrar, Straus and Giroux 2017), 153–54.

47. Stephen Schulhofer, Tom Tyler, and Aziz Huq, "American Policing at a Crossroads: Unsustainable Policies and the Procedural Justice Alternative," *Journal of Criminal Law & Criminology* 101 (2011): 335–74, especially 345–49 (summarizing research finding that voluntary cooperation with authorities depends more strongly on perceived fairness than on fear of sanctions).

48. Aziz Huq summarizes the empirical literature on "stop, question and frisk" policies, concluding that it "remains largely predicated on a mere guess about the effect of intensive street stops on violent crime levels." "The Consequences of Disparate Policing: Evaluating Stop-and-Frisk as a Modality of Urban Policing," *Minnesota Law Review* 100 (2017): 2397–480 at 2421. Moreover, as Huq astutely notes, the important question is not whether stop-and-frisk policies reduces crime, but how this policy compares to other policing techniques that might be adopted instead, such as hot-spot policing. See also Franklin E. Zimring, *The City That Became Safe: New York's Lessons for Urban Crime and Its Control* (Oxford University Press 2012), 144–47.

I do not deny that if aggressive stop-and-frisk policing turns out to be more effective at reducing crime than feasible alternatives, this would be a powerful reason in favor of retaining the practice. However, the aim of anti-deference is not merely to protect access to central capability by reducing crime. It is to protect *effective* access to central capability—access on terms that reflect one's standing as an equal. Even if discriminatory policing does lower the crime rate, it would tend to have the effect of requiring those targeted by the policy to show deference to the police in order to be able to make use of public space. These individuals would effectively be regarded as a threat to be managed rather than as coequal citizens. This is inconsistent with the commitment to status equality that is at the heart of the political ideal of anti-deference.[49]

This argument is a qualified one. Since what is at issue here is the differential allocation of a burden in creating a public good, the views of those being asked to bear a heavier burden carry significant weight. If the targeted minority groups largely support stop-and-frisk policing—perhaps on the basis of the (potential) benefit it is alleged to produce—that would weaken the characterization of racial profiling as subordination. Even so, however, it might not render that characterization entirely inapt. It may be that the reason stop-and-frisk produces such benefits (again assuming, perhaps counterfactually, that it does) is because of past discrimination against the minority community. For example, higher rates of criminal offending in minority communities may be causally connected to social oppression by the very majority group that now seeks to impose higher costs on the minority group as a result of that higher rate of offending. If so, even if members of the oppressed group come to favor aggressive stop-and-frisk policing as the lesser of two evils, there might well still be reason to characterize the use of such policing as subordination. This is because its justification would rest on the assumption of an oppressive social relationship.[50]

The anti-subordination principle reflects the idea that criminal justice institutions are not reducible to a means for efficiently deterring and

---

49. See Huq, "The Consequences of Disparate Policing: Evaluating Stop-and-Frisk as a Modality of Urban Policing," sections I.C–D.

50. This argument is owed to Kasper Lippert-Rasmussen, "Racial Profiling versus Community," *Journal of Applied Philosophy* 23(2) (2006): 191–205. Lippert-Rasmussen's paper is a response to Mathias Risse and Richard Zeckhauser, "Racial Profiling," *Philosophy & Public Affairs* 32(2) (2004): 131–70. For Risse's reply, see "Racial Profiling: A Reply to Two Critics," *Criminal Justice Ethics* 26(1) (2007): 4–19.

preventing crime. The criminal law and its associated institutions are part of an overall ensemble of public institutions oriented toward fostering relations of democratic equality among their constituents. Crime is obviously dominating. But the criminal law should not itself be a source of domination. Public institutions committed to the political ideal of anti-deference could not approve efforts to prevent crime that operate by terrorizing people in the exercise of the basic prerogatives of civic membership. That would be to substitute public domination by officials for private domination by criminals.

Optimality. Equal political voice and the restriction on public humiliation operate as constraints on a criminal justice system. Denial of political equality, just like policies or actions that reinforce degrading status hierarchies, are *per se* inconsistent with the idea of a society of peers. However, while I have emphasized the connection between status equality and distributive justice—that one's standing as an equal depends upon sufficiently robust access to a range of central capabilities—the connection between those capabilities (housing, movement, employment, and so forth) and equal status is less direct, and more subject to trade-offs, albeit of a restricted kind. Because of the criminal law's distinctive reliance on harsh sanctions that themselves amount to serious invasions of central capability, there is a strong presumption against criminal punishment even in the face of noncompliance. I accept Pettit and Braithwaite's suggestion that, given the clear impact of criminal punishment on central capability, the burden of proof should lie squarely on proposals to employ criminal justice interventions.[51] That presumption is only defeated if imposing harsh sanctions on rule violators optimally promotes effective access to central capability for all, when compared to other feasible alternatives (including doing nothing.) Optimality thus has the following structure: because impairing a person's effective access to central capability is to impair an aspect of that person's status as an equal, it should in all cases be difficult to justify. Only the potential impairment of central capability for others is sufficiently weighty to defeat that presumption.

As I propose to understand it, this part of anti-deference is an aggregative standard, in that it aggregates the overall impact of a criminal justice

51. John Braithwaite and Philip Pettit, *Not Just Deserts: A Republican Theory of Criminal Justice* (Clarendon 1990) . See also Norval Morris, *Madness and the Criminal Law* (University of Chicago Press 1983).

intervention across both potential victims and potential criminals alike. It is in that respect situated within the consequentialist tradition of social theory. That said, the account is, strictly speaking, non-consequentialist in nature. That is because I start from a universal right to equal status, one that I do not attempt to defend on consequential grounds.

The literature comparing aggregative and non-aggregative approaches to social theory is expansive, and it is not my intention to enter that debate here. In brief, my reasons for preferring an aggregative approach have to do with the difficulties that non-aggregative theories tend to face in coming to grips with uncertainty and risk, both of which seem endemic to public policy generally; as well as with what I believe to be their unattractive implications in the context of the criminal justice policy specifically.

Consider Scanlon's suggestion to compare, in a strictly pairwise manner, the moral urgency of a person burdened by a decision to do A, as compared to the urgency of a person burdened by a decision to do B.[52] Comparing these claims in a pairwise manner restricts attention to the moral quality of the burdens imposed, rather than the number of people affected. For instance, Scanlon asks whether we ought to briefly stop a television broadcast watched by millions in order to disentangle someone who is suffering excruciating pain after having fallen into the broadcasting equipment. The urgency of rescuing the person who has fallen into the equipment is qualitatively more urgent that that of someone whose television program is interrupted, suggesting that we should effectuate the rescue, regardless of how many people are inconvenienced.

So far, so good. But consider what this non-aggregative approach would imply in the context of criminal justice. A person's claim to be protected from violent crime—murder or rape, for instance—is very urgent indeed. It is plainly more urgent than another person's claim not to be subject to observation by the authorities. After all, while you may find it annoying or intrusive if you are observed by a police officer on the street, that complaint is nevertheless much less urgent than that of someone who is seriously assaulted or raped. A strictly pairwise comparison of these claims would suggest that any amount of police observation would be acceptable if it prevents even one person from being victimized in that way.[53]

---

52. T.M. Scanlon, *What We Owe to Each Other* (Harvard University Press 1998), 235–36.

53. A plausible compromise position accommodates aggregation by discounting the marginal weight of each additional claim (perhaps asymptotically), implying that although the lesser complaints of *n* people might in some cases outweigh the greater complaint of one, it

This implication is unattractive. It makes it too easy to justify sweeping policies of mass surveillance and aggressive policing. Perhaps living in a police state would decrease the violent crime rate marginally, and perhaps the complaint of a victim of a violent crime is, when considered in a strictly pairwise comparison, more serious than the complaint of someone who has a police officer permanently stationed outside her front door. But I am not confident that we should conclude that it would be permissible, much less morally required, for the state to station a police officer outside everyone's home, even if doing so would decrease crime. It seems natural to regard the objection to mass surveillance as having something to do with the overall impact of those policies when replicated across a society generally.[54]

Of course, there are a great many ways in which we might aggregate claims. My preferred approach is a finitely weighted rule that prioritizes the claims of the worst off, with the priority represented along a dimension of relative weight rather than more categorically.[55] The upside of accommodating aggregation in this way is that it avoids the kinds of "cliffs" that result from threshold views such as leximin or sufficientarianism, which prohibit imposing trivial losses on people just below some welfare threshold, even when doing so would create substantial benefits to a large number of people, including those just above that same welfare threshold. However, the downside is the same as the upside: this form of prioritarian aggregation allows that a trivial benefit to the fabulously well-off, supposing there are enough of them, could in principle justify imposing quite a serious loss on someone who is significantly worse off.[56]

---

is not the case that two complaints of a given seriousness are counted as exactly twice as serious as one. This view is considered by Victor Tadros: see "Controlling Risk," in *Prevention and the Limits of the Criminal Law*, ed. Andrew Ashworth, Lucia Zedner, and Patrick Tomlin (Oxford University Press 2013), 133–55.

54. This line of objection particularizes a critique that Barbara Fried, among others, has raised in a more general way to non-consequentialist moral theory; see "What *Does* Matter? The Case for Killing the Trolley Problem (or Letting It Die)," *Philosophical Quarterly* 62(248) (2012): 505–29 especially 512. That said, it addresses only one type of non-aggregative view; there are many others, which may not be damaged by the kind of concern I raise in the text. Hence, the line of thought given here is, at best, merely suggestive.

55. For a thorough overview of the literature, and defense of prioritarianism, see Mathew Adler, *Well-Being and Fair Distribution: Beyond Cost-Benefit Analysis* (Oxford University Press 2011).

56. For discussion of combining the appealing concern for the worst off in leximin with the appealing concern for social welfare in more thoroughly aggregative views, see Marc

On balance, the advantages of avoiding ad hoc policy cliffs strike me as fairly substantial, while the downside risks of finitely weighted prioritarian aggregation seem manageable. The weight assigned to the claims of the worst off can be adjusted so as to strike the most appealing set of trade-offs for the most probable sorts of cases. Perhaps truly intolerable outcomes can be ruled out of the prioritarian calculus by assigning an appropriately stringent weight to the claims of the worst off, or by acknowledging some deontologically grounded constraint. For instance: one might restrict the range of possible sentences available to a sentencing court by appeal to rights against being treated in certain ways. Capital punishment, torture, life imprisonment without the possibility of parole, and long periods of solitary confinement might simply be ruled out from the outset. Consequently, a finitely weighted prioritarian approach can be brought arbitrarily close to a leximin distributive principle without the need to draw a bright line between people just below and just above some threshold of moral concern.

The optimality principle has two implications for the criminal law that are worth noting explicitly. First, it is inconsistent with most expressivist theories of punishment. Consider, for instance, Husak's claim that, far from being the law of last resort, the criminal law should in some cases be the law of *first* resort. This is because, according to Husak, the criminal law is the uniquely appropriate means for publicly condemning wrongdoing.[57] What appears to be decisive for Husak, as well as others who have defended expressivist theories of punishment, from Nozick to Hampton to Brudner, is the thought that there is an independent and non-derivative reason for valuing the expressive condemnation of criminal acts. On this view, the expressive condemnation of wrongdoing has intrinsic value, regardless of whether or not punishment in fact contributes to protecting people's basic interests. It is a way of respecting or vindicating a person's rights, regardless of whether it also protects her interests.

Fleurbaey, Bertil Tungodden, and Peter Vallentyne, "On the Possibility of Nonaggregative Priority for the Worst Off," *Social Philosophy and Policy* 26(1) (2008): 258–85.

57. Doug Husak, "The Criminal Law as Last Resort," *Oxford Journal of Legal Studies*, 24 (2) (2004): 207–35 at 220–27. See also Jean Hampton, "Punishment, Feminism, and Political Identity: A Case Study in the Expressive Meaning of Law," *Canadian Journal of Law & Jurisprudence* 11(1) (1998): 23–45 at 36–37; Joshua Kleinfeld, "Reconstructivism: The Place of the Criminal Law in Ethical Life," *Harvard Law Review* 129(6) (2016): 1485–565.

Economizing on punishment should lead us to reject this argument. To rely on criminal punishment solely to send a message is tantamount to locking up some people in order to make other people *feel* safer, even when doing so does not make them *actually* safer. People's subjective experiences are certainly important, but it is hard to see how they could be sufficiently important to justify imposing such serious costs on others. By punishing purely to send a message, public institutions would be stripping some people of the basic prerogatives of equal civic membership without materially advancing the security of those prerogatives for others.[58]

Perhaps expressing condemnation through punishment can be cashed out consequentially, in terms of inducing greater levels of cooperation in the future. As I noted in Chapter 2, there is a fair amount of evidence suggesting that cooperation is enhanced by sanctioning defectors. However, this account assigns a derivative rather than intrinsic value to expressive punishment. It is derived from the significance of public condemnation of wrongdoing to making it the case that one's rights and interests are adequately protected, not from an alleged intrinsic value in expressing condemnation through punishment. When regarded in this light, expressive condemnation is a permissible basis for imposing criminal sanctions only because, and insofar as, sanctions of that kind are the optimal means of sustaining cooperation with institutions and social rules that are worthy of our support. Expressive condemnation of wrongdoing is not, in other words, on its own a sufficient basis for imposing criminal sanctions.

The second implication of optimality concerns abolitionism about the criminal law. Philosophical abolitionism is a minority view, and for good reason.[59] I noted in Chapter 2 that punishment is an important

58. For similar observations, see my "Equality, Assurance and Criminalization," *Canadian Journal of Law & Jurisprudence* 27(1) (2014): 5–26; Benjamin Ewing, "The Political Legitimacy of Retribution: Two Reasons for Skepticism," *Law & Philosophy* 34 (2014): 369–96; Victor Tadros, "Criminalization and Regulation," in *The Boundaries of the Criminal Law*, ed. R.A. Duff, Lindsay Farmer, S.E. Marshall, Massimo Renzo, and Victor Tadros (Oxford University Press 2011): 163–90; Malcolm Thorburn, "Constitutionalism and the Limits of the Criminal Law," in *The Structures of the Criminal Law*, ed. R.A. Duff et al., (Oxford University Press 2011), 96; and Nathan Hanna, "Say What? A Critique of Expressive Retributivism," *Law & Philosophy* 27(2) (2008): 123–50. Here, I am arguing that expressive condemnation is not sufficient to justify the criminal law. For reasons given in Chapter 5, I also believe that it is not necessary.

59. For a recent defense, see David Boonin, *The Problem of Punishment* (Cambridge University Press 2008).

element in the evolution of cooperation. This suggests that there may be conditions when punishment is not only permissible, but morally required. Punishment is morally obligatory if it is a necessary step in stabilizing the patterns of social cooperation required of just societies. The rule of law, once established, may counsel reducing reliance on punishment. But it may take some degree of willingness to punish rule-violators to get the rule of law off the ground. Punishment may similarly be required if social conditions are such that there is no other feasible way of protecting people from serious violence, as may be the case in contexts of failed states and extreme civil unrest. These judgments are notoriously uncertain. But that is the point: the justifiability of a system of punishment in a given social context is highly contingent, and seems unlikely to be appropriate for categorical armchair judgments one way or the other.

That said, there is a kernel of truth to abolitionism. There might be reason to believe that much, even most, criminal punishment might not be justifiable *here and now*—that is, in the context of institutionally dense administrative states. It might be feasible for states of this kind to secure universal and effective access to central capability without relying, or relying nearly as much, on criminal justice interventions. These kinds of states have the developed legal, political, and regulatory institutions that make it possible for the state to respond to crime in increasingly less destructive ways, in part by intervening earlier (e.g., through universal education, early childhood education and the like), in part through more effective regulation (e.g., of access to weapons and alcohol), and in part through more sophisticated forms of ex post response to crime (e.g., through mental health counseling and treatment, drug courts, restorative justice initiatives, and the like.[60]) Even when outright abolition isn't on the table, the institutional capacity of the administrative state nevertheless suggests that punishment should often be relied upon only

60. See Mark W. Lipsey and Francis T. Cullen, "The Effectiveness of Correctional Rehabilitation: A Review of Systematic Reviews," *Annual Review of Law & Social Science* 2007 (3): 297–320 at 314 (reviewing meta-analyses of rehabilitation in correctional settings and finding that "rehabilitation treatment is capable of reducing the re-offense rate of convicted offenders and that it has greater capability for doing so than correctional sanctions"); Francis T. Cullen and Cheryl Lero Jonson, "Rehabilitation and Treatment Programs," in *Crime and Public Policy*, ed. James Q. Wilson and Joan Petersilia (Oxford University Press 2011), 293–344.

in narrowly defined contexts and as a backup once other means have failed.[61] Whether modern administrative states could effectively displace all, or most, of the work currently done by criminal justice institutions is obviously an open empirical question. However, if it proves to be possible to protect effective access to central capability through non-punitive means, then the best thing to do about the criminal law might be to get rid of it.

Inclusive aggregation. I have proposed evaluating criminal justice interventions from the point of view of prioritarian aggregation. The decision to rely on the criminal law to enforce a given legal norm should be evaluated in terms of its overall impact on effective access to central capability, with priority for the interests of those whose access to those capabilities is least secure. This principle is grounded in an interpretation of the ideal of a society of equals as one in which each person may access the basic prerogatives of civic membership on terms befitting a peer. This ideal supports a qualification on the optimality principle, namely that in assessing the impact of a criminal justice intervention, public institutions generally should not consider it easier to justify invading someone's capabilities on the ground that he has committed a crime, no matter how serious. The method of aggregation should in this sense be inclusive.

Inclusive aggregation is a controversial principle, largely because it seems to marginalize the moral significance of guilt to punishment.[62] To be clear, inclusive aggregation is a requirement of equal *consideration*, not of equal *treatment*. It does not rule out criminal punishment; it only rules

61. For an excellent discussion of the narrow role of coercive institutions in a broader panoply of institutions devoted to promoting rule compliance, see Mark Kleiman, *When Brute Force Fails: How to Have Less Crime and Less Punishment* (Princeton University Press 2009).

62. Among those who reject it are Mitch Berman, "Punishment and Justification," *Ethics* 118 (2008): 258–90; Boonin, *The Problem of Punishment*, 48; Joel Feinberg, *Harm to Others: The Moral Limits of the Criminal Law* (Oxford University Press 1984), 189; and Daniel Farrell, "Deterrence and the Just Distribution of Harm," *Social Philosophy and Policy* 12(2) (1995): 220–40 at 224. Robert Nozick once characterized this view as "bizarre." *Anarchy, State & Utopia* (Basic Books 1974), 62. Others have found it less bizarre: see Sharon Dolovich, "Legitimate Punishment in Liberal Democracy," *Buffalo Criminal Law Review* 7 (2004): 307–442, especially 361–63, 368; and David Hoekema, "The Right to Punish, and the Right to Be Punished," in *John Rawls' Theory of Social Justice*, ed. H Gene Blocker and Elizabeth Smith (Ohio University Press 1980): 239–69 at 252. Dolovich and Hoekema draw the connection between inclusive aggregation and Rawls more explicitly, and in a more general way, than I do here. Although he doesn't use this terminology, John F. Pfaff appears to endorse a similar principle: see *Locked In* (Basic Books 2017), 179–80.

out discounting the interests of potential criminals in deciding how a legal rule is to be enforced. Society must surely enforce its rules, but how those rules are justifiably enforced should be assessed against the egalitarian concern to protect *each* person's status as an equal.

The argument for inclusive aggregation starts with the egalitarian principle that criminals do not forfeit their entitlement to equal respect and concern by virtue of having committed a crime, no matter how serious. But if so, then it follows that public institutions may not permissibly discount A's interests relative to B's because it turns out that A has committed a crime whereas B has not.[63] By deeming a guilty person's interests as of lesser worth than the claims of others, public institutions would in effect be deeming that person to be of lesser worth than those others. Hence, the egalitarian principle that requires public institutions to refrain from stigmatizing those who have committed crimes as being of lesser worth also requires them to consider equally the interests of potential criminals and victims alike in deliberations about criminal justice policy.[64]

But why should we accept the egalitarian principle that criminals do not forfeit their equal status by virtue of having committed a crime? Here, I can do no better than refer to Sharon Dolovich's observation that it would be too unrealistic to assume that even well-meaning individuals with a developed sense of justice would not sometimes fail to act appropriately. As Dolovich notes, temptations and pressures to commit criminal acts arise from a wide variety of natural and social contingencies, many of them beyond any individual's control and, moreover, contingencies to which even the best of us might well be subject. To the degree that, as Dolovich puts it, we cannot reasonably be confident that we cannot *always* avoid temptation, anger, impulsivity, desperation, and other motives for crime, it would seem reasonable to endorse the egalitarian premise that those

63. Consider the "importation model" accepted, according to Thomas Ugelvik, as the official policy of Norwegian prisons: the institutions of the welfare state, from schools to libraries to the healthcare system are imported into the prison such that a prisoner's status is maintained while in custody. Prisoners are "acknowledged as citizens with important citizen's rights, even when they are serving a custodial sentence. The prison is part of the society around it." Ugelvik, "Prisons as Welfare Institutions?," 394.

64. Compare Peter Ramsay's democratic account: "A Democratic Theory of Imprisonment," in *Democratic Theory and Mass Incarceration*, ed. Albert Dzur, Ian Loader, and Richard Sparks (Oxford University Press 2016), 85–113. The account I sketch is less Hegelian than Ramsay's, but is similarly based on a conception of political equality as the basic democratic commitment.

who commit crimes should not be treated as a class apart, but simply as what they are: ordinary, fallible people.[65]

It is perhaps worth recalling that crime is not simply the natural result of millions of independent choices by abstract and unencumbered individuals. Public institutions not only define when and how individuals will be sanctioned for violating a given legal rule, but they also contribute to defining the social circumstances under which individuals perceive the options that are realistically open to them, choose their actions, and plan their lives. Insofar as there are social determinants of crime over which public institutions exercise influence—education level, socioeconomic status, employment, and so forth—there is reason to view responsibility for crime as broadly shared rather than purely as a matter of individual fault. Given our shared decisions about how to shape those institutions, those who foreseeably go on to commit crimes can hardly be treated as having made an entirely unencumbered choice to exclude themselves from the political community, a decision for which they alone bear the blame. Egalitarians can hardly disavow collective responsibility for the bad things people do if they do them because of the state's failure to sustain the conditions of free and equal membership.[66]

Taken together, these two thoughts—the ubiquity of crime, and shared responsibility for the environment determining its incidence—support the egalitarian principle, and suggest that public institutions should not discount the interests of the guilty in determining how best to protect people from crime.[67] The egalitarianism implicit in the egalitarian principle is Rawlsian in this sense: just as for Rawlsians there is "no prejusticially given distributive share deserved by the intelligent and able that it is the job of our system of distributive justice to hand out," I am suggesting that there is also "no prejusticially given suffering

---

65. Dolovich, "Legitimate Punishment in Liberal Democracy," 364–78.

66. See Tommie Shelby, "Justice, Deviance and the Dark Ghetto," *Philosophy and Public Affairs* 35(2) (Spring 2007): 126–60 at 152; Jeffrie Murphy, "Marxism and Retribution," *Philosophy and Public Affairs* 2(3) (Spring 1973): 217–43; Matt Matravers, *Justice and Punishment* (Oxford University Press 2000), 265–67; Kelly, *Limits of Blame*.

67. For contrasting views, see Christopher Wellman, "The Rights Forfeiture Theory of Punishment," *Ethics* 122(2) (2012): 371–93 (arguing that it is permissible to punish people who have committed crimes regardless of whether doing so secures any valuable public purpose); Hampton, "Punishment, Feminism, and Political Identity," 43 (arguing that because we should favor the interests of the innocent over the guilty, "we have to choose a criminal code that is committed to retribution").

that is deserved by the criminal offender that it is the job of our system of retributive justice to ensure he gets."[68] Rather, in designing public institutions—including criminal justice institutions—each person is entitled to equal respect and concern, abstracting from who in particular has turned out to have committed a crime and who has turned to have suffered an injury.

It is certainly true that a principle of inclusive aggregation gives rather less significance to individual responsibility in the evaluation of criminal justice policy than some would like. However, for reasons that I explore more fully in Chapter 7, it would be unwarranted to conclude that inclusive aggregation fails to respect people's choices. The argument I have given for inclusive aggregation does not depend upon the supposition that people who commit crimes do not voluntarily choose to act as they do, nor have I claimed that a variety of reactive attitudes—perhaps including resentment and blame—might not sometimes be appropriately oriented at those who victimize others.[69] Rather than denying that people are responsible for what they do, inclusive aggregation reflects the thought that giving in to the temptation to crime is an inevitable risk of shared social life that public institutions should strive to mitigate in ways that reflect our shared stake in how each other's lives go.

What does this mean concretely? Consider the following case. President Obama once proposed providing universal access to early childhood education across the United States. The proposal was supported by a number of decades-long longitudinal studies that indicated that providing early childhood education would reduce future criminal offending, particularly

---

68. Matt Matravers, "Mad, Bad or Faulty? Desert in Distributive and Retributive Justice," in *Responsibility and Distributive Justice*, ed. C. Knight and Z. Stemplowski (Oxford University Press 2011), 136–51 at 150. See also Matravers, "Political Theory and the Criminal Law," in *Philosophical Foundations of Criminal Law*, ed. R.A. Duff and Stuart P. Green (Oxford University Press 2011), 81.

69. There are limits to inclusive aggregation. For instance, it may permit favoring the interests of victims (or potential victims) as a tiebreaker, that is in cases when an equivalent harm must fall on one side or the other. Under those conditions, it does not seem unfair to ask those who create a situation of danger to bear the costs of meliorating that risk. My thanks to David Enoch and Re'em Segev for a very helpful conversation on this point. The case of people who, in some consistent way, cannot be relied upon to accept basic reciprocity—sociopaths, for instance—raises another qualification for inclusive aggregation. For discussion of this issue, see Dolovich, "Legitimate Punishment in Liberal Democracy," 361–62.

among the disadvantaged.[70] Although Obama's proposal focused on early childhood education, there is evidence that improving the quality of education later in life also has a significant negative effect of criminal offending.[71] Similar results have been reported with summer employment for unemployed youth: even relatively low intensity ex ante treatment can have a significant and long-term negative impact on future crime.[72] Obama's proposal presented the following choice: expend resources on a prosocial intervention now, or do nothing and wait for those children to grow up and commit crimes, and then punish them for doing so at that point. In short: *schools, now* or *prisons, later.*

How should we approach this choice? In particular, how should we think about the interests of the children who, absent early childhood education, will go on to commit crimes later in life and are subsequently punished for doing so? If we are entitled to discount the interests of those who commit crimes, then their interests should be excluded from deliberation about whether to support universal early childhood education. While it is true that these children will be treated more harshly by *prisons, later* than under *schools, now*, their interests turn out to be less worthy of protection precisely because of the crimes they will have committed. Hence, as far as their interests are concerned, we are entitled to regard the choice between *schools, now* or *prisons, later* as one of moral indifference.

Inclusive aggregation suggests, in contrast, that the interests of the children who, absent the intervention, will go on to commit crimes and

70. J. Heckman, S, Hyeok Moon, R. Pinto, P. Savelyev, and A. Yavitz, "The Rate of Return to the High/Scope Perry Preschool Program," *Journal of Economics* 94(1–2) (2009): 114–28; C. Belfield, M. Nores, S. Barnett, and L. Schweinhart, "The High/Scope Perry Preschool Program: Cost-Benefit Analysis Using Data from the Age-40 Followup," *Journal of Human Resources* 41(1) (Winter 2006): 162–90. President Obama's statement in support of expanding access to early childhood education can be found here: https://www.whitehouse.gov/the-press-office/2013/02/13/fact-sheet-president-obama-s-plan-early-education-all-americans.

71. D. Deming, "Better Schools, Less Crime?," *Quarterly Journal of Economics* 125 (2011): 2063–115 at 2065 (finding that "a treatment of between 1 and 4 years of enrollment in a higher quality public school led to large and persistent reductions in young adult criminal activity"); L. Lochner and E. Moretti, "The Effect of Education on Crime: Evidence from Prison Inmates, Arrests, and Self-Reports," *American Economic Review* 94(1) (2004): 155–89.

72. Sara Heller, "Summer Jobs Reduce Violence among Disadvantaged Youth," *Science* 346(6214) (December 5, 2014): 1219–23. Heller found that even a modest level of part-time employment led to a significant, and long term, decline in violent offending. Young people in the treatment groups had a decrease in violent crime arrests of 43 percent relative to those in the control group (1220). Moreover, the decrease in violent crime arrests persisted well after the end of the employment period (1221).

subsequently enter the criminal justice system have a claim of justice to *schools, now* over *prisons, later.* That policy better respects their status as equals—their entitlement to the protection of their central capabilities—than one that waits for them to commit crimes and then punishes them for doing so. It insists that even those who are (or will be) guilty of criminal acts are entitled to equal consideration in the design of public institutions.[73]

3.4 On Guilt and Innocence

My aim in this chapter has been to provide one example of how a fully political standard of justification for the criminal law could be spelled out. Beyond noting how it draws from widely shared ideals about democratic equality, I have not sought to provide a foundational defense of anti-deference. However, one family of concerns is so prevalent that it merits comment even in this context. As I have noted, my approach is aggregative in that it evaluates outcomes according to the degree to which they protect effective access to central capabilities, without discounting the interests of the guilty vis-à-vis those of the innocent. However, even restricted aggregation inevitably opens the door to worries about sacrificing the innocent at the altar of the greater good. Under this heading, one might worry that however much it values the interests of the guilty, the approach I have sketched does not take sufficiently seriously the interests of the *innocent.*

The perennial selling point for retributivism is the clarity with which it grounds the claim that only the guilty may be punished. The appeal of this "negative" retributive claim appears substantially broader and deeper than the more controversial "positive" retributive claim that the guilty are to be punished. An approach to the criminal law that sees the criminal law as an instrument for promoting social welfare may appear to be at odds

---

73. If the state knows that, absent treatment T, you will eventually end up committing crime C, making you liable to punishment P, it then faces a choice between the social cost of providing T as opposed to the social cost of C and the consequent punishment P. Since, by hypothesis, T is less destructive of effective access to central capability than P, it follows trivially that $T < (P + C)$. But that inequality does not follow if we are entitled to apply a discount factor, d, to P on account of your guilt in committing C; in that case, possibly $T \geq [(d)(P) + C]$. If, as some have proposed, the guilty have no claim against proportionate punishment ($d = 0$), then the question reduces simply to whether the social cost of prevention is greater than the social cost of crime.

with the negative principle. From the political trials of the Star Chamber to the criminalization of sodomy, the criminal law has often been used to oppress people who do not fit into this or that ideal of a just society.[74] My embrace of an even loosely aggregative approach to criminal justice is subject to the same worry. It might seem to suggest that we are entitled to punish whomsoever we wish, so long as doing so achieves some overarching social good, such as maximally protecting effective access to central capability. Yet it is a fixed judgment that the innocent should not be punished, even in the name of an otherwise noble social ideal. A focus on individual moral fault, whatever else its defects, at least ensures that the criminal law cannot be turned into a general purpose means for molding people and institutions to conform to some overarching vision of the good society.

The rights of the innocent are, obviously, of central moral importance. However, I suspect that these rights provide a rather less powerful objection to consequentialist approaches to punishment than is sometimes supposed. The worry about punishing the innocent might be understood in at least four different senses. First, it might be understood in terms of systematically punishing people who have not violated any determinate legal rule. Second, it might be understood in terms of opportunistically punishing people who have not violated a legal rule. Third, it might be understood in terms of punishing people who have not engaged in morally wrongful conduct. Finally, it might be understood in terms of punishing people who committed a wrong, but were not culpable in doing so—that is, as a worry about strict liability. I address each of these versions in turn.

First, the principle might be understood in a minimal, positivist sense: people ought not be criminally punished unless they engage in conduct that violates some legal rule fixed in advance. Punishing the innocent is objectionable because it amounts to punishing people who have not violated some determinate legal rule.

A public law conception straightforwardly accommodates this thought. On a public law conception, the criminal law is a generically coercive rule-enforcing institution, one that operates by threatening to impose costs on noncompliance with a legal rule. This function would be entirely undermined if sanctions were systematically imposed without regard to whether someone had complied with the rule. The use of ex post

---

74. For instance, in slave-owning societies: see Michael Hindus, *Prison and Plantation: Crime, Justice, and Authority in Massachusetts and South Carolina, 1767–1878* (University of North Carolina Press 1980).

punishment to secure legitimate expectations must be sensitive to responsibility, in the sense of only punishing the guilty, if it is to provide the assurance that I have argued is its basic function.[75] The significance of guilt, in this respect, is not contingent upon the content of the law that is putatively being enforced. Even if it is a bad law, there is value in ensuring that it is only applied to people who actually flout its requirements. Suppose the law prohibits helping an elderly person cross the street. It would be wrong to punish someone who deliberately flouted the law, but it would be a further and different wrong to punish someone who wasn't even doing *that*. Applying an unjust law unfaithfully makes it impossible to predict when you will be liable to punishment, whereas if it is applied faithfully, at least you can know when you will and will not be liable.

A more difficult question concerns the *opportunistic* punishment of people who did not violate some legal rule—if punishing *this* person on *this* occasion might reasonably be expected to yield a better outcome than not, regardless of whether he actually broke the law. It seems that what we want is not a contingent explanation about how a given case fits into an overall pattern, but one that is grounded in the wrong done in *this individual case*. The examples that motivate this thought typically involve officials acting outside the law (hanging the innocent man to quiet the mob, etc.) This suggests that the underlying question concerns the moral status of opportunistic punishment, i.e. punishment that would secure a substantial benefit even though not authorized by law. Suppose, for instance, that someone acts in a morally reprehensible manner, but in a way that law does not actually prohibit. Perhaps he ought to have foreseen that his action would harm another, but if the law does not require him to have foreseen it, then it would be objectionable for an official to nevertheless punish him for that failure. What seems objectionable about it is that the official acts opportunistically, in that the official acts outside the law, albeit to secure a desirable outcome.

Can anti-deference explain what's wrong with opportunism by public officials? I think it can. When an official overrides the law in this way, she treats that law as less than fully authoritative: she treats it as open to renegotiation on a case-by-case basis in a way that, by hypothesis, the law itself does not contemplate. But that seems antidemocratic. When a public official decides to make an exception to the law as written, or to exceed the

75. See Matravers, "Political Theory and the Criminal Law," 80.

powers that the law grants her, she to that extent denies others equal opportunity for influence over the law. She claims for herself the authority to determine whether the law should be L, or L^+ (i.e., L plus the opportunistic exception she wishes to make). It is not that L^+ is necessarily a worse law than L; for all we know, L^+ might be morally better than L. It might be the rule that the legislature should have endorsed, as opposed to the one it did endorse. The problem is that L^+ is not *public* law.[76] In taking it upon herself to apply L^+ instead of L, the official usurps the entitlement of each person subject to the law to have an equal opportunity for influence over the law. Instead, the official unilaterally decides to replace L with L^+. This is a wrong that applies to each instance in which an official prioritizes her private judgment over democratically legitimate law. Notably, it is not contingent upon an estimate of whether allowing occasional deviations will or will not maximize the good. It is a concern about the integrity of the law that is not reducible to the law's substantive moral value.[77]

It could, of course, be the case that the law itself acknowledges an exception, requiring an official to apply L, but allowing her to apply L^+ under certain circumstances. An official who applies L^+ under those circumstances would not be acting opportunistically, since her doing so would be contemplated under public law. She would only be acting opportunistically if she were to apply L^+ under circumstances in which she is not legally authorized to do so. But whether the law should countenance such an exception is a question of the law's substantive moral value, rather than one of opportunism. No account of criminal law can prevent legislatures from enacting flawed laws; and, more to the point, the account I suggest provides a substantive criterion for evaluating whether a given law *is* flawed.[78]

Consider in this context the landmark Canadian case, *Frey v Fedoruk*.[79] Frey was caught trespassing and "peeping" at a woman while she was at home. As the criminal code at the time did not prohibit peeping, Frey was

---

76. I am presuming that L *is* legitimate public law. If it is not, then there is a deeper problem than opportunism in enforcement.

77. This argument draws from Kolodny, "Rule over None II." It also has some parallels to David Estlund's treatment of the "Nuremburg defense," that is, that one should be excused from wrongdoing because one was simply following orders. See "On Following Orders in an Unjust War," *Journal of Political Philosophy* 15(2) (2007): 213–34 at 228–29.

78. For a sophisticated treatment of exceptions in the law, see Luis Duarte D'Alemeida, *Allowing for Exceptions: A Theory of Defences and Defeasibility in Law* (Oxford University Press 2015).

79. [1950] SCR 517.

charged with breach of the Queen's peace. True, nothing in the written law specifically prohibited Frey from peeping, but his actions would have been widely condemned in his community as morally odious. What objection could there be to making an exception to the law as written by prosecuting Frey? Citing concerns about undue discretion and uncertainty in the criminal law, the Supreme Court of Canada concluded that wrongfulness alone is not sufficient to empower the state to prosecute. The court insisted—correctly, in my view—that the exercise of the state's criminal law power must be constrained by the rule of law, rather than rest solely on an official's judgment, however plausible, about the morality of someone's conduct. The structure of *Frey v Fedoruk* parallels that of the hoary old chestnut about hanging an innocent man in order to still the baying mob: an accused who is known to be innocent in law, but who finds himself in circumstances where making an exception and punishing him might reasonably be thought to be of moral value. The answer to the chestnut parallels the answer in *Frey*: punishment beyond what the law authorizes is antidemocratic and contrary to a system of public law.

To be sure, the wrongfulness of denying others an equal opportunity for influence is not an all-things-considered statement about what officials must always do. Clearly, it would be wrong to frame an innocent man of murder. But it is not so clear that an official ought inevitably to cleave to her publicly defined duties, come what may. My claim is not that it is always the case that an official must do her legal duty. When an official must do her duty, and when she permissibly departs from it, is a challenging question, and probably not amenable to categorical resolution. I do not aim to contribute to resolving that question here. My aim, rather, is to explain, from within the parameters of anti-deference, why there is a unique kind of wrong that inheres in each case in which an official substitutes her private judgment for democratically legitimate law and, in that sense, punishes the innocent. This argument explains why the opportunistic punishment of someone who has not broken the law is objectionable, even apart from its consequences: doing so robs each person subject to the law of an equal say over the law that applies to him.[80]

The third version of the punishment of the innocent objection rests on a moralized interpretation of what it means for innocent people to be punished: you are innocent if what you did was not *morally* wrong. This principle, in turn, can be given one of two glosses. The first construes moral

80. I am indebted to Ekow Yankah for helpful discussion of these points.

wrongfulness as a matter of the actus reus of the crime: what you did was morally wrong if it would have wrong even if positive law did not prohibit it. In other words, criminal punishment is only permissible with respect to *mala in se* crimes. This is an implausibly demanding conception of what it means to punish the innocent. Public institutions bring about a significant change in the moral landscape. They render it permissible to do things to people that it would not otherwise be permissible to do (e.g., take their property in the form of taxes), and to require people to do things that they would not otherwise be required to do (e.g., settle disputes through the justice system). If this is true, then it follows that pre-politically wrongfulness cannot be a per se constraint on the operation of public institutions. So although anti-deference does not restrict punishment to people who commit pre-politically wrongs, that is a feature, not a bug.[81]

Finally, and more plausibly, one might interpret moral wrongfulness in mens rea terms: what you did was morally wrong if you broke the law, and did so with a suitable degree of awareness about the nature of your conduct. Hence, you are "morally" innocent if you lacked mens rea with respect to one or more of the actus reus elements of the crime. The concern about protecting the innocent, on this interpretation, boils down to a concern about the use of strict liability in the criminal law, a trend that is often associated with the growth of the administrative state.

There is indeed reason to be concerned about the overuse of strict liability in the criminal law. Yet this concern is consistent with the framework of anti-deference. After all, by restricting criminal sanctions to knowing and voluntary violations, public institutions allow people to control their exposure to criminal sanctions. In effect, they insure people against one kind of harm (harms emanating from the state) by insuring others against a different kind of harm (harms emanating from *them*). It seems plausible to regard control over whether one will be punished as part of what it means to have effective access to central capability. Thus, the value of providing people with the ability to control when the state will invade those capabilities by providing them with a fair opportunity to comply with the law's demands is readily accommodated within the perspective of anti-deference.[82]

---

81. I defend this point more fully in Chapter 6.

82. See H.L.A. Hart, "Legal Responsibility and Excuses," collected in H.L.A. Hart, *Punishment and Responsibility: Essays in the Philosophy of Law*, 2nd ed. (Oxford University Press 2008); Rawls, *A Theory of Justice*, 241; Erin Kelly, "Criminal Justice without Retribution," *Journal*

Perhaps, however, the worry about punishing the morally innocent—in the sense of a prohibition on strict liability—is meant to be of a more categorical nature than a commitment to anti-deference is capable of supporting. Fair opportunity finds support from within the perspective of anti-deference, but by the same token it finds its limits there too. Rawls once asked us to suppose that

> Members of rival sects are collecting weapons and forming armed bands in preparation for civil strife. Confronted with this situation, the government may enact a statute forbidding the possession of firearms . . . And the law may hold that sufficient evidence for conviction is that the weapons are found in the defendant's house or property, unless he can establish that they were put there by another. Except for this proviso, the absence of intent and knowledge of possession, and conformity to reasonable standards of care, are declared irrelevant.[83]

In such a scenario, Rawls concluded, waiving the fair opportunity principle—as the contemplated strict liability statute does—would nevertheless be justified, as "the risks to their liberty on any other course would be worse." Some have taken Rawls to task for this passage. Thomas Pogge, for instance, has argued that similar reasoning would open the door to strict liability as a way of dealing with drunk drivers, drug runners, rapists, and others.[84]

On this point, I am inclined to think that we should side with Rawls. After all, the imagined case is one in which there is very good reason to think that people cannot effectively be protected from serious victimization short of some kind of strict liability regime. It is, in other words, a case in which the threat to liberty from victimization by third parties clearly outweighs the threat to liberty from abrogating the fair opportunity principle by, in essence, shifting the burden of proof onto an accused

---

of Philosophy 106(8) (2009): 440–62 at 449–51. For a critique of the fair opportunity principle, see Alan Brudner, *Punishment and Freedom: A Liberal Theory of Penal Justice* (Oxford University Press 2009), 70–75.

83. Rawls, *A Theory of Justice*, 242.

84. Thomas Pogge, "Three Problems with Contractarian-Consequentialist Ways of Assessing Social Institutions," *Social Philosophy and Policy* 12(2) (1995): 241–66 at 259.

to explain himself. A categorical insistence on proof of subjective fault in every instance is immune to a balancing of harms, and hence would have us prefer even dramatically higher rates of victimization rather than punish people who could not establish their good reasons for acting as they did. Yet if it is possible that one's liberty might be more greatly impaired in a world where one faced an extremely high risk of victimization than in a world with a much lower risk on account of a strict liability enforcement regime, then the very value that speaks in favor of the fair opportunity principle would under such circumstances also speak in favor of its limitation.

As it happens, Pogge's concerns about relaxing the rules of subjective fault for rapists describes fairly precisely the trajectory of sexual assault law in Canada. In an early case, *R v Pappajohn*, the Supreme Court of Canada affirmed the traditional common law principle that true crimes require subjective fault, holding that an honest but mistaken belief in the complainant's consent would defeat liability for sexual assault—indeed, even a completely unreasonable belief would defeat liability, so long as it was sincerely held.[85] Over the span of twenty years, with some legislative intervention and prodding by feminists, the Supreme Court gradually came around to the view that someone who wishes to defend himself against a sexual assault charge by claiming that he thought the complainant was consenting had to have taken reasonable steps to ascertain consent, the proof of which steps (at least enough to lend the claim an "air of reality") lies in the first instance on him.[86] As a result, in Canada, sexual assault—a "true crime" if ever there was one—is not only essentially an objective fault offense, it is in some respects a strict liability offense. If you intentionally touch someone in what a court regards as a sexual manner, and that person does not subjectively consent to the touching, you have committed sexual assault unless *you* can establish an air of reality to your perception that the complainant was consenting. This will typically require you to show that you formed your belief on the basis of an affirmative expression of consent; that you honestly and truly believed that her conduct evinced willingness is not sufficient. Feminists roundly perceived this shift in the law of sexual assault to be a major victory, given how

85. *R v Pappajohn*, [1980] 2 S.C.R. 120.

86. *R v Ewanchuk*, [1999] 1 S.C.R. 330.

difficult it is to prove beyond a reasonable doubt that someone did not genuinely believe that "no" meant "convince me" or "try harder."

Suppose that by making sexual assaults much easier to prosecute, these reforms significantly lower the rate of sexual assaults in Canada. That should count in favor of the rule. To be weighed against it is the loss of fair notice to those people who did in fact genuinely believe that the complainant was consenting but cannot raise sufficient evidence to establish the reasonableness of that belief. Hence, the question is whether the social gains that flow from making sexual assault easier to prosecute justify placing an onus on the initiators of sexual contact to affirmatively ascertain consent. My aim is not to speculate about how this particular exercise in balancing interests comes out. My point is that it *is* an exercise in balancing interests.

3.5 Conclusion

This chapter has sought to sketch an example of what it would take to provide a fully political justification of the criminal law, thereby establishing the viability of a public law conception of the criminal law as outlined in Chapter 2. I started with an interpretation of public institutions as a way of establishing and maintaining a society of equals, one in which each person can lead a life as a peer among peers. This interpretation is democratic, egalitarian without being equalizing, and focused on a form of freedom—effective access to central capability—as its currency of evaluation. A capability is central if it is required for a person to live in that society as a peer, and a person has effective access to it when she can exercise that capability without an objectively reasonable fear of interference from others. By stabilizing public institutions committed to the ideal of anti-deference, the criminal law plays a vital role in securing the conditions under which, in Pettit's memorable phrase, anyone can look anyone else in the eye without fear, shame, or deference.

Given this interpretation of the political morality of public institutions, I then asked what it would take to establish that institutions committed to the ideal of anti-deference would approve the use of the criminal law as a means of enforcing their rules and policies. I defended four claims. First, the criminal law should be democratic law, in the sense that it ought to be the outcome of a process that provides those who are subject to it with an equal opportunity to weigh in on its content and operation. Second, the criminal law ought not be used in a way that corrodes the expectations of reciprocity and trust in public institutions, paradigmatically by entrenching attitudes of social subordination. Third, it should be used when, but only when, a convincing case has been made that nothing short of criminal sanctions for noncompliance will optimally protect effective access to central capability for all. Fourth, in making that case, public institutions are not entitled to discount the rights and interests of criminals. Equal status is non-waivable, or at least not waived by crime. The overall ideal that emerges is of a criminal law that supports public institutions in fostering the conditions of democratic equality, and that does so by means that are evidence-based, substantively and procedurally democratic, and protective of central capability for all.

Having sketched these principles, I now turn to applying them. Accordingly, in the next chapter I consider perhaps the single most pressing issue in contemporary American criminal law: the problem of mass incarceration.

4

Mass Incarceration and the Theory of Punishment

"Besides, Revenge without respect to the Example, and profit to come, is a triumph, or a glorying in the hurt of another, tending to no end; (for the End is alwayes somewhat to Come;) and glorying to no end, is vain-glory, and contrary to reason; and to hurt without reason, tendeth to the introduction of Warre; which is against the Law of Nature; and is commonly stiled by the name of *Cruelty*."[1]

"There is the feeling of a Kantian imperative behind the word 'deserts.' Certain things are simply wrong and ought to be punished. And this we do believe."[2]

4.1 Introduction

At approximately 700 people in state custody per 100,000 adult residents, the United States incarcerates far more people than any other nation. The United States now incarcerates at a rate that is five times higher than a generation ago, and about five to ten times higher than is the norm in other liberal societies.[3] The United States incarcerates over 20 percent of the world's inmate population—over 2 million individuals—despite

1. Thomas Hobbes, *Leviathan*, chapter XV, Noel Malcolm, ed. (Clarendon Press 2012), 233.

2. Willard Gaylin and David J Rothman, "Introduction," in *Doing Justice: The Choice of Punishments* (Report of the Committee for the Study of Incarceration), ed. Andrew von Hirsch (Hill & Wang 1976), xxxix.

3. Steve Redburn, Jeremy Travis, and Bruce Western, eds., *The Growth of Incarceration in the United States: Exploring Causes and Consequences* (The National Academies Press 2014), 13; see also Roy Walmsley, ed., *World Prison Population List*, 10th ed. (International Centre for Prison Studies 2013), available at: http://images.derstandard.at/2013/11/21/prison-population.pdf.

having less than 5 percent of the world's population.[4] In recent years, it has become conventional to refer to the anomalously high American incarceration rates as reflecting a policy of "mass incarceration," and law, public policy, and criminology journals are filled with discussions of the evils of mass incarceration, its causes, and what can be done to mitigate it.[5] Many commentators believe that these kinds of ultra-high incarceration rates represent a serious injustice, and that the United States should strive to reduce its inmate population by a significant degree.

The question I consider in this chapter concerns the phenomenon of mass incarceration, but in a somewhat oblique way.[6] I do not propose to ask whether the United States acts unjustly in incarcerating as many people as it does. I will simply assume that mass incarceration is unjust. This is a relatively uncontroversial assumption, since most theorists, criminologists, economists, and commentators appear to agree that the United States now incarcerates too many people, and that this is a serious moral wrong. I will also assume that a philosophical theory of punishment should, among other things, specify the conditions under which criminal punishment is just or unjust. Hence, I will assume that a philosophical theory of punishment should, when applied to the United States, offer an explanation of what makes the incarceration rate in the United States unjust. Of course, any such explanation will depend on a wide range of empirical facts and assumptions, all of which may be more or less contestable. But in general I think it is uncontroversial that a philosophical theory of punishment should provide criteria to help us judge whether any given system of punishment is just or unjust. Even proponents of "rational reconstruction" in legal theory typically suggest that their accounts do not simply rationalize the status quo, but give us a vantage point from which to evaluate it.

The claim I defend in this chapter is that an adequate theory of punishment for the United States must be open to considering the aggregate

4. For population figures, see United States and World Population Clock, available at http://www.census.gov/popclock; for incarceration figures, see Walmsley, *World Prison Population List.*

5. There is by now an extensive literature across sociology, criminology, economics, history, politics, and law on mass incarceration. For a brief overview of the literature on the political context in which mass incarceration developed in the United States, see Redburn, Travis, and Western, eds., *The Growth of Incarceration in the United States,* ch. 4.

6. By "mass incarceration," I shall simply mean: incarceration at or above the rate currently prevailing in the United States, that is, roughly 700 per 100,000 adults.

costs and benefits of a system of punishment. It cannot be based purely on individual rights; it cannot be what I shall call a "strictly deontological" theory of punishment. Strictly deontological theories of punishment would tolerate any arbitrarily high rate of incarceration so long as each person incarcerated is guilty and receives a proportionate sentence for his or her crime. The conclusion I ultimately defend is that you can either affirm that the United States currently incarcerates too many people, or you can affirm a strictly deontological theory of punishment. But you cannot affirm both.

For a theory of punishment to provide a plausible metric for deciding how much punishment is enough requires that it take into account its aggregate social costs, relative to the gains fairly attributable to a system of punishment. Families, neighbors, community members, potential offenders, and potential victims alike all share in these costs, and just penal institutions must be able to explain why punishing this much, and no less, is plausibly consistent with publicly avowable principles of justice. I shall argue that the framework of anti-deference, introduced in Chapter 3, satisfies this criterion, whereas strictly deontological theories do not.

The argument is structured as follows. I start by briefly characterizing strictly deontological theories of punishment. I then turn, in Section 4.2, to arguing that strictly deontological theories cannot explain the injustice of mass incarceration. I consider objections in Section 4.3, and step back to draw broader lessons for the theory of punishment in Section 4.4.

4.2 Strict Deontology and Social Cost

A "strictly deontological theory of punishment" includes any theory that (1) purports to provide an explanation of when it is permissible to punish those who commit crimes, and that (2) does so in terms that exclude consideration of the expected costs and benefits of punishment. "Costs" and "benefits" should be understood generically: whether in terms of utility, social resources, capabilities, welfare, or so forth. I use the term "permissible" as follows: if it is permissible for A to do X, then A has, in general, all the justification she needs to do X; it would not be unjust for A to do X. In particular, because of clause (2), it would not be unjust even if the costs of doing X outweigh the benefits. If you prefer to understand "permissible" to include the logical possibility of "permissible, but unjust," then you can simply rephrase clause (1) of my definition accordingly. In that case, you should understand clause (1) as: "purports to provide a comprehensive, all things considered explanation of when punishment would be justified."

What does it mean to say that strictly deontological theories categorically exclude consideration of the social costs of punishment from affecting its permissibility? It means that you can have all the justification you need (all you need to make it morally permissible) to punish someone without considering whether any good would come from doing so. You may take the social costs and benefits of punishment into account if you wish, but whether you do so is strictly up to you. Hence, a strictly deontological theory does not simply insist that deontological constraints must be respected to render punishment permissible. It goes further and claims that if the constraints are respected, then punishment *is* permissible: satisfying deontological constraints is necessary *and* sufficient to establishing that punishing someone is permissible. Consequently, "hybrid" theories of punishment are not strictly deontological in my sense, since these theories make satisfaction of deontological side-constraints into merely a necessary, rather than sufficient, condition for the permissibility of punishment.

It is worth emphasizing that strictly deontological theories are not necessarily retributive theories, and that retributive theories are not necessarily strictly deontological theories. First, retributive theories can take a teleological form, in which retribution is simply another good to be promoted. Second, strict deontology does not necessarily depend on retribution as a reason for punishment. For instance, Kit Wellman's strong rights forfeiture theory claims only that it is permissible to punish someone who has forfeited his right not to be punished. It is noncommittal as to what positive reasons we have (retributive or otherwise) to punish anyone. Therefore, a theory can be strictly deontological without being retributivist. Of course, there *are* retributive forms of strict deontology. Strictly deontological retributivists claim that, as Mitch Berman puts it, "punishment is justified because doing so is right—something we have reason, or ought, to do—and where its rightness is not derivative of its being valuable."[7] However, this is a further commitment, not one that flows from a strictly deontological theory per se.

---

7. Mitchell Berman, "Two Kinds of Retributivism," in *Philosophical Foundations of the Criminal Law*, ed. R.A. Duff and Stuart P. Green (Oxford University Press 2011), 433–57 at 452.

You may wonder who defends a strictly deontological theory of punishment. Here are four contemporary versions. First, consider Wellman's recent defense of a rights forfeiture theory. According to Wellman, whatever good punishing someone may achieve, we are only permitted to punish that person if he has forfeited his right against punishment, as normally people have a strong right not to be treated in the way that punishment inevitably treats them. A person forfeits his right not to be punished by committing a crime. Therefore, we may only permissibly punish those who have committed crimes.[8] However, rights forfeiture theory is not necessarily a strictly deontological theory. Wellman helpfully distinguishes between "weak" and "strong" variants of rights forfeiture: the weak variant holds that rights forfeiture is necessary but not sufficient to explain the permissibility of punishment, whereas the strong variant holds that it is both necessary and sufficient. Rights forfeiture theory in its weak form is not a strictly deontological theory. This is because, on a weak rights forfeiture theory, it might be that we are only permitted to punish someone when she has forfeited her right against punishment *and* doing so also furthers some important social aim. Hence, while a weak form of rights forfeiture theory does purport to provide an explanation of the permissibility of punishment as required by (1), it need not do so in terms that exclude an assessment of the social costs of punishment, as required by (2). On the other hand, strong rights forfeiture theory—the version Wellman defends—is a strictly deontological theory. This is because it holds that rights forfeiture is sufficient to make punishment all-things-considered permissible, making consideration of the social costs of punishment strictly irrelevant. As Wellman puts it, if someone has forfeited her right against punishment, we may punish her whether or not doing so furthers some important social aim.[9]

Second, Arthur Ripstein has defended a rigorously Kantian form of strict deontology. According to Ripstein, "[u]nless the right to punish is

---

8. Christopher Wellman, "The Rights Forfeiture Theory of Punishment," *Ethics* 122(2) (2012): 371–93; see also Wellman, *Rights Forfeiture and Punishment* (Oxford University Press 2017), ch. 2.

9. Wellman, "The Rights Forfeiture Theory of Punishment," 375 n.7. In a later work, Wellman concedes that state punishment "would not be justified unless the criminal legal system secured vitally important goods that would be unavailable in its absence." He nevertheless insists that "a punishment that serves no other purpose might nonetheless be morally permissible." *Rights Forfeiture and Punishment*, 23; compare Wellman, "Rights and State Punishment," *Journal of Philosophy* 106(8) (2009): 419–39, especially 428–30.

inherent in the idea of a rightful condition, no good consequences could authorize it." Conversely, insofar as the right to punish is inherent in the idea of a rightful condition, then "its justification does not depend on those consequences."[10] Ripstein is thus committed to the claim that the right to punish inherent in the Kantian "rightful condition" is both necessary and sufficient to justify punishment, and that the consequences of punishment are strictly immaterial. For Ripstein, public law "constitutes a system of equal freedom in which no person is subject to the choice of another,"[11] and punishment is required to "hinder hindrances to freedom"[12]—that is, criminal acts—and even if "the incentives provided by law would be empirically unnecessary . . . [punishment] would still be required."[13] Indeed, on Ripstein's view, in upholding public right, the sovereign is ***obligated*** to punish every crime she comes across. Failing to punish is "strictly speaking inconsistent with the rightful condition," and hence would be "wrong in the highest degree," and even "a single exception" would be a renunciation of the law's own principle.[14]

Third, although Alan Brudner takes issue with Ripstein's Kantianism, Brudner's Hegelian theory is itself a variant of strict deontological theory. Brudner explicitly denies that punishment can be "justified in prospective terms as a means to furthering socially desirable ends."[15] He rejects a Hartian-style mixed theory, according to which socially beneficial consequences of punishment provide the affirmative reason in favor of punishment. The "beneficial effects of punishment" cannot be regarded,

---

10. Arthur Ripstein, *Force and Freedom: Kant's Legal and Political Philosophy* (Harvard University Press 2009), 301.

11. Ripstein, *Force and Freedom*, 306.

12. Ripstein, *Force and Freedom*, 55.

13. Ripstein, *Force and Freedom*, 307.

14. Ripstein, *Force and Freedom*, 320–21. To be fair, Ripstein attempts to constrain the maximalist tendencies of his Kantian view by insisting that he is not taking "any specific position about what public resources should be devoted to crime detection, or where those resources should be focused." However, it is hard to see what motivates the distinction between investigation (entirely discretionary) and prosecution (entirely mandatory): if it is such an affront to the law to allow even a single crime to go unpunished, why is it not equally an affront if crime that could easily be detected (and hence punished) were allowed to go undetected (and hence unpunished)? Perversely, this suggests that the state could decide to underfund policing and crime detection precisely *so that* it could avoid acquiring the rigorous Kantian duty to punish criminals once detected.

15. Alan Brudner, *Punishment and Freedom* (Oxford University Press 2009), 38.

Brudner claims, as a public reason in favor of punishment, and hence whatever good is achieved by punishment carries no justificatory significance.[16] On Brudner's view, a criminal renders himself vulnerable to punishment because by intentionally denying someone else's rights he implicitly denies his own, and as a result he has no basis for complaint when the state violates *his* rights by punishing him.[17] The substantive justification for state punishment, according to Brudner, is that it is required to make manifest that the criminal's implicit claim to an unlimited liberty of action is "aporetic," and thereby "to vindicate the truth . . . that the only valid claims of permission to act are those that can be validated by equal ends."[18] On Brudner's view, actual concrete punishment of the criminal is positively required to make this manifest precisely because, by actualizing his claim to unlimited freedom in external conduct, the criminal clothes his egoistic principle in a false veneer of legal validity. Far from being a means of promoting the public good, punishment is justified because it expressively denies the wrongdoer's own denial of rights. Hence, Brudner's view is a strictly deontological theory: it holds that punishment is permissible—indeed, required—under conditions that make no mention of punishment's contribution to public welfare, but that instead turn only on the expressive vindication of rights.

Finally, and perhaps surprisingly, Antony Duff has recently defended a form of retributive theory that implies strict deontology.[19] According to Duff, "what gives criminal punishment its meaning and the core of its normative justification is its relationship, not to any contingent

---

16. Brudner, *Punishment and Freedom*, 42.

17. Brudner, *Punishment and Freedom*, 37–41. Unlike Wellman, Brudner views punishment as a rights violation rather than as a rights forfeiture. Malcolm Thorburn defends a view reminiscent of Brudner's: see "Punishment and Public Authority," in *Criminal Law and the Authority of the State*, ed. Antje du Bois-Pedain, Magnus Ulväng, and Petter Asp (Hart 2017), 7–33.

18. Brudner, *Punishment and Freedom*, 46. See also Jean Hampton, "Correcting Harms vs Righting Wrongs: The Goal of Retribution," *University of California Los Angeles Law Review* 39 (1991): 1659–702 at 1686.

19. R.A. Duff, "Retrieving Retributivism," in *Retributivism: Essays on Theory and Policy*, ed. Mark White (Oxford University Press 2011), 3–18. Martha Nussbaum has expressed doubts about Duff's choice of a strictly deontological starting point for his account of punishment; see Martha Nussbaum, *Anger and Forgiveness* (Oxford University Press 2016), 188–89. In more recent work, Duff seems to take a softer line, arguing that guilt alone is not sufficient to justify punishment. See Antony Duff, *The Realm of Criminal Law* (Oxford University Press 2018), ch. 7.

future benefits that it might bring, but to the past crime for which it is imposed." This, according to Duff, is the "core retributivist thought."[20] Just as individuals have standing to call friends, family, and colleagues to account in the case of ordinary transgressions, the political community has standing to call citizens to account in the case of public wrongs. Calling those who commit public wrongs to account is not done because it furthers other goals that we might have; rather, it is *constitutive* of the respect due to citizens. Failure to pursue and prosecute a wrongdoer betrays an attitude of indifference to the victim, and perhaps to the perpetrator as well. Criminal punishment is a way for the community and wrongdoer to show that they are appropriately engaged with the victim's injury by demanding a "formal, forceful expression of apology."[21] Showing respect for the agency of the victim justifies us in calling the wrongdoer to account through punishment, and this reason for punishment is categorically insensitive to the expected social cost of punishment. Hence, insofar as calling a wrongdoer to account provides a sufficient reason for punishing someone—which it must, since it is allegedly constitutive of showing respect, something we presumably have sufficient reason to do—it follows that Duff's retributivism is strictly deontological.

In contrast to Wellman's noncommittal form of strict deontology, Ripstein's, Brudner's, and Duff's theories are both strictly deontological and retributive. They go beyond the claim that punishment is only permissible when someone has forfeited his or her rights, and insist that there is a positive retributive requirement to punish: to uphold the rightful condition, to expressively deny the denial of rights, or to show respect for those whose rights were wrongfully invaded. Strictly deontological retributivism would not allow us to tell one victim that we are not going to devote the resources to investigating, prosecuting, and punishing the person who assaulted him because we have a better use for those resources. Even if we do have a "better" use for the resources, to fail to call his assailant to account just *is* to fail to show him sufficient respect (uphold the rightful condition, allow a denial of rights to stand unchallenged, etc.) That is

20. Duff, "Retrieving Retributivism," 3. Or, as Nozick once put the point, the consequential goods achieved by punishing wrongdoers—reform, deterrence, or incapacitation, say—are merely an "especially desirable and valuable bonus" rather than "part of a necessary condition for justly imposed punishment." Robert Nozick, *Philosophical Explanations* (Harvard University Press 1983), 374.

21. Duff, "Retrieving Retributivism," 18.

what it means for punishment to be constitutive of respect for the victim. Presumably, it is not the case that we are permitted to respect victims less than we otherwise would simply because there are more of them. If we design our institutions such that we know in advance that a great many perpetrators—indeed, with respect to some crimes, the large majority of them—will never be called to account for their crimes, then victims of unpunished crimes have a powerful deontological claim that they are not being taken sufficiently seriously. Their objection remains even if people who are at risk of becoming unemployed, sick, or unable to access a tolerably good education would *also* have claims if resources were diverted from those programs to fund a fully enforced criminal justice regime.

4.3 Strict Deontology and Mass Incarceration

Strictly deontological theories, retributive or otherwise, cannot explain why the United States currently incarcerates too many people. The argument can be presented as follows:

1. The United States today unjustly incarcerates too many people.
2. According to a strictly deontological theory, punishment is justified (i.e., is permissible all things considered) if it does not violate relevant deontological constraints.
3. The current American incarceration rate is not the result of widespread violation of deontological constraints.
4. Hence, a deontological theory of punishment cannot explain why the United States unjustly incarcerates too many people.

Note again that I am simply assuming that (1) is true. The second step of the argument flows from the logical structure of a deontological theory of punishment. Step (3) requires more elaboration, and I will focus most of my attention on it.

First, however, I pause to clarify the nature of premise (1). To be sure, the argument would be more ambitious if it were stated unconditionally; that is, if it purported to show that some specified rate of incarceration, *n*, is *necessarily* unjust, unjust in all possible worlds. However, I doubt any such claim can be sustained, at least for any plausible value of *n*.[22] This

22. What is a plausible value of *n*? It is worth bearing in mind that even in the United States today the incarceration rate is less than 1 percent, and that in most other Anglophone

is because for any plausible value of n, whether it is just to incarcerate that many people depends on a wide range of social facts. What might be an unjustly high rate of incarceration in modern Sweden might not be unjust in post-revolutionary China, or even in the contemporary United States. To put it slightly differently, consider a theory of punishment as a function that takes a range of factors (crime rates, sentencing norms, legal traditions, etc.) as inputs and returns an estimate of the maximum permissible rate of incarceration as an output. Call that estimate n_{MAX}. No plausible theory of punishment treats n_{MAX} as a constant; rather, its value is sensitive to the values that are assigned to the relevant inputs.[23]

Hence, premise (1) would be too strong if it required a theory of punishment to show why a *specific* rate—say 700 people in custody per 100,000 adults—is per se unjust, regardless of social context. Premise (1) is therefore more contingent, and applies specifically to the incarceration rate in the contemporary United States. That said, the more interesting question is *which* inputs a theory treats as relevant in setting n_{MAX}. Strictly deontological theories have a particularly limited set of relevant inputs, essentially those having to do with guilt and the proportionality of the sentence imposed, to the exclusion of factors having to do with (for instance) crime rates and the relative marginal cost of incarceration. Strictly deontological theories focus on the quality of individual transactions, ignoring the aggregate benefits and burdens of a system of punishment.

One way of framing the conclusion (4) that I defend is that strictly deontological theories too sharply restrict the range of relevant inputs in determining n_{MAX}. In contrast, theories of punishment that are open to

countries, the rate is closer to 0.01 percent. It is hard to imagine what a society that incarcerated even 10 percent of its population would look like, and it may well be the case that under social conditions where one would find such a rate—perhaps conditions of civil war or insurrection—normal theories of justice would simply fail to apply.

23. To illustrate, consider the following simplified example. Suppose your theory of punishment says that the single input factor that is relevant to determining whether punishment is permissible is guilt: if someone is guilty of a crime, then it is permissible to punish him. Suppose, further, that in society S there is only one crime, C, and people who are convicted of committing C invariably serve one year in prison. In this case, the value of n_{MAX} is straightforwardly estimated: it is simply the number of people who commit C in a given year. After all, if the state were to investigate, prosecute, and convict every single person who commits C, then the number of instances in which C is committed would determine the actual incarceration rate, and given that time served for C is one year, at any given time n_{MAX} should correspond to the number of instances of C in the previous year. Any higher rate of incarceration, and S would inevitably either be incarcerating innocents or imposing disproportionate punishments. The point is that C is a variable, not a constant.

consequential considerations can appeal to a range of aggregative inputs in estimating n_{MAX}. They can, for instance, consider the expected aggregate costs of incarceration—the harms imposed directly on those incarcerated, the collateral consequences on families and communities, and the opportunity costs to society of time wasted languishing in prison—as well as its expected benefits, such as the reduction in criminal offending. When the marginal benefits from incarceration are declining relative to its social cost, then a theory that is open to aggregative reasons will plausibly set n_{MAX} at the inflection point where further reliance on incarceration entails more harm than good. An interpretation of n_{MAX} along these lines could provide a plausible explanation of why the United States unjustly incarcerates too many people. Plausibly, in expanding its custodial population from approximately 120 per 100,000 to over 700 per 100,000, the United States has come to incarcerate so many people that the marginal cost of incarceration outweighs marginal benefits.

In contrast, the strongly individualistic character of strictly deontological theories implies that it is equally permissible to punish any person who has committed a criminal act, whether he is the first person or the nth person to do so, for any arbitrarily large value of n. Hence, insofar as a deontological theory purports to show that it is permissible to punish *any* criminal wrongdoer, it shows that it is permissible to punish *all* of them—regardless of the costs of doing so. Punishing that many people may be pointless or even counterproductive. But strictly deontological theories are united in rejecting those types of concerns from bearing on the permissibility of punishment: they tell us that we are permitted to punish regardless of whether doing so "is necessary to promote some important aim."[24] Hence, for a strictly deontological theory to explain why the United States today incarcerates too many people, it must do so by showing how the United States' elevated incarceration rate is a result of a widespread violations of a relevant deontological constraint, a violation that can be made out on a case-by-case basis.

Accordingly, I now turn to examining proposition (3), that the current American incarceration rate is not the the result of widespread violation of deonotological constraints. The paradigmatic deontological constraints on punishment are that punishment be restricted to people who are actually guilty of true crimes, and be administered in proportion to their

24. Wellman, "Rights Forfeiture Theory of Punishment," 375 n.7.

culpability. Is it the case that the American incarceration rate is so anomalously high because the United States punishes factually innocent people, criminalizes morally innocent conduct, or imposes disproportionate sentences? There is reason to be skeptical. Recent empirical work suggests that America's elevated incarceration rate stems largely from increases in the rates at which people who are guilty of uncontroversial crimes are prosecuted for felony offenses, and given relatively short custodial sentences as a result. This research suggests that the United States could actually incarcerate many more people than it currently does without punishing high numbers of factually innocent people, over-criminalizing, or imposing disproportionate sentences.

Factual guilt. I start with the proposition that only those who are actually guilty of a crime should be punished. Suppose the United States were to fully respect this constraint, or at least as well as can reasonably be expected (since some errors will be inevitable.) Would respecting this constraint bring the incarceration rate down significantly? No. While wrongful convictions are a serious problem, it is very unlikely that they are sufficiently numerous to contribute in any meaningful way to the scale of incarceration in the United States.[25] In fact, the United States could dramatically *raise* incarceration rates while fully respecting the constraint against punishing the innocent. The reason is simple: there are a great many crimes that go unpunished. A profoundly important fact about criminal justice in the United States is that, even with the highest incarceration rate in the world, and even with respect to so-called core offenses such as assault, sexual assault, theft, and burglary, the criminal law in the United States is not even remotely close to being fully enforced. In 2007, roughly 61 percent of murders and non-negligent manslaughters known to police resulted in arrests or were otherwise considered "solved." Those rates go down substantially for other crimes: comparable figures for rape are 42 percent, for robbery 26 percent and for burglary and car theft 13 percent.[26] Considered in the aggregate, clearance rates for violent crime have hovered around 45 percent for several decades, and the comparable figure

25. For an estimate, in the context of capital rape-murders, see D Michael Risinger, "Innocents Convicted: An Empirically Justified Factual Wrongful Conviction Rate," *Journal of Criminal Law & Criminology* 97(3) (2007): 761–806.

26. Sourcebook of Criminal Justice Statistics Online, Table 4.19.2007: Offenses Known to Police and Percent Cleared by Arrest, available at: http://www.albany.edu/sourcebook/pdf/t4192007.pdf (accessed May 11, 2018).

for property crimes is roughly 15 percent.[27] These are, moreover, clearance rates, not conviction rates—that is, they represent the rate at which police consider a crime "solved," not the rate at which someone has actually been called to account for the crime through prosecution and punishment. When we turn to convictions, we see that in state courts in 2004, approximately 68 percent of murder and non-negligent manslaughter arrests resulted in convictions, while only about 16 percent of motor vehicle theft arrests and 44 percent of burglary arrests resulted in convictions.[28] As a rough, back-of-the-envelope calculation, these figures together suggest that about 43 percent of murders and non-negligent manslaughters, 6 percent of burglaries, and 2 percent of motor vehicle thefts ultimately resulted in convictions. These figures are concededly rough, since they do not account for people who are convicted through a process commencing with a summons rather than an arrest, nor do they account for crimes that are considered cleared but that do not result in an arrest. On the other hand, these rates are sensitive only to crimes known to police, and there is evidence that a great deal of crime goes unreported—in some categories, such as assault (65 percent), sexual assault (86 percent), and domestic violence (90 percent), a majority to an overwhelming majority of crime is not reported.[29] These figures appear broadly consistent with contemporary and historical trends in the United Kingdom.[30]

In short: there are *many* more instances of people forfeiting their rights against criminal punishment by committing crimes than there are instances of criminal punishment actually being imposed. The very high rate of attrition between the rate at which crimes are committed and the rates at which they are punished suggests that there is quite an extensive

---

27. Sourcebook of Criminal Justice Statistics Online, Table 4.21.2007: Percent of Offenders Known to Police Who Were Cleared by Arrest, available at: http://www.albany.edu/sourcebook/pdf/t4212007.pdf (accessed May 11, 2018).

28. Sourcebook of Criminal Justice Statistics Online, Table 5.0002.2004: Felony Convictions and Sentences and Rate per 100 Arrests, available at: http://www.albany.edu/sourcebook/pdf/t500022004.pdf (accessed May 11, 2018).

29. See David Kennedy, *Deterrence and Crime Prevention: Reconsidering the Prospect of Sanction* (Routledge 2009), 45.

30. See Andrew Ashworth and Mike Redmayne, *The Criminal Process*, 4th ed. (Oxford University Press 2010), 156–57 (estimating that "no more than 2 percent" of the eight most frequently committed offenses in the United Kingdom result in a conviction). For historical evidence, see Peter King, *Crime, Justice, and Discretion in England 1740–1820* (Oxford University Press 2005), 11–12, 132–34 (reporting estimates from the late eighteenth and early nineteenth centuries that only 1–10 percent of property crimes were prosecuted).

degree of headroom in criminal justice inputs before the constraint of factual guilt kicks in as a limiting factor. For instance, if my back-of-the-envelope calculations are any guide, American criminal justice institutions could prosecute ten times as many domestic assaults, sixteen times as many burglaries, and fully fifty times as many car thefts while still punishing only the guilty. So although people who are wrongfully convicted clearly have powerful claims about how they have been treated, the injustice of mass incarceration cannot be chalked up to lots of innocent people being punished for crimes they did not commit.

Criminalization. Deontological theories of punishment do not simply claim that it is right (or all-things-considered permissible) for the guilty to be punished proportionately. They also typically claim that what it is to be guilty is, within some range, not purely a matter of positive law. People do not forfeit their rights or deserve punishment simply because the legislature says they do. Rather, they forfeit their rights or deserve punishment when the acts they perform are *appropriately* or *rightly* criminalized. Thus, even if it is conceded that the United States is mostly punishing guilty people, in the sense of people who have contavened some positive criminal law, perhaps the United States has criminalized conduct that it is simply inappropriate to criminalize in the first place. Perhaps overcriminalization of this sort explains why the United States incarcerates too many people.

By far the most significant area of criminal law that might plausibly be thought of in these terms is the so-called "war on drugs." Indeed, it is sometimes claimed that the war on drugs explains America's experiment with mass incarceration.[31] If this claim were true, and if a convincing case could be made that criminalizing narcotics violates some deontological constraint on criminalization, then perhaps deontological theorists would be able to explain why the United States should have a much lower incarceration rate. Deontological theorists could claim that while there would be no injustice in prosecuting literally every instance of every crime, it turns out there are many fewer such instances than we thought, at least once we take into account the malign influence of the war on drugs.

Unfortunately, the claim that the war on drugs explains mass incarceration is unsupported by the evidence. For over two decades, the percentage of people imprisoned for a drug offense in the United States has been fairly stable at about 20 percent—significant, but not enough

---

31. See, e.g., Michelle Alexander, *The New Jim Crow* (The New Press, 2010).

to explain the fivefold increase in incarceration rates over the last generation.[32] The majority of people in state prisons are there because they committed violent crimes; in fact, there are about as many people in state prisons for homicide (14 percent of state inmates) as there are for drug offenses (16 percent). If we factor in property offenses, nearly three-quarters (72.6 percent) of state prisoners are in custody because of traditional offenses.[33] While it *is* true that stripping out people convicted of drug crimes would lower incarceration rates, it would not bring rates anywhere near what they were for most of the twentieth century, or as low as they are in any of the United States' usual comparator countries.[34] And while it is also true that there was a sharp increase in the proportion of people incarcerated for drug offenses during the 1980s, that was a sharp increase from a very low baseline: in 1980, state prisons housed only 19,000 drug offenders, compared to over 170,000 violent offenders and nearly 90,000 property offenders. By 2009, the number of drug offenders in state prisons grew by roughly an additional 220,000 people, but the number of violent offenders grew by over 500,000, and the number of property offenders by almost 172,000.[35] In fact, over half of the growth in prison populations from 1980 to 2009 is explained by growth in the number of incarcerated violent offenders, and if we factor in property offenses, we account for fully two-thirds of the growth.[36] As John Pfaff has noted, "[e]ven

---

32. In 2012, drug offenders made up approximately 16 percent of the state prison population. E. Ann Carson, *Prisoners in 2013* (Bureau of Justice Statistics, 2013), 15, tbl. 13, available at: http://www.bjs.gov/content/pub/pdf/p13.pdf; see also John F. Pfaff, "The War on Drugs and Prison Growth: Limited Importance, Limited Legislative Options," *Harvard Journal on Legislation* 52(1) (2015): 173–220; Pfaff, *Locked In: The True Causes of Mass Incarceration—and How to Achieve Real Reform* (Basic Books 2017), ch. 1; James Forman, Jr, "Racial Critiques of Mass Incarceration: Beyond the New Jim Crow," *New York University L.aw Review* 87(1) (2012), 47–48.

33. Carson, *Prisoners in 2013*, 15, tbl. 13. The Marshall Project, a news organization focused on criminal justice issues in the United States, has put the Bureau of Justice Statistics online in the form of an interactive website, which the reader can manipulate to see how many violent offenders would have to be released in order to cut America's incarceration rate by 50 percent. Note that even with a 50 percent reduction, the United States would still be the most punitive developed country on the planet. Available at: https://www.themarshallproject.org/2015/03/04/how-to-cut-the-prison-population-by-50-percent.

34. See Redburn, Travis, and Western, eds., *The Growth of Incarceration in the United States.*

35. Pfaff, "The War on Drugs and Prison Growth," tbl. 1A.

36. See John Pfaff, "Escaping from the Standard Story: Why the Conventional Wisdom on Prison Growth Is Wrong, and Where We Can Go from Here," *Federal Sentencing Reporter* 26(4) (2014): 265–70, 265–66.

if we released every offender currently serving time for a drug conviction, the US prison population would remain above 1 million, and the racial composition of its prisons would not shift much"—specifically, the prison population would go from 1.4 million to 1.1 million, and the percentage of black prisoners would decline two percentage points, to 36 percent.[37]

This is not to say that the so-called "war on drugs" is morally insignificant, or that it has not wrought huge swaths of largely pointless devastation through the lives of a great many people. It would also be overstating the case to say that the war on drugs has had a negligible impact on American incarceration rates. It is, for instance, possible that drug offenses may matter to incarceration rates more indirectly: it may be that the war on drugs has a given large number of people criminal records, resulting in longer sentences for subsequent, non-drug offenses. It is also possible that the war on drugs has made drug markets more dangerous, and hence more criminogenic. But in terms of actual drug incarcerations, it is reasonably clear that while they are non-negligible, they cannot explain the phenomenon of mass incarceration. The impact of incarceration for drug offenses on the incarceration rate is far overshadowed by the impact of prosecutions for traditional "core" crimes, violent crime in particular.

To put the point more generally, the implicit hypothesis underlying the thought that over-criminalization explains overpunishment is the proposition that increasing criminalization causes increasing incarceration. But it is not obvious why this would be true. After all, crimes do not prosecute themselves. Hence, it is not obvious why simply expanding the number of options available to prosecutors should expand the number of people who are incarcerated, holding resources and priorities constant. What the statistics regarding violent crime and property offenses suggest is that the set of crimes for which people are actually sent to prison have remained fairly stable even as incarceration rates have exploded. Growth in incarceration

---

37. John Pfaff, "The Micro and Macro Causes of Prison Growth," *Georgia State University Law Review* 28(4) (2012): 1239–73 at 1270; Pfaff, "The Causes of Growth in Prison Admissions and Populations," Working Paper No. 1884671 (2011), 22–24, available at: https://ssrn.com/abstract=1990508. Blumstein and Beck similarly acknowledge that drug offenses do not explain the bulk of the explosion in incarceration rates. Alfred Blumstein and Allen J. Beck, "Reentry as a Transient State between Liberty and Recommitment," in *Prisoner Reentry and Crime in America*, ed. Jeremy Travis and Christy Visher (Cambridge University Press 2005), 50, 78. But see Blumstein and Beck, "Population Growth in U.S. Prisons, 1980–1996," in *Prisons*, ed. Michael Tonry and Joan Petersilia (University of Chicago Press 1999), 17, 21.

appears to have largely been driven by increased numbers of prosecutions for a relatively stable number of offenses, not over-criminalization per se.[38]

Harsh sentencing. Finally, it might be thought that it is American criminal justice institutions' proclivity for meting out disproportionately harsh sentences that explains why its custodial population is so large.[39] There are, of course, many instances of headline-grabbing sentences that many people believe to be disproportionate. However, these kinds of ultra-harsh sentences do not seem to be what drives the United States' ultra-high incarceration rate. What appears to be doing most of the work is an increased willingness on the part of American prosecutors to file felony charges that carry some amount of prison time, rather than a routine demand for extremely long sentences.[40]

Pfaff has recently analyzed data from eleven states from the National Corrections Reporting Program from 1982 to 2003, and found that, when examining median and 75th percentile prisoners, time served has actually been stable, or in some cases even declining, in this period.[41] Median time served ranged from about six months (California) to about two years (New Jersey); at the 75th percentile, time served ranged from about one year (California) to about four (Virginia). In a subsequent paper, Pfaff bolsters this conclusion with data drawn from all fifty states. Actual release rates from state prisons over the last three decades closely parallel a hypothetical invariant release schedule, according to which half of all prisoners are released within a year, and three-quarters within five years, with only 1 percent remaining incarcerated after eleven years. For most inmates, the amount of time served has not materially increased during the last three decades, even as the incarceration rate has shot up.[42]

---

38. Pfaff, *Locked In*, 156–57; my thanks to Elizabeth Brown for discussion of this point.

39. For a discussion of sentencing in the United States in comparison to other Western jurisdictions, see James Q. Whitman, *Harsh Justice: Criminal Punishment and the Widening Divide between America and Europe* (Oxford University Press 2005), especially ch. 2. My discussion in this section is indebted to Pfaff, *Locked In*, ch. 2.

40. For prisoners released in 2012, the median time served for violent crimes was twenty-eight months, twelve months for property crimes, and thirteen months for drug offenses. See Carson, *Prisoners in 2013*, 8, tbl. 17.

41. John Pfaff, "The Myths and Realities of Correctional Severity," *American Law and Economics Review* 13(2) (2011), 499–504. The states in question are California, Colorado, Illinois, Kentucky, Michigan, Minnesota, Nebraska, New Jersey, South Dakota, Virginia, and Washington.

42. John Pfaff, "The Causes of Growth in Prison Admissions and Populations," available at http://web.law.columbia.edu/sites/default/files/microsites/criminal-law-roundtable-2012/

It is worth noting that, while many states have ultra-harsh repeat offender laws, with the exception of California, they appear to be rarely used.[43] Prosecutorial discretion generally means that there are ways around most harsh sentencing laws. Indeed, since the way around them is often through a guilty plea to another offense with a lower sentence, it is possible that what these laws do is to enhance the ability of prosecutors to efficiently send guilty people to prison rather than ramp up time served—an outcome to which retributivists can hardly object.

While time served has been relatively flat, Pfaff presents evidence that points to an increase in the rate at which prosecutors file felony charges, rather than arrest rates, conviction rates, or harsher sentencing, as the more significant contributor to prison population growth in the United States. Since the increase in felony charges presumably comes from cases that prosecutors in previous generations would have dismissed or treated as misdemeanors, it appears that, as Pfaff puts it, "despite the attention paid to three-strike laws, TIS [truth in sentencing laws], and the like, the predominant locus of increased punitiveness over the past ten to fifteen years still appears to be at the low end, not the high."[44] This suggests in turn that a jurisdiction that does not utilize extraordinarily harsh sentencing outcomes as a general matter may still incarcerate an extraordinary number of people largely by virtue of growth in its custodial inputs. This is a source of growth that, deontological theories are unable to meaningfully limit. It is, Pfaff writes, "[c]hanging decisions

files/Pfaff_New_Admissions_to_Prison.pdf, at 30–32 (accessed May 11, 2018). As Pfaff puts it, "sanctioning severity does not appear to have changed much at all between 1977 and the early 2000s; to the extent that there has been any change since then, it has been in the direction of *leniency*." (4) For contrary views, see Blumstein and Beck, "Population Growth in U.S. Prisons, 1980–1996" and Blumstein and Beck, "Reentry as a Transient State between Liberty and Recommitment." Pfaff's findings are based on two data sets, not utilized by other studies, that allow Pfaff to disaggregate prison admissions per arrest into its component parts, namely felony filings per arrest, convictions per filing, and prison admissions per conviction. Pfaff, "The Micro and Macro Causes of Prison Growth," 1245.

43. Franklin Zimring, Gordon Hawkins, and Sam Kamin, *Punishment and Democracy: Three Strikes in California* (Oxford University Press 2001), 20–21. As Zimring has noted elsewhere, the federal "three strikes" law was applied 35 times in the four years after its enactment, whereas the California statute—enacted the same year as the federal statute—was applied over 40,000 times. Indeed, the California statute "has resulted in nine times as many prison terms as all of the 26 other three strikes laws in the United States combined." Franklin Zimring, "Imprisonment and the New Politics of Criminal Punishment," *Punishment & Society* 3(1) (2001): 161–66, 163.

44. Pfaff, "The Myths and Realities of Correctional Severity," 504.

in prosecutors' offices about when to file charges" that "appear to be the primary—at times, seemingly almost the sole—driver of prison growth, at least since the mid- to late-1980s."[45]

To be fair, by most accounts, America's experiment with mass incarceration began a full decade earlier, so Pfaff's analysis may well miss factors that were more operative in those earlier years than subsequently. That said, an earlier study found a similar pattern from the 1970s to 1988, suggesting that, even as America's experiment with mass incarceration was ramping up, time served was actually going down slightly, but was more than compensated for by an increase in prison admissions.[46]

It is, in any case, quite plausible that incarceration rates in the United States would typically be more sensitive to prosecutorial activity than to crime rates. This is due to the low rate at which crimes are prosecuted. Suppose, for instance, that one out of ten criminals is prosecuted. Even a modest 5 percent increase in the prosecution rate, from 10 percent to 15 percent, would result in a 50 percent increase in indictments. In contrast, a 5 percent rise in the crime rate would yield only a 0.5 percent impact on indictments, since only one out of ten cases is being prosecuted to begin with. Consequently, the institutional structure of the criminal law, with persistently low rates of prosecution relative to crime, means that prosecutorial charging decisions have a disproportionately large effect on the rate of inputs into the criminal justice system.[47] Hence, for a theory of punishment to come to grips with the phenomenon of mass incarceration, it should have some measure for estimating appropriate levels of prosecutorial activity. This is a distinct concern from proportionality in sentencing, and not one, prima facie, that lends itself to individualistic moral analysis. (It might be the case that too many prosecutions would be bad for society, but is it the case that every criminal has a right to expect no more than an *n* percent chance of being prosecuted for his or her crime?[48])

To summarize: holding crime rates constant, the United States could dramatically raise the rate at which people are placed into the criminal

---

45. Pfaff, "The Causes of Growth in Prison Admissions and Populations," 7.

46. Patrick Langan, "America's Soaring Prison Population," *Science* 251(5001) (March 29, 1991): 1568–73.

47. See King, *Crime, Justice, and Discretion in England 1740–1820*, 12.

48. See Hamish Stewart's recent attempt to articulate a deontological account of the wrong of mass incarceration. See "The Wrong of Mass Punishment," *Criminal Law and Philosophy* (2016), doi:10.1007/s11572-016-9409-2.

justice system without running afoul of the deontological constraint against punishing the innocent. Moreover, even if the United States refused to incarcerate people for drug crimes, its incarceration rate would still be anomalously high, since the large majority of people who are in custody are there for traditional *mala in se* crimes. Finally, ultra-harsh sentences do not explain why the American incarceration rate is as high as it is. To the contrary, there is some reason to believe that the major cause of growth in the American incarceration rate is that more people are facing (not obviously disproportionate) custodial sentences for the (mostly traditional) crimes they (actually) commit. Hence, mass incarceration in the United States does not appear to be the result of systematic violation of any of the usual deontological constraints. This suggests, in turn, that a strictly deontological theory cannot explain why the United States incarcerates too many people. Absent a more complete account of the deontological constraints that limit the degree to which a society may permissibly punish the guilty, punishment theorists face a choice: either they can endorse the claim that the United States unjustly incarcerates too many people, or they can endorse a strictly deontological theory of punishment. What they cannot do is endorse both.[49]

I stress that I am not criticizing deontological theories of punishment for being unable to resolve the type of fine-grained "policy" question that philosophical theories in general should not be expected to answer. What I am criticizing them for is their inability to get a grip on one of the most basic issues in criminal justice, which is how much of it there should be. A theory of punishment that cannot provide a plausible framework for deciding whether it would be a good idea to quintuple the size of the incarcerated population does not have an *incomplete* answer to this question; it has *no* such answer. That is a serious failing in a theory that is

49. In subsequent writing, Wellman distinguishes between the institutional and interactional levels of justification, and suggests that whereas a strongly deontological justification applies at the interactional level, when it comes to justifying institutions a more consequentialist approach is warranted. Christopher Wellman, *Rights Forfeiture and Punishment* (Oxford University Press 2017), 53. Wellman's reason for thinking that consequential considerations do not apply at the interactional level is that punishing an innocent person in order to protect rights would impose an unreasonable burden on that person. But this is an odd reason for restricting the level at which consequential considerations apply, rather than restricting the conditions under which they are permissibly acted upon. After all, it is hard to see how the burden of wrongful punishment is rendered more reasonable by virtue of being imposed by an institution rather than by an individual. Conversely, if punishment is only permissible at the institutional level when doing so will do some good, why should it not also be permissible at the individual, interactional level under the same restriction?

ostensibly meant to help us evaluate our actual criminal justice institutions and practices.

4.4 Proportionality, Crime Rates, and Value Pluralism

I now turn to consider objections. First, one might object that even relatively short custodial sentences are disproportionately harsh for many crimes. There are two difficulties with this line of thought. First, while the concept of proportionality could, of course, be modulated so as to hit any exogenously specified incarceration rate, doing so would plainly drain proportionality of independent moral content. It would simply be a means for ensuring that the incarceration rate doesn't exceed some arbitrarily specified value for n_{MAX}, rather than a substantive factor in determining how much punishment is appropriate in a given case. Second, once we leave behind the realm of the outrageous—boiling oil for bicycle thieves, as Philip Pettit and John Braithwaite once put it—it becomes very hard, if not impossible, to be specific about what counts as a proportionate punishment. Indeed, deontological theorists often concede as much. For instance, while Wellman insists that a person who commits a crime only forfeits his claim against a proportionate punishment, he is at pains to note that what is required for a punishment to be proportionate is very hard to determine. As he notes, "the most sophisticated retributivists routinely shy away from offering precise punishments for specific crimes," and he too declines to offer a "simple formula for determining which specific rights are forfeited by any given crime."[50]

I do not mean to suggest that proportionality is a meaningless ideal. My claim is rather that the ideal of proportionality in punishment is, to borrow a Rawlsian slogan, "political, not metaphysical."[51] The norm of proportionality is made meaningful by the decisions of appropriately constituted institutions, not by abstract moral reflection. We have considered judgments—for instance, that life imprisonment for petty

50. Wellman, "The Rights Forfeiture Theory of Punishment," 386–87; *Rights Forfeiture and Punishment*, 32; see also Andreas von Hirsch, *Deserved Criminal Sentences* (Bloomsbury 2017), ch. 5.

51. See Emmanuel Melissaris, "Toward a Political Theory of the Criminal Law: A Critical Rawlsian Account," *New Criminal Law Review* 15(1) (2012): 146–48. Metaphysical conceptions of proportionality remain current in the literature; see, e.g., Greg Roebuck and David Wood, "A Retributive Argument against Punishment," *Criminal Law and Philosophy* 5(1) (2011): 73–86.

theft is wrong—and these judgments provide a reasonably solid basis for judging a sentencing regime that routinely produces those kinds of outcomes to be in that respect unjust. But within these very broad limits, what proportional punishment consists in is determined by the operation of appropriately constituted institutions, institutions that may be informed by particular cultural beliefs, legal traditions, and so forth.[52] If we are unsure about the sentences our institutions generate, we have reason to take a hard look at the design of those institutions to ensure that they are not dominated by perverse incentives, capture, and short-term political gain. Even if they aren't, it may still be the case that the sentences they generate are pointlessly long, inflicting more harm than benefit. But that does not show that they are therefore disproportionate.

Second, proponents of strictly deontological theories may bite the bullet and claim that mass incarceration *is* permissible. Perhaps this is not as unpalatable as it sounds. Suppose, a philosopher might suggest, that half of the population steals a kidney from the other half of the population, and that all of the kidney thieves are promptly captured, prosecuted, and imprisoned for a proportionate amount of time. What would be the injustice in that? After all, everyone in prison is guilty, and is serving a proportionate punishment. Isn't that exactly what punishment is for?[53]

Again, I have simply been assuming that mass incarceration is unjust. My question is only whether strictly deontological theories can explain why that might be. What I have been suggesting is that, in effect, if you are moved by the kidney example, then perhaps you should be more sanguine about mass incarceration than is typically the case. After all, the kidney example and mass incarceration in the United States today share some important similarities. The overwhelming majority of people in jails and prisons are in fact guilty, they are guilty of mostly uncontroversial crimes, and are, in the main, serving sentences that are not obviously disproportionate. Since mass incarceration is not composed of mass violation of individual rights, there is, by this reasoning, no objection to mass incarceration.

Biting the bullet in this way is consistent with my overall conclusion, which is that strictly deontological theories cannot explain what is

---

52. See Nicola Lacey and Hanna Pickard, "The Chimera of Proportionality: Institutionalising Limits on Punishment in Contemporary Social and Political Systems," *Modern Law Review* 78(2) (2015): 216–40 at 219–20, 227.

53. I owe this example (and this objection) to Kit Wellman.

wrong with mass incarceration, not that mass incarceration is wrong. To be clear, for reasons given below, I believe mass incarceration *is* wrong. But this is for reasons that are unavailable to a strictly deontological theorist. In any case, this bullet is sufficiently unpalatable that I suspect few will be tempted to bite it. Under mass incarceration conditions, what the state is doing is punishing lots of guilty people. If there is no moral objection to punishing any one of those individuals, it's hard to see, on an individualistic framework, where the moral objection to punishing all of them comes from. Yet there *is*, or so I assume, a moral objection to punishing them all. (Taken individually, each of the hypothetical kidney thieves plainly deserves punishment. Does that necessarily make it permissible for public institutions to give it to them? *All* of them?)

I have been stressing that strictly deontological theories cannot explain what is wrong with mass incarceration. The situation for strictly deontological retributivism is even worse. From that point of view, there is some positive reason to punish the guilty so long as doing so does not violate anyone's rights. Suppose that the wrongness of mass incarceration is consistent with respecting rights at the individual level. What does that suggest? It suggests that we should regard mass incarceration in the United States as a model for other countries to emulate. On this view, the United States does a better job than any other country in ensuring that the guilty are punished, and it does so without violating individual rights. True, punishing that many people does not further any valuable social aims, and in fact hinders many of them. But that is, by deontological lights, morally irrelevant. Hence, while most deontological retributivists deny that there is a *duty* to punish all criminals, they nevertheless seem to be implicitly committed to the view that so long as it violates no individual rights, mass incarceration of the guilty should not be regarded as a deep moral failure, but instead celebrated as a milestone in vindicating the rights of victims. Proponents of strictly deontological theories of punishment have not tended to endorse this line of thinking. But it seems baked into the logic of their position.

Third, it might be observed that even if a strictly deontological theory cannot explain why the United States incarcerates too many people, a deontological theorist can still explain why its criminal justice system is unjust in many other respects. I am, of course, happy to concede this point. After all, I am not suggesting that deontological theorists cannot explain why American criminal justice institutions are unjust in *any* respect.

There are lots of reasons those institutions are unjust, and many of these reasons have little or nothing to do with the scale of those institutions.

Note, however, that a concern with the scale of criminal justice may turn out to have implications for at least some of these issues. Suppose that American criminal justice institutions are unjust in part because the custodial population is disproportionately comprised of racial minorities. Should this inequity be remedied by incarcerating fewer guilty minority defendants, or should it instead be remedied by incarcerating more guilty white defendants? From the point of view of comparative equality, either strategy would be acceptable. However, if you believe that the United States already incarcerates too many people, then you will have reason to favor the decarceration strategy. Conversely, if you think that there are no valid moral objections to punishing someone (proportionately) for a crime that he committed, then you should regard the choice between incarcerating fewer minority criminals and incarcerating more white criminals as equally good options. If you think that punishing the guilty is constitutive of respect, the rightful condition or expressively repudiating wrongs, then you will have reason to favor the inflationary strategy.

Finally, it might be argued that my account has wrongly portrayed deontological punishment theorists as oddly single-minded—obsessed with punishing the guilty to the exclusion of all else. But nothing prevents strictly deontological theorists from recognizing value pluralism, such that any deontological reason we have to punish is qualified by the many competing demands that citizens can legitimately make on each other.

I concede that I am indeed portraying deontological theorists as morally single-minded. But I deny that this is an unfair characterization. As I have explained, strictly deontological theories cannot explain what is wrong with mass incarceration in the United States because they exclude the expected social costs and benefits of a system of punishment from the outset. Those theories make the permissibility of punishment turn entirely on one set of moral considerations to the exclusion of others, namely whether punishment does any good for anyone. That, or so it seems to me, is tantamount to denying a powerful source of competing demands on the morality of punishment. That is what it is to be morally single-minded.

Of course, it is always possible to imagine that there are further, strictly deontological, constraints that would permit a deontological theory of punishment to be appropriately critical of mass incarceration. Thus, Wellman points out that rights forfeiture is not always sufficient to render punishment permissible, "because there may be other factors which ground obligations."[54] For instance, if A has promised B that she will not punish C even if C does forfeit his rights, then it would not normally be permissible for A to punish C, even if he does forfeit that right. However, while Wellman's example of third-party promises of immunity may be probative in individual contexts, it seems unlikely to explain why the United States has unjustly incarcerated hundreds of thousands, if not millions, of people over the last several decades.[55] So we need some other deontological constraint to explain why, given that millions of people have forfeited their rights by committing crimes, we are nevertheless obligated to punish only a small fraction of them. Given the inadequacy of standard deontological constraints on punishment to explain what is wrong with mass incarceration, it hardly seems unfair to shift the burden onto deontological theorists to state what those further conditions are supposed to be. These further conditions should explain why the United States today, despite punishing only a small fraction of the guilty, nevertheless punishes too many people; and they should do so without introducing the very considerations of social costs that strict deontology is committed to excluding as irrelevant.[56]

4.5 Anti-deference and Mass Incarceration

Why it is that strictly deontological theories are unable to explain how committed we should be to punishing the guilty? As I see it, the basic

54. Wellman, "The Rights Forfeiture Theory of Punishment," 375 n.7. See also Larry Alexander and Kimberly Ferzan, with Stephen Morse, *Crime and Culpability* (Cambridge University Press 2009), 7–10. Tellingly, although Alexander and Ferzan initially introduce the idea of deserved punishment as entailed by respecting people's choices (6), their discussion of "moderate" retributivism transforms deserved punishment into just another type of value to be pursued, to some optimal level, by the social planner. This, I think, confuses a teleological and a deontological conception of desert. See *Crime and Culpability* at 13 (characterizing desert as a "deontological side constraint.")

55. As it happens, there is a legal device that operationalizes roughly the kind of promise Wellman envisions, which is a prosecutor's offer of immunity in exchange for cooperation with an ongoing investigation. It is unlikely that the United States incarcerates too many people because too many of these promises have been reneged on.

56. Hamish Stewart has recently tried to offer just such an account; 'The Wrong of Mass Punishment," *Criminal Law and Philosophy* (2016), doi:10.1007/s11572-016-9409-2. While I agree with Stewart that a policy of relentless prosecution and punishment is hard to square with the ideals of a free society, Stewart does not explain why such a policy is not permitted by a Kantian theory of punishment. Indeed, Ripstein explicitly claims that punishing criminals is positively *required* by the "rightful condition," such that any exceptions would be wrongful and a betrayal of the law. Ripstein, *Force and Freedom* at 320–21. Rather than a vindication, Stewart's argument thus appears to be a reductio of a Kantian approach to punishment.

problem is that strictly deontological theories are exclusively focused on the rights of individuals, and hence are led to ignore the social costs of an overall *system* of punishment. As a result, they have no means for cost containment: they lack the resources for distinguishing between what makes it justifiable to punish the first criminal and the nth criminal, for any arbitrarily large *n*.

This is a surprising flaw in a theory ostensibly designed to assess social institutions. Evidently, it would be implausible to assess the fairness of other large social institutions, such as healthcare, education, the tax code, and so forth exclusively by looking at individual transactions. We do not determine, for instance, what the marginal tax rate should be for people in your income bracket by asking how much of your income you "deserve" to keep, while ignoring broader questions of what would make for a fair and efficient income tax structure. Nor, for that matter, do we decide how much healthcare, education, transportation, or police services to provide you without considering the broader social cost of providing that level of service. Since individualism is implausible in these other contexts, why does it seem to have such a grip on us when we are thinking about crime and punishment? What makes it plausible to insist, as Duff and Wellman do, that the permissibility of punishment has nothing to do with the "contingent future benefits" that might flow from punishment, or whether punishment under some set of circumstances is "necessary to promote some important aim"?[57]

I suspect the answer has to do with a thought I considered in Chapter 2—namely, that what a person deserves by way of punishment for crime is individually determinable, whereas what a person deserves by way of her fair share of the social product is not. The idea is that, unlike taxes, healthcare, education, and so forth, the criminal law exemplifies private interpersonal morality. On such a conception, comparing the overall social costs and benefits of a system of punishment is beside the point, morally speaking, since each person's culpability is determined on an individual basis.

Contrast this view to an account of criminal law as public law. On that kind of view, the moral standards that apply to the criminal law are simply specific applications of broader political principles—principles that embody our reasons for valuing public institutions generally. That is the force of

57. Duff, "Retrieving Retributivism," 3; Wellman, "The Rights Forfeiture Theory of Punishment," 375, n.7.

holding the criminal law to a fully political standard of justification. Hence, from a public law point of view, what it is for an individual to be fairly treated by the criminal justice system should not be explained in purely individualistic terms, but should be assessed against the legitimate expectations engendered by institutions that operate according to publicly avowable principles of justice. Just as how much income a person deserves to keep, or how much healthcare she deserves to receive are determined, in part, by reference to the costs to others of adopting the corresponding policy, what a person deserves by way of punishment is determined by considering whether others could reasonably be expected to bear the costs of imposing it.[58]

The political ideal of anti-deference, elaborated in Chapter 3, provides an illustration of this type of approach. The political ideal of anti-deference suggests that we have reason to value public institutions insofar as they protect each person's access to central capability on a non-discriminatory and non-hierarchical basis. Access to these capabilities is constitutive of equal social standing. But because criminal punishment tends itself to undermine effective access to central capability, there is a strong reason not to have more of it than necessary—that is, more than necessary to protect those capabilities for all. Punishment, as the invasion of central capability, is permissible when it is part of a strategy that optimally protects central capability on a universal and inclusive basis, but not otherwise. In other words, we have reason to value punishing the guilty to the extent, but only to the extent, that failing to punish would itself jeopardize universal access to central capability.

Because of how essential central capabilities are to a person's equal standing in society, those whose lives are thereby affected by the operation of criminal justice institutions—for instance, because they are incarcerated, or because they are at risk of being victimized by others—are owed an explanation of why they ought to agree to have their lives affected in that way. Since incarceration will certainly invade effective access to a wide swath of central capabilities, it is not enough to show that the legal rule that the sanctions are used to enforce is designed to protect central capability; it must also be shown that nothing less than a system of custodial sanctions of that kind will do to ensure that the rule is adequately respected. That, in turn, is cashed out in terms of protecting universal access to central capability, including access by those who we believe to

58. "Sensitivity to social cost is a familiar theme in the distributive justice literature. See, e.g., Ronald Dworkin, *Sovereign Virtue* (Harvard University Press 2002)

have violated the rule. If those conditions are met then public institutions will be able to say, to potential victims and wrongdoers alike: true, *you* have had your liberty impaired, but no other policy could have treated you better while still respecting each person's entitlement to equal consideration of *their* liberty.

In quintupling the size of its custodial population over the last generation, it is plausible that the United States has crossed that line. Clearly, this is a judgment call, and no amount of social science evidence could be fully determinative.[59] That said, it seems plausible to believe that while *some* level of criminal punishment is required to stably protect each person's effective access to central capability, by punishing as many guilty people as it does, the United States has now well overshot any reasonable estimation of that mark. Why? Because it is, at the very least, doubtful that increased punishment on that scale has been effective at deterring crime; because the lifetime costs to people who have served time behind bars, and to their families and communities, are staggeringly high; because there are non-punitive means of managing the risk of violent crime that build, rather than destroy, capability; and because the level of policing and punishment that some communities are now forced to tolerate have seriously eroded the expectations of reciprocity and trust that lie at the foundation of continued social cooperation. In other words, the proposition that the United States currently punishes too many people can be vindicated by appeal to the aggregate social impact of punishing that many people, including the guilty. The political ideal of anti-deference explains what is wrong with mass incarceration precisely in terms of the "contingent future costs" of punishment on that scale. What is wrong with mass incarceration in the United States is that it is excessive with respect to the "important social aim" of protecting each person's basic interests on terms befitting social and political equals.

59. For an overview, see Pfaff, *Locked In*, ch. 4. On the scale of punishment relative to crime, see Holger Spamann, "The U.S. Crime Puzzle: A Comparative Perspective on U.S. Crime and Punishment," *American Law & Economics Review* 18(1) (2016): 33–87 (finding that mass incarceration is largely ineffective at preventing crime); Franklin Zimring, *The City That Became Safe* (Oxford University Press 2011), 187–89 (noting that NYC's massive crime decline in the 1990s and 2000s was accompanied by decreasing rates of incarceration); Redburn, Travis, and Western, eds., *The Growth of Incarceration in the United States*. On the collateral consequences of punishment, see sources cited in Chapter 6; non-punitive alternatives for managing crime, Chapter 7; and the corrosive effect of aggressive policing on trust, Chapter 3.

I conclude with three observations. First, no normative theory of criminal justice, including this one, should be expected to generate unique and determinate answers to detailed questions about this or that policy initiative. However, in contrast to deontological theories, the political ideal of anti-deference at least suggests a relevant moral principle, if no doubt contestable in application, for addressing these kinds of questions. If it turns out that quintupling the size of the custodial population does not optimally protect the likelihood that everyone—including those held in custody—will enjoy effective access to central capability when compared to other reasonably feasible institutional arrangements, that would be a reason not to do so, and potentially a reason to undo it if has already been done. A plausible theory of punishment must have a way of accommodating empirical evidence about the conditions under which we should expect punishment in general, and custodial sanctions in particular, to be an effective means in achieving the ends that public institutions are meant to promote. The evaluation of these conditions cannot afford to ignore the social cost of a system of punishment.[60] A theory of punishment need not necessarily take the evidence amassed by sociologists, economists, and criminologists about the extraordinarily high net social costs of mass incarceration to be decisive, but it cannot afford to completely ignore it, either.

That said, although I have characterized the political ideal of anti-deference in very general terms, it cannot be meaningfully applied without appeal to context-specific evidence. It is a more particularized, jurisdiction-specific, and historically contingent approach to thinking about the morality of punishment than is perhaps typical in the literature. The prevailing interpretation of the central capabilities at a given

60. For just one example, a theory of punishment that takes seriously the task of determining when the use of custodial sanctions is appropriate, and when it has become excessive, must be sensitive to what we know about how people respond to the possibility of sanction. See, for instance, William Spelman, "What Recent Studies Do (and Don't) Tell Us about Imprisonment and Crime," *Crime and Justice* 27 (2000): 419–94; Redburn, Travis, and Western, eds., *The Growth of Incarceration in the United States*, Chapter 5. Naturally, what we conclude from an estimate of the elasticity of crime to punishment depends in part upon broader commitments in the theory of justice—how we assess the social value of reducing crime as against the costs of punishment, as well as how we assess the resulting distribution of social advantage across the population. The need for an overarching normative theory is apparent when considering that punishment is not the only way to reduce criminal offending; other means, such as increasing the male high school graduation rate, also appear to reduce offending, though at different rates, and with a different distribution of social costs and benefits. See Lance Lochner and Enrico Moretti, "The Effect of Education on Crime: Evidence from Prison Inmates, Arrests and Self-Reports," *American Economics Review* 94(1) (2004): 155–89.

place and time, the historically determined form of democratic control, the evidence with respect to crime rates, the relative impact of custodial sanctions, the availability of alternatives and the opportunity cost of punishment, for instance, are all indispensable inputs in thinking about what level of incarceration might be permissible in a given context.

Finally, one might think that my argument is a roundabout way of defending a utilitarian theory of punishment. But this is not so. There are many ways of describing the public good, and the specific approach of classical utilitarianism—maximizing aggregate welfare or preference satisfaction—is but one of them. There are many others.[61] As I have emphasized, anti-deference is prioritarian and capability-based, rather than maximizing and welfarist. Indeed, not only is anti-deference not utilitarian; it is not even consequentialist in the usual understanding of the term. The basic value of social equality is based on a principle universal moral equality, and I have made no effort to ground that principle in any kind of felicific calculus. The democratic and egalitarian credentials of anti-deference are grounded in a picture of the kind of government that is appropriate to a society of moral equals, not in anticipation of better outcomes overall. That said, it *is* part of my argument that a normative theory of criminal justice that takes seriously the aggregate costs and benefits of those institutions cannot afford to be as austerely abstract as strictly deontological theories tend to be. To be sure, strictly deontological theories of punishment can hardly be faulted for being uniquely immune to facts. That seems to be a widely shared problem in thinking about the criminal law generally. However, the inability of strictly deontological theories of punishment to come to grips with evidence-based policy is consistent with a moralizing approach that focuses on the criminal law as the expression of moral sentiment and/or the vindication of abstract rights, while marginalizing the net social cost of a system of punishment. Behind the deontologist's appeal to abstract rights and their vindication stands the emotional call to strike back at those we fear and resent.[62]

---

61. Pettit and Braithwaite's republican theory of punishment, for instance, is expressly consequentialist but not at all utilitarian. See John Braithwaite and Philip Pettit, *Not Just Deserts: A Republican Theory of Criminal Justice* (Oxford University Press 1987).

62. Recall the history of California's notorious "three strikes" law, which is both harsher and broader than habitual offender laws in other states: the law was initially drafted by the father of a murder victim, and gained political traction after a paroled repeat violent offender kidnapped, sexually assaulted, and murdered a twelve-year-old girl. It was precisely *not* the product of a careful, cold-blooded look at the costs of enacting a three strikes law. Indeed,

4.6 Conclusion

There is a fair amount of irony to the argument I have mounted. Theories of punishment that focus on the consequences of a system of punishment are often thought to be unprincipled because they are allegedly consistent with excessive punishment and the trampling of people's rights in the name of crime reduction. The irony is that it is actually strictly deontological theories that lack the resources to constrain the growth of the carceral state. Despite their emphasis on constraining punishment, it is strictly deontological theories that turn out to have a problem with punishment maximalism. Refusing to so much as consider punishment's "contingent future benefits" or its contribution to an "important social aim" may appear principled in the context of the individual case, but it is much more problematic when used as a justification for ignoring the aggregate impact of hundreds of thousands, or even millions, of decisions to impose proportionate punishment on plainly guilty people. Ignoring aggregation in this broader context yields the result that where the net social costs of a generalized practice are steeply rising, the fact that they are not obviously decisive in the individual case will mask quite extreme costs when enacted as general social policy, costs that no one would think it reasonable to incur if presented with the policy in the aggregate. Yet because of their systematic exclusion of social cost, this is precisely what strictly deontological theories entail.

When the aggregate costs of incarceration are worth bearing, and when they are not—as well as what it means to share in bearing those costs as equals—are questions that cannot be answered simply by observing that a penal system only punishes the guilty, and then only proportionately. It requires instead a theory that takes seriously the political character of criminal justice institutions, and especially their role as public institutions that create and allocate crucial forms of social advantage. What is wrong

later efforts merely to fund a *study* of the law's impact were vetoed by the governor. Why bother? After all, if we are entitled to punish wrongdoers regardless of (as Duff puts it) the "contingent future benefits" from doing so, and regardless of (as Wellman puts it) whether doing so is "necessary to promote some important aim," then evidence about what good might be achieved by more punishment is simply beside the point. Zimring, Hawkins, and Kamin archly note that popular support for California's law "could be the opposite of an instrumental justification, in which people believe that the legislation is appropriate only because it is effective. Instead, it is often the case that belief in the effectiveness of a penal statute is rooted in the citizens' conviction that the law is appropriate. Since the penal measures *feel* right, they must be working well." Zimring, Hawkins, and Kamin, *Punishment and Democracy*, 221.

with mass incarceration is not that it necessarily tramples individual rights, for one could devise a system of mass incarceration that assiduously respected the moral rights of each of the millions of guilty people it punished. What is wrong with mass incarceration is that it disfigures millions of lives for little to no end, thereby imposing extraordinary costs on people in a way that is inconsistent with publicly avowable principles of justice. Hence, if it is to be both satiable and relevant to the evaluation of public institutions, a theory of punishment should start with a conception of criminal punishment as the subject matter of a political theory of justice, rather than simply private morality writ large.

5

Reasons to Criminalize

5.1 Introduction

In Chapter 2, I defended an account of criminal law as public law. In Chapter 3, I articulated a democratic and egalitarian standard of political justification—the political ideal of anti-deference—as a way of giving normative content to a public law conception. In the last chapter, I argued that because anti-deference considers the aggregate social cost of a system of punishment, it provides a more plausible framework for thinking about punishment than accounts that seek to explain the permissibility of punishment in exclusively individualistic terms. My aim in this chapter is to show how the public law conception in general, and the model of anti-deference in particular, can be extended to questions about the scope of the criminal law. I start by considering, in Sections 5.2 and 5.3, the connection between the private right conception and what I shall refer to as a "subject matter" based approach to criminalization. In Sections 5.4 and 5.5 I sketch a contrasting approach to criminalization, from a public law point of view in general and the point of view of anti-deference in particular.

5.2 Direct Prohibitions, Wrongfulness, and Core Criminality

From the point of view of criminal law as the vindication of private rights, criminal punishment is an outgrowth of a moral practice familiar from everyday life. Just as punishment in everyday life targets moral wrongdoing, so too does punishment under the criminal law. A very natural thought about criminalization flows from this general idea, to wit: only conduct that is independently morally wrongful should be criminalized (the "wrongfulness principle"). On this view, the criminal law is an intrinsically condemnatory institution, and for its condemnation of X to be truthful, it must be the case that X is a type of act worthy of condemnation—for instance, because it is a violation of someone's moral rights. "[W]hat is distinctive of criminal law," as Antony Duff puts it, is that it "purports to define, and provide for the condemnation of, certain kinds of moral wrong," and hence "to justify the criminal law's content we must therefore show that what it defines as crimes are indeed wrongs of the appropriate kind."[1] While many different measures might be taken to prevent or discourage people from engaging in wrongdoing—measures that might respond to or shape conduct that has not yet ripened into wrongful action—the criminal law is only engaged once wrongdoing is actually present. The distinctive morality of the criminal law is backward-looking condemnation for what has been done, rather than a forward-looking attempt to see what might still be salvaged.

The wrongfulness principle is an instance of what I shall call a *subject matter* approach to the theory of criminalization. On a subject matter approach, a theory of criminalization consists of one or more principles that identify the types of conduct that are the permissible objects of criminalization by reference to a shared moral property (for instance, that it causes harm to others, violates a right, or is otherwise wrongful.)[2] Whether a type of action exemplifies that property is intrinsic to the type of conduct in question, and can be discerned by considering its instances in the abstract. One need not know much about law, institutions, social traditions, or other contextual facts to know that murder, rape, and theft are harmful, violate rights, and are morally wrongful. From the perspective of a subject matter approach, to criminalize conduct is to attach a label to conduct because that conduct exhibits, intrinsically rather than contextually, a distinctive moral property.

The wrongfulness principle enjoys wide popularity. For instance, Doug Husak defends such a view. He asks: "What else but morality would anyone think the law *should* enforce? No alternatives are

1. Antony Duff, *Answering for Crime: Responsibility and Liability in the Criminal Law* (Hart Publishing 2007), 81.

2. Glanville Williams described this as a "material definition" of criminal law: "The Definition of Crime," *Current Legal Problems* 8(1) (1955): 107–30.

viable."[3] Husak has even suggested that endorsing the wrongfulness principle in some form is a categorical requirement for any acceptable theory of criminalization.[4]

Wrongfulness, understood in this way, reflects a long-standing way of thinking about crime and the criminal law: as a matter of common sense and everyday moral judgment, rather than technical expertise and professional judgment. This view of crime and the criminal law predates the rise of the lawyer-dominated trial, the centralization of enforcement and punishment, and the systemization of the law: it is, in that sense, a premodern view of the criminal law. Consequently, and perhaps unsurprisingly, it has trouble coming to terms with the characteristic development of modern law, namely the rise of the regulatory state. As Peter Ramsay has noted, so-called *mala prohibita* offenses present an enduring puzzle for a conception of the criminal law as the vindication of private right.[5] The problematic status of *mala prohibita* offenses may reflect Blackstone's construal of crimes as "public wrongs," in the sense of an injury to the public rather than, as had traditionally been the case, in terms of procedure, jurisdiction and remedy. On that view, *mala prohibita* must be wrongs to be crimes (which they surely are, at least sometimes), but their wrongfulness must

---

3. Doug Husak, *Ignorance of Law: A Philosophical Inquiry* (Oxford University Press 2016), 34.

4. Husak, "*Malum Prohibitum* and Retributivism," in *The Philosophy of Criminal Law: Selected Essays* (Oxford University Press 2010), 411; see also Husak, *Overcriminalization: The Limits of the Criminal Law* (Oxford University Press 2008), 73–76; and Husak, *Ignorance of Law*, 37. Many others have endorsed the wrongfulness principle in some guise or another. See, e.g., Andrew Simester and Andreas von Hirsch, *Crimes, Harms and Wrongs: On the Principles of Criminalisation* (Hart 2011), 19–30; Grant Lamond, "What Is a Crime?, " *Oxford Journal of Legal Studies* 27(4) (2007): 609–32 at 627; R.A. Duff, "Towards a Modest Legal Moralism," *Criminal Law and Philosophy* 8 (2014): 217–35; Kit Wellman, "Rights Forfeiture and *Mala Prohibita*," in *The Constitution of the Criminal Law*, ed. R.A. Duff, Lindsay Farmer, S.E. Marshall, Massimo Renzo, and Victor Tadros (Oxford University Press 2013), 77–96 at 79; R.A. Duff et al., *The Trial on Trial: Volume 3* (Hart Publishing 2007), 54. The current popularity of the wrongfulness principle is a manifestation of what Jeremy Horder has called the "counter-reformation" in criminal law theory: "Bureaucratic 'Criminal' Law," in *Criminalization: The Political Morality of the Criminal Law*, ed. R.A. Duff, Lindsay Farmer, S.E. Marshall, Massimo Renzo, and Victor Tadros (Oxford University Press 2014), 101–3. Recently, some theorists have begun to challenge wrongfulness as a constraint on criminalization. See Andrew Cornford, "Rethinking the Wrongfulness Constraint on Criminalisation," *Law and Philosophy* 36 (2017): 615–49; Tadros, *Wrongs and Crimes*, ch. 17.

5. See Peter Ramsay, "The Responsible Subject as Citizen: Criminal Law, Democracy and the Welfare State," *Modern Law Review* 69(1) (2006): 29–58 at 32; Lindsay Farmer, *Making the Modern Criminal Law: Criminalization and Civil Order* (Oxford University Press 2016), 17; Nicola Lacey, *In Search of Criminal Responsibility: Ideas, Interests, and Institutions* (Oxford University Press 2016), 126.

be explained in a manner distinct from *mala in se* crimes.[6] The challenge in this respect is accounting for the wrongfulness of *mala prohibita* in a way that does not wind up rendering the *mala in se/mala prohibita* distinction ultimately otiose. This is because the legitimacy of *mala prohibita* offenses rest upon an account of the legitimacy of the state; but once this is on offer, it is not clear why such an account would not similarly extend to *mala in se* offenses, which are, after all, also creatures of public law. In this connection, one might recall Nicola Lacey's observation that the rise of the regulatory state has presented a "persistent legitimation problem for criminal law," a problem only partially eased by a reconceptualization of responsibility in terms of choice rather than character.[7] This "legitimation problem" is rooted in the historical distinction between justice (law) and police (administration), out of which the *mala in se/mala prohibita* distinction arises. But, as Mireille Hildebrandt points out, this distinction has little applicability to modern societies which have subjected vast and intricate bureaucracies to the rule of law.[8]

Since most contemporary theorists are reluctant to conclude that the state may not use the criminal law to enforce otherwise legitimate regulatory ends, a significant amount of attention has been dedicated to explaining how so-called *mala prohibita* crimes can be brought within the rubric of the wrongfulness principle. I shall consider some of the currently popular arguments regarding the wrongfulness of *mala prohibita* (grounded in an alleged duty to obey fair laws) shortly. First, however, it is worth considering how the problematic status of regulatory offenses is connected to an intuitive, but flawed, way of thinking about criminal law. For these purposes, Joel Feinberg's approach is paradigmatic. In particular, I am concerned with the approach Feinberg—one of the twentieth century's leading liberals—took to determining what a theory of criminalization is a theory *of*. In a brief passage in *Harm to Others*, Feinberg noted that he would limit his attention to the criminal law as a system of "direct prohibitions." On his account, a direct prohibition is the use

---

6. Blackstone's account was not stable, as it could not explain why every private injury was not also a public wrong. See David Lieberman, "Mapping Criminal Law: Blackstone and the Categories of English Jurisprudence," in *Law, Crime and English Society, 1660–1840*, ed. N. Landau (Cambridge University Press 2002), 139–61 at 153–56.

7. Lacey, *In Search of Criminal Responsibility*, 126.

8. Mireille Hildebrandt, "Justice and Police: Regulatory Offenses and the Criminal Law," *New Criminal Law Review* 12 (2009): 43–68, 60–1.

of the law to prohibit some type of conduct outright rather than merely regulating how it is performed, where that prohibition is based on a "primary" rather than "derivative" reason.[9] A primary reason for punishing X arises out of the character of X considered "quite independently of the legal statute that prohibits it." We do not need a law to tell us that murder is wrong, for instance. A derivative reason for punishing X, in contrast, arises out of X's status as a violation of a legal rule. A direct prohibition, then, is a legal prohibition that is motivated in the first instance by primary reasons: where the decision to authorize punishment is taken not merely as a "last resort," but rather "is clearly *for* something other than (or in addition to) mere disobedience to authority as such, and it can be specified what punishment is for independently of the rules of legal institutions set up for some purpose."[10] Feinberg's theory of criminalization, developed at length in *The Moral Limits of the Criminal Law,* is focused exclusively on the criminal law as a system of direct prohibitions.

Yet Feinberg was by no means unaware that the criminal law had important roles beyond that of directly prohibiting antisocial conduct. Indeed, he explicitly noted the criminal law's role in stabilizing the operation of public institutions.[11] He did not suggest that there was anything illegitimate or unimportant about the criminal law operating in this manner. So why did Feinberg restrict his attention to direct prohibitions, while ignoring the criminal law's broader role in enforcing cooperation with legal rules?

Feinberg's answer appears to rest on the worry that taking into account the criminal law's rule-enforcing role would make the kind of theory of criminalization he wanted to defend impossible. Taking seriously the criminal law's role in stabilizing public institutions would mean that a theory of criminalization "would wander over the entire range of economic and political policy."[12] But this is a curious observation. If, as Feinberg recognized, the criminal law has an important rule-enforcing

9. Joel Feinberg, *Harm to Others* (Oxford University Press 1984), 19–21.

10. Feinberg, *Harm to Others,* 21.

11. Feinberg, *Harm to Others,* 20.

12. Feinberg, *Harm to Others,* 21. Feinberg also suggests that "direct prohibitions" are generally "a more drastic and serious thing than its main alternatives" on account of the severity of criminal punishment (23). This might be a reason to focus on more severely graded crimes—felonies rather than misdemeanors, for instance. It is not clear that it is a reason for focusing on direct prohibitions to the exclusion of other uses of the criminal law.

function, and if, as Feinberg also recognized, an adequate theory of criminalization would therefore have to be integrated with a broader way of thinking about public policy, then the appropriate conclusion would seem to be: so be it. The theory of criminalization would be but an application of a broader theory of the appropriate use of legislative power generally. After all, given that enforcing cooperation with legal rules is an important function of the criminal law, focusing only on direct prohibitions crimes would produce at best a very partial theory of criminalization. Oddly, however, Feinberg appears to have given little further thought to the matter. This is a striking omission, as the very idea that there might *be* distinctive "moral limits" to the criminal law turns on isolating a subset of the criminal law and ignoring those parts that are caught up in the "entire range of economic and political policy." If the criminal law cannot be isolated from the regulatory state, then the only meaningful "moral limits" on the criminal law are the ones that apply to the regulatory state in general. The harm principle would not be limited to critique of outdated morals offenses: it would be a principle regulating *everything* the state does. Yet Feinberg has little more to say on the point.

The decision to focus on direct prohibitions is consequential. Consider the way in which the criminal law is used to enforce civil, political, and social rights. Under federal law in the United States, it is a criminal offense to injure, intimidate or interfere with someone to prevent her from voting, or more generally, from "participating in or enjoying any benefit, service, privilege, program, facility, or activity provided or administered by the United States," or indeed, from participating in any such program or activity "receiving Federal financial assistance."[13] Can the moral status of interfering with someone who seeks to make use of a state-provided benefit, service, privilege, program, facility, or activity be assessed "independently of the rules of legal institutions set up" to provide it, as Feinberg requires of a direct prohibition? It is hard to see how, at least without

13. 18 U.S.C. § 245(b) (1968). A further provision criminalizes interfering with public school students, workers, interstate travel, or the use of public accommodations generally, when such interference is motivated by racial, ethnic, religious, or nationalistic animus. This provision presents an interesting hybrid case. On the one hand, one might plausibly understand this provision to prohibit the manifest immorality of discriminatory interference. On the other hand, the statute's focus on education, labor, interstate travel, and public accommodations suggests that one might also interpret it as focused on regulating access to a range of public institutions. Under the former interpretation, the statute is a direct prohibition, whereas it is not under the latter interpretation. For a brief history of this statute, see Randall Kennedy, *Race, Crime and the Law* (Vintage Books 1998), 67–69.

appeal to a wide range of commitments regarding "economic and political policy" that Feinberg sought to exclude from a theory of criminalization. This too is obscured by a conception of the criminal law as a system of direct prohibitions. An account of the morality of the criminal law that excludes consideration of the "entire range of economic and political policy." More generally, in a democratic society of any complexity, the moral status of much of what government does will be determined in part by whether it represents a reasonable conclusion to a fair political process. This too is obscured by a conception of the criminal law as a system of direct prohibitions.

To be fair, Feinberg's approach to the theory of criminalization was not unprecedented. He was in a way following in the footsteps of James Fitzjames Stephen. Writing in the mid-nineteenth century, Stephen noted that the criminal law was filled with a great variety of offenses, relating to matters as diverse as education, family support, labor regulation, environmental protection, and public health. Stephen gave scant attention to these offenses, on the grounds that they did not pertain to the "criminal law properly so called, but are merely the sanctions by which other branches of the law are, in case of need, enforced."[14] Writing a century later, Feinberg continued Stephen's approach by dismissing large parts of the criminal law by philosophical fiat.

Conversely, Feinberg's exclusive focus on direct prohibitions was also not foreordained. Glanville Williams—in a paper that appeared a few decades before Feinberg's *Harm to Others*—had insisted that neither crime nor criminal law could be defined by reference to a particular subject matter. According to Williams, crime, and the criminal law, had to be defined with reference to the kind of process set up to respond to legal claims of various kinds—for instance, a process initiated by public officials and culminating, upon success by the moving party, with punishment.[15] As Jeremy Horder observes, "for Williams, there could be no 'essence' of crime in a world, as he saw it, dominated by *mala prohibita*, 'with the close social and economic regimentation that seems to be an inseparable part of modern society.' "[16] Like Feinberg, Williams

---

14. Sir James Fitzjames Stephen, *A History of the Criminal Law of England*, vol. 3 (MacMillan & Co. 1883), 266. My remarks here draw from Jeremy Horder, "Bureaucratic 'Criminal' Law," 103.

15. Williams, "The Definition of a Crime," 123.

16. Horder, "Bureaucratic 'Criminal' Law," 103–4.

realized that the criminal law had long been enmeshed in the regulatory state; but unlike Feinberg, Williams did not marginalize the significance of this fact in his account of criminal law.

Focusing on "direct prohibitions" as the paradigmatic case can make it appear as if the criminal law has a distinctive subject matter, namely a subset of intrinsically wrongful acts. Focusing on direct prohibitions achieves this by defining away all those cases in which the criminal law's rule-enforcing function is front and center. As a result of this narrowed focus, it can seem as if the task of a theory of criminalization lies in characterizing more precisely the nature of that subset of manifest wrongdoing that is the proper subject matter of the criminal law.[17] But taking a broader view of the criminal law's role in enforcing legal rules generally calls into question the idea that the criminal law *has* an intrinsic subject matter. This broader view suggests that the moral limits of the criminal law should be found not in *what* is being regulated, but in *how*: not in the moral quality of some act considered in isolation, but in the principles governing when it is appropriate to rely on ex post sanctions to ensure robust and ongoing social cooperation.[18]

5.3 Does the Criminal Law Have a "Core"?

Feinberg did not provide a convincing reason for focusing "almost exclusively" on the criminal law as a series of direct prohibitions on manifest wrongdoing. This does not mean that there is no such reason. Is there one? Plainly, the public law conception suggests not. But let us consider some other possibilities.

First, might it be the case that traditional *mala in se* crimes form the core of the criminal law in some quantitative sense? That seems unlikely. A focus on direct prohibitions cannot be justified on the ground that it is even remotely close to an accurate portrayal of the criminal law in practice. Consider the case of American criminal justice. By any measure, American criminal law is concerned with enforcing manifest wrongdoing to only a very limited extent. One way of assessing this is to note that only a very

17. See, for instance, Grant Lamond's account of the "nature of crime" as blameworthy wrongdoing that is a particularly grave instance of disrespect for a shared value. "What Is a Crime?," 627.

18. For another critique of subject-matter-based principles of criminalization, see Victor Tadros, *Wrongs and Crimes* (Oxford 2017), ch. 5.

small number of offenses—the various forms of assault, sexual assault, homicide, reckless endangerment, perhaps robbery and a few others—are plausibly construed as manifestly wrong. In comparison, federal law has been estimated to recognize approximately 4,000 distinct offenses carrying criminal sanctions.[19] This number represents only the provisions contained in the United States Code, and does not include the regulations promulgated by myriad federal regulatory agencies that formally rely on the threat of criminal sanctions to enforce their rules. Taking those into account, there may be "more than 10,000 regulatory requirements or proscriptions carrying criminal sanctions."[20] Surprisingly, it is unclear just how many criminally enforceable regulations are in force; some have reported figures of 300,000 or more, though this is little more than conjecture.[21] Even if this estimate is off by two orders of magnitude, it would nevertheless still be the case that so-called true crimes constitute a vanishingly small fraction of federal criminal law. (It is hard to generalize about state law, at least absent a more systematic accounting of what different states have criminalized, whether directly, by regulation, or by delegation to municipalities).

Note that this is neither a uniquely American phenomenon nor a particularly recent one. As Novak has emphasized, criminal sanctions have long been used to enforce a wide variety of regulatory aims, from transportation to alcohol consumption to building codes.[22] Looking beyond the United States, Chalmers and Leverick have reported that of 3,155 new crimes created by legislation in the UK in the years 1997–1998 and 2010–2011, a grand total of 31—or about 1 percent—were categorized as traditional criminal law offenses. In contrast, there were nearly 1,000 new

---

19. See John S. Baker, Jr, "Measuring the Explosive Growth of Federal Crime Legislation *Engage* 5(2) (2004), available online at http://www.fed-soc.org/publications/detail/measuring-the-explosive-growth-of-federal-crime-legislation. Ronald Gainer has estimated that there are approximately 3,300 federal offenses. "Federal Criminal Code Reform: Past and Future," *Buffalo Criminal Law Review* 2(1) (1998): 45–159 at 67.

20. Gainer, "Federal Criminal Code Reform," 74.

21. Thomas B. Leary, "The Commission's New Option That Favors Judicial Discretion in Corporate Sentencing," *Federal Sentencing Reporter* 3(3) (1990): 142–44 at 144, n.10 (citing Stanley S. Arkin, Comments at the George Mason Conference on Sentencing of the Corporation (October 25, 1990)).

22. William Novak, *The People's Welfare: Law and Regulation in Nineteenth-Century America* (University of North Carolina Press 2002), 15–16; see also Markus Dubber, *The Police Power: Patriarchy and the Foundations of American Government* (Columbia University Press 2005).

agriculture-related offenses, 400 health- and safety-related offenses and about 200 new offenses related to environmental protection and food production.[23] Admittedly, during this period there were approximately 350 new offenses in the category of "terrorism/international sanctions," many of which presumably would qualify as manifest wrongdoing. Yet even if we include every single new terrorism offense as a *mala in se* offense—surely an overly generous estimate, given the breadth of these offenses—it is still the case that nearly 90 percent of the newly created crimes in this period appear to be some form of "regulatory" offense.

Alternately, one could look not at criminal law itself, but at how that law is enforced on the ground. Even supposing that property offenses are *mala in se* (though, for reasons suggested below, this is far from obvious), of the approximately 8.2 million arrests made in 2010, only about a quarter were for violent crimes or property crimes.[24] Measured by police conduct, the bread and butter of American criminal justice is not conduct such as serious assault (less than 4 percent of arrests), much less homicide (less than 0.01 percent) or rape (less than 0.2 percent). Rather, it is conduct such as driving under the influence (about 10 percent), drug abuse (about 12 percent), and a variety of public order offenses related to alcohol, vagrancy, and disorderly conduct (about 13 percent). A similar pattern is found if we look at convictions rather than arrests. Fewer than half of convictions are for violent or property offenses; drug convictions alone comprise nearly twice as many felony convictions as all the categories of

---

23. James Chalmers and Fiona Leverick, "Quantifying Criminalization," in *Criminalization: The Political Morality of the Criminal Law*, ed. R.A. Duff, Lindsay Farmer, S.E. Marshall, Massimo Renzo, and Victor Tadros (Oxford University Press 2014), 54–79 at 65–66, tables 2.1 and 2.5. Chalmers and Leverick also report that in these periods the large majority (nearly 80 percent) of newly enacted crimes were required in order to implement an international obligation: see table 2.4. Horder similarly reports that of the 440 criminal offenses enacted in the UK in 2008, "perhaps as few as 30 . . . were aimed at private individuals," with a plurality of the rest directed at business regulation: see "Bureaucratic 'Criminal' Law," 115.

24. See Bureau of Justice Statistics, *Sourcebook of Criminal Justice Statistics Online*, Table 4.6.2010, available online at http://www.albany.edu/sourcebook/pdf/t462010.pdf (accessed May 13, 2018). My calculations reflect a broader view of what counts as a "violent" or "property" crime than the Bureau of Justice Statistics does, as they include non-aggravated assaults and non-forcible sex offenses. Going by the BJS's own account of "violent" and "property" offenses reduces the proportion of violent and property offense arrests to about 17 percent of the total. "Violent" crimes include murder and non-negligent manslaughter, forcible rape, robbery, aggravated assault, arson, other assaults, and sex offenses (other than the already-included forcible rape, but excluding prostitution).

violent crime combined.[25] Finally, given that the largest portion of criminal justice expenditures is spent on corrections, one might suspect that, if anywhere, incarceration would reflect a priority for crimes plausibly construed as manifest wrongdoing. And, indeed, incarceration is more heavily concentrated on so-called core criminal offenses than other arrests or convictions, although a significant proportion of offenders (approximately 27 percent) are imprisoned for drug or public-order-related offenses, and if property offenses are not counted as *mala in se* offenses, leaving violent offenses as the primary category of *mala in se* crimes, then the proportion of people imprisoned for *mala in se* offenses sinks to about one out of two.[26] (I consider the question of whether we really want to count pure property offenses as inherently wrongful shortly.) When local jails and federal prisons are factored in, that proportion sinks further to approximately one out of three.[27]

Finally, these figures likely significantly overstate the degree to which the criminal justice docket is concerned with manifest wrongdoing, because they are based exclusively on *felony* convictions. The criminal law's rule-enforcement function is nowhere more evident than in misdemeanor cases, and misdemeanor prosecutions have been estimated to outnumber felonies by an order of magnitude.[28] For instance, driving with a suspended license—a common misdemeanor—is frequently caused by the defendant's failure to comply with more mild sanctions (fines) used to enforce a variety of substantive rules, from parking offenses to the care and insurance of one's car to failure to pay child support. Although little

---

25. See Bureau of Justice Statistics, *Sourcebook of Criminal Justice Statistics*, Table 5.44.2006, available online at http://www.albany.edu/sourcebook/pdf/t5442006.pdf (accessed May 13, 2018).

26. See Bureau of Justice Statistics, *Sourcebook of Criminal Justice Statistics*, Table 6.0001.2010, available online at http://www.albany.edu/sourcebook/pdf/t600012010.pdf (accessed May 13, 2018).

27. See John Schmitt, Kris Warner, and Sarika Gupta, *The High Budgetary Cost of Incarceration*, Table 3 (Center for Economic and Policy Research, June 2010), available at http://www.cepr.net/index.php/publications/reports/the-high-budgetary-cost-of-incarceration/.

28. This is based on a recent estimate by the National Association of Criminal Defense Lawyers, which used the caseload statistics from twelve states to extrapolate a national rate of approximately 10.5 million misdemeanor prosecutions per year. See R.C. Boruchowitz, M.N. Brink, and M. Dimino, *Minor Crimes, Massive Waste: The Terrible Toll of America's Broken Misdemeanor Courts* (April 2009), available at http://www.nacdl.org/public.nsf/defenseupdates/misdemeanor/$FILE/Report.pdf. See also Alexandra Natapoff, *Misdemeanors*, *Southern California Law Review* 85 (2012): 101–63.

systematic data is available about the millions of misdemeanor cases processed each year, common offenses include conduct such as minor thefts, loitering, public intoxication, under-age possession of alcohol, and minor drug offenses.[29] It is likely that only a small fraction of misdemeanor offenses concern what may plausibly be thought to be independently wrongful conduct. This suggests that including the millions of misdemeanor cases processed by criminal justice institutions each year is likely to make the already small proportion of criminal justice activity directed at inherently wrongful conduct smaller still.

To be sure, these numbers should not be taken too strictly, as the concepts of "direct prohibition" and *mala in se* are not susceptible to uncontroversial application. Are criminal prohibitions on drunk driving a direct prohibition on the manifest wrongdoing of jeopardizing others through dangerous driving, or is it rather a prophylactic rule designed to reduce the risk of accidents by establishing an easily verified norm of general applicability? (Could they be both? Consider that Canadian law criminalizes *both* impaired driving *and* driving with over 80 milligrams of alcohol per 100 milliliters of blood.[30]) Is drug possession manifestly wrong? What about trafficking? Could trafficking be manifestly wrong even if consuming drugs is not, or would it be better in that case to understand it as a form of regulatory offense aimed at regulating conditions of import and sale? Depending on how one answers these questions, one might wish to include drug offenses as a form of direct prohibition. And unsurprisingly, what we consider to be manifestly wrong is historically and culturally conditioned. For instance, in early English law, rape was considered to be a type of *property* offense, and to the extent that property is a legally constituted concept, the status of rape as manifestly wrong in that society would be cast into doubt.[31]

I have given the benefit of the doubt to the direct prohibition theory by including property offenses as a form of manifest wrongdoing. One might well question this assumption. While pure property offenses such as theft are obviously wrong, it is not clear that their wrongness can be explained apart from their role in undermining a legally constituted set

29. See Bouruchowitz, Brink, and Dimino, *Minor Crimes, Massive Waste.*

30. *Criminal Code*, R.S.C. 1985, ss. 253(1)(a) and (b).

31. The deep contingency of how the common law has conceived of many allegedly core crimes is a theme in the work of Lindsay Farmer; see *Making the Modern Criminal Law*, part III.

of expectations that we have reason to value. Arguably, what offenses such as theft are about is protecting the set of legal institutions that we conventionally consider to constitute "property," rather than preexisting rights whose invasion would be plainly wrong in any just legal regime. If property offenses enforce a set of expectations about property ownership and use, then explaining their legitimacy will depend upon an account of justice in public institutions rather than an account of natural rights. Taking property from someone else without that person's consent only wrongs her if her expectation to have exclusive control over its disposition is itself legitimate, and whether it is legitimate depends upon whether the institutions and practices engendering that expectation are just. In Rawlsian jargon, private law is part of society's basic structure, and hence answerable to the political principles that apply to the basic structure.[32] As such, the criminalization of pure property offenses would have to be subject to the same norms of justice that apply to other parts of the basic structure, rather than standing solely on the fact that we intuitively regard them as morally wrong. At the very least, construing pure property offenses as crimes simply in virtue of their (alleged) status as manifest wrongdoing would require a robust account of the prepolitically morality of property, one sufficiently powerful to crowd out the obvious socioeconomic effects of enforcing one set of property rights over another.[33] It is worth noting that the proportion of criminal justice activity devoted to enforcing property crimes is substantially larger than that devoted to enforcing violent crimes.[34]

Many people think that the United States, along with other countries, suffers from an epidemic of "overcriminalization."[35] Regardless of

---

32. There are more than twice as many arrests for property offenses as for violent offenses: Bureau of Justice Statistics, *Sourcebook of Criminal Justice Statistics Online*, Table 4.6.2010, available online at http://www.albany.edu/sourcebook/pdf/t462010.pdf (accessed May 13, 2018). Felony convictions for property convictions (28 percent) similarly outnumber convictions for violent offenses (18 percent): Bureau of Justice Statistics, *Sourcebook of Criminal Justice Statistics*, Table 5.44.2006, available online at http://www.albany.edu/sourcebook/pdf/t5442006.pdf (accessed May 13, 2018).

33. See Samuel Scheffler, "Distributive Justice, the Basic Structure and the Place of Private Law," *Oxford Journal of Legal Studies* 35(2) (2015): 213–35.

34. See Liam Murphy and Thomas Nagel, *The Myth of Ownership: Taxes and Justice* (Oxford University Press 2002). My thanks to Leora Dahan-Katz and Miri Gur-Arye for encouraging me to address this point more squarely.

35. See Husak, *Overcriminalization*.

whether this is true, one might argue that the theory of criminalization is meant to be a normative theory.[36] Therefore, we cannot simply conclude from the fact that there is a gap between what our favored theory says is permissibly criminalized and what is actually criminalized that the theory must be defective. The argument here, however, is not simply that representing the criminal law as a system of direct prohibitions on independently wrongful conduct is not a perfectly accurate depiction of the criminal law. My point is that a theory of criminalization focused on manifest wrongdoing cannot claim authority—as an account of "true" or "paradigmatic" criminal law—on the basis of its general fidelity to existing law or practice. If direct prohibitions on manifest wrongdoing constitute the core of the criminal law, it would have to be for some other reason.

For instance, one might try to salvage the thought that the criminal law is essentially a set of direct prohibitions by arguing that direct prohibitions form the moral core of the criminal law in a more abstract sense, in that they are *functionally*, if not numerically, the standard way in which the criminal law operates. One way of fleshing out this thought is to argue that the criminal law seeks to categorically prohibit certain types of conduct, rather than merely set prices or rules for how the conduct is to be engaged in, as may perhaps be true of, say, tort law or administrative law.[37] Perhaps there isn't a clear division between criminal prohibitions and tort or administrative regulations in every case, nor is it necessarily the case that categorically prohibiting conduct will always be de facto more effective at eliminating unwanted conduct than, say, some kind of private liability or tax. The thought, rather, is that the meaning of a categorical prohibition on X is different than the meaning of taking steps to ensure that there is less of X, or that X should occur only within certain limits or if

36. It is not entirely clear how recent a phenomenon this is; certainly, the criminal law has for a long time included many types of conduct that go well beyond so-called "core" crimes. See, e.g., Darryl Brown, "History's Challenge to Criminal Law Theory," *Criminal Law & Philosophy* 3 (2009): 271–87; see also James Chalmers, "Overcriminalization by Numbers," *Current Legal Problems* 67 (2014): 483–502 at 495 (noting that there is "surprisingly little evidence" to support the claim "that the rate of criminalization has increased in recent decades in the UK.") Lindsay Farmer has noted that use of the criminal law to backstop a wide variety of legislation was common in Scotland by the 1830s onward; in a notable passage, Farmer singles out the development of the automobile as "one of the most important developments for the modern criminal law." *Criminal Law, Tradition and Legal Order* (Cambridge University Press 2005), 122–23. See also Horder, "Bureaucratic 'Criminal' Law" (tracing complaints about overcriminalization back to the late eighteenth century, and noting difficulties in establishing that recent years have in fact witnessed higher rates of criminalization).

37. See, e.g., *R v Wholesale Travel Group*, [1991] 3 SCR 154.

certain conditions are met. If so, then it would make sense to focus on the use of the criminal law in cases where it is engaged in "direct prohibitions" on conduct, even if we acknowledge that the criminal law also has ancillary functions as well. A proposal along these lines seems intuitive, in that it mostly tracks ordinary English usage. Often, for instance, when people discuss the "criminalization" of prostitution, drug use, physician-assisted suicide, or other topics, what they have in mind is not *any* legal regulation of those activities, but only an express "thou shalt not . . . " prohibition on engaging in that conduct. Consider, for instance, the contrast between heroin and prescription medications: in common usage, only the former is "criminalized," although if someone without the appropriate licenses dispenses or transacts in prescription medications, that action could potentially result in a criminal prosecution.[38]

Despite its intuitive appeal, this proposal turns out to be unconvincing upon further analysis. Pretty near any legal regime can be described alternately as "prohibitory" or "regulatory," contingent upon the level of generality at which the targeted conduct is specified. Of course, no one is in favor of even just a little bit of murder. But if we instead look at killing more broadly, then it is clear—for example, through the law of self-defense—that the law does not embody a categorical prohibition on killing but permits it under certain limited conditions. This suggests that although the law criminalizes murder, at a broader level of generality it merely regulates killing. The same would go for sex: the law criminalizes rape but merely regulates sex. It does not claim that sex is per se impermissible, but only sex under certain conditions. In other words, murder and rape may look like absolute prohibitions if we focus only on the specific offense-creating provision, whereas a broader point of view reveals them to be part of an overall regulatory scheme. This would, paradoxically, exclude murder and rape as instances of true criminal law. Conversely, perhaps hunting out of season and unlicensed possession of a firearm look more like "regulatory" offenses only because we have in mind their place in a broader scheme of rules. If, however, we focus on the specific conduct targeted by the offense-creating provision, then they may start to

38. See for example Chapter 13, Subchapter 1, Part C (Registration of Manufacturers, Distributors and Dispensers of Controlled Substances) of the United States' *Controlled Substances Act*. The unauthorized sale or transfer of prescription drugs could also contravene section 5(1) of the Canadian *Controlled Drugs and Substances Act*, provided the drugs were listed under Schedules I– IV of the *Act*.

look like absolute prohibitions. When we criminalize unlicensed possession of a firearm, are we suggesting that we shall tolerate only a moderate amount of unlicensed possession? Or is the thought that *no one* legitimately possesses a firearm absent prior legal authorization? Surely the latter.[39]

Absent some principled reason to prefer one or another level of generality in describing conduct, we should reject the idea that the criminal law is essentially prohibitory rather than regulatory in function. One might claim that the criminal law is a condemnatory institution that categorically prohibits wrongdoing. But one might just as well say that the criminal law is a regulatory institution, one that works by prohibiting certain defined types of act or omission in more or less specific contexts.[40]

Finally, one might argue that there is a privileged role for *mala in se* offenses because those types of offenses are fundamentally at odds with basic features of free and equal citizenship. In Chapter 3, for instance, I stressed the difficulties in ensuring that the criminal justice system does not become a source of domination. But *mala in se* crimes are themselves dominating. Surely, public institutions devoted (as I have suggested they should be) to protecting people from domination would have particularly strong reasons to criminalize acts that themselves amount to domination. Other types of crime might diminish or impair social cooperation, but not so directly, and not so viscerally, as paradigmatic *mala in se* offenses. So isn't it the case, on the very view I espouse, that something very much like the traditional *mala in se* offenses have a special status in a theory of criminalization?

It is unquestionably the case that traditional *mala in se* offenses are typically dominating. But that does not warrant the conclusion that the appropriate response, morally speaking, to people who dominate others is to dominate them in return, namely by criminalizing what they do and punishing them for doing it. To the contrary, that is a substantive, and controversial, principle of political morality. It is, moreover, one that is

39. One might be tempted to recast the prohibition/regulation distinction in terms of the distinction between common law and statute. But it is just not clear why we should think that courts do not regulate and that legislatures do not prohibit. Recall that the criminal law (including so-called core offenses) is in many jurisdictions a creature of statute.

40. Nicola Lacey, "Criminalization as Regulation: The Role of Criminal Law," in *Regulating Law*, ed. Christine Parker, Colin Scott, Nicola Lacey and John Braithwaite (Oxford University Press 2004), 144–67.

potentially inconsistent with anti-deference, which insists that criminal justice interventions be calculated to optimally protect everyone from domination. Anti-deference is inconsistent with automatically, as it were, responding to instances of private domination with public domination. Hence, even though traditional *mala in se* offenses are often plausibly construed as attacks on free and equal citizenship, that characterization alone does not establish what, if anything, the state ought to do to protect people from those attacks.[41]

As Lindsay Farmer has noted, criminal law theorists have devoted disproportionate attention to a small number of atypical crimes, the law of homicide in particular. Criminal law theory, Farmer observes, has become ever more singularly fixated on manifest wrongdoing by individuals qua individuals even as the criminal law has become increasingly less individualistic and more attuned to the needs of large, complex, and institutionally dense societies.[42] What explains this disconnect between what legal theorists are interested in and what the criminal law actually looks like? Perhaps part of the explanation is that the norms of interpersonal morality seem to provide a secure basis from which to criticize existing law.[43] However, the norms of interpersonal morality are not the only way to ground a normative theory of criminalization. One might, for instance, start with a conception of justice in public institutions. Adopting such a perspective would naturally lead one to consider when just institutions would approve the use of the criminal sanction to enforce their laws and policies. This would provide a basis for critical evaluation of the criminal law. But it would not lead one to regard the large majority of existing criminal statutes as not "true" criminal law because they do not amount to direct prohibitions on manifest wrongdoing.

---

41. Consequently, I am skeptical that there is a duty to criminalize and punish wrongdoing, as some have suggested. See A.P. Simester and Andreas von Hirsch, *Crimes, Harms and Wrongs* (Bloomsbury 2014) at 197–8; Arthur Ripstein, *Force and Freedom* (Harvard University Press 2009), ch. 10; and Alon Harel, "The Duty to Criminalize," *Law & Philosophy* 34 (2015): 1–22. My thanks to Arthur Ripstein for encouraging me to develop the points considered in this, and the previous, paragraph.

42. Farmer, *Criminal Law, Tradition and Legal Order*, ch. 5, especially 141, 167–72.

43. See, for instance Kit Wellman's insistence that the inescapable starting point of a theory of punishment are our independent moral rights against being punished. See "The Rights Forfeiture Theory of Punishment," *Ethics* 122(2) (2012): 371–93 and "Rights Forfeiture and *Mala Prohibita*."

5.4 Criminalization from a Public Law Point of View

What does the theory of criminalization look like from a public law point of view? Two claims are particularly salient: first, the decision whether to criminalize X is subject to justification under a fully political standard. Second, any subject-matter-based constraints must themselves be justified under that standard, rather than as a matter of the freestanding morality of the criminal law. After considering these claims in general terms, I sketch how they would apply in the context of the so-called harm principle.

In Chapter 2, I argued that the most basic function of the criminal law is to stabilize cooperation with public institutions, and that a fully political standard is the appropriate standard to apply in determining how well criminal law performs this function. A fully political standard of justification holds that

(7) The criminal law is worth supporting if and only if:
  a. the institutions whose rules it enforces are worth supporting, and
  b. its use in a particular context would be consistent with the principles that make those institutions worth supporting in the first place.

Under a fully political standard, deciding whether it is appropriate to criminalize X requires determining whether doing so stabilizes cooperation with worthwhile institutions, that being the basic point of using the criminal law to enforce public rules; and, if so, further determining whether the use of criminal sanctions to achieve that end would be consistent with our reasons for considering that institution to be worth supporting in the first place. This latter calculation would necessarily include consideration of the potential for intrusive surveillance, police harassment, excessively onerous compliance requirements, and the other ancillary effects of criminally enforcing a rule. For instance: should we support criminalization of assault? Is it the case that worthwhile public institutions would seek to protect people from assault? Presumably. Is it also the case that the reasons those institutions are worthwhile—that they support free and equal citizenship, respect rights, promote the public good, and so forth—are consistent with using criminal sanctions as a means for achieving that end? Possibly, contingent upon the other means open to us for protecting people from assault.

What it takes to satisfy a fully political justification depends on what you believe to be the most plausible moral framework for evaluating public institutions. A consequentialist approach will generally favor granting such permission only when doing so optimally promotes a given maximand. A rights-based approach will generally favor granting such permission only when doing so respects rights. A contractarian theory will evaluate public institutions as the possible objects of public willing.[44] And so forth. In the next section, I consider how the specific framework I favor, the political ideal of anti-deference, would fill in the general contours of a public law approach to criminalization. For the moment, however, I am concerned with general features of this approach that should apply irrespective of whatever specific framework one favors.

What is the status of subject-matter constraints under a public law approach to criminalization? A public law approach will only contain subject-matter constraints to the degree that those constraints are part of a more general theory of justice. What it will not contain are subject matter constraints based on the inner morality of the criminal law. This is because there is no inner morality to the criminal law. There is only the ordinary political morality that governs the public use of coercive force.

This is not to say that there can be no subject-matter constraints on a public law approach. Perhaps some types of subject matter constraint might be defended from within a public law perspective as part of a more general view of justice. For instance, political liberalism is often associated with the view that there are "private" areas of one's life—for instance, matters of conscience, association, and sexuality—that are fenced off from state regulation by a range of privacy-protecting rights. On a view of this kind, there is indeed a significant subject-matter constraint on the criminal law. But this is simply because the state may not permissibly set public policy in these areas, so there are no legitimate public rules to *be* criminally enforced.

To take a different example, one might view natural rights as a general constraint on state action, in which case they would also provide a subject matter constraint on the criminal law. Consider Wellman's account of

44. See for instance Susan Dimock, "Contractarian Criminal Law Theory and *Mala Prohibita* Offenses," in *Criminalization: The Political Morality of the Criminal Law*, ed. R.A. Duff, Lindsay Farmer, S.E. Marshall, Massimo Renzo, and Victor Tadros (Oxford University Press 2014), 151–82. My view owes much to Dimock, though I reject the wrongfulness and desert principles, both of which she accepts.

rights forfeiture. On Wellman's view, people have natural rights that any legitimate state is bound to respect. These rights, however, can be forfeited by violating another person's natural rights. In this case, the state is at liberty to inflict proportional harms on the rights violator if it wishes to, for instance by punishing him.[45] Insofar as criminalizing X authorizes the state to punish you (punishment that would normally count as violating your rights) if you do X, then Wellman's view supports a subject-matter constraint of the following kind: only those acts that amount to a forfeiture of your natural right not to be punished in that way may permissibly by criminalized. If you only forfeits your right against punishment through conduct that violates rights, then the state may only criminalize conduct if it violates rights.[46] After all, if it would be illegitimate for the state to actually punish you for X-ing, then arguably it would also be illegitimate for the state to *threaten* to punish you for X-ing—that is, to criminalize X-ing.[47] This is a subject-matter constraint on the content of the criminal law, but again it is one that is drawn from a broader theory of the legitimate use of public coercion rather than something putatively special about the criminal law.

Not every political theory that recognizes natural rights will generate a subject-matter-based constraint. Wellman's rights forfeiture theory creates a subject-matter constraint on the criminal law because it views the permissibility of punishing someone as conditioned on whether that person's own conduct respects rights. But not every right, or every theory of rights, is conditioned in this way. First, some rights might not be subject to forfeiture. For instance, the right against being tortured is plausibly of this kind. Perhaps other rights are like this too, such as rights against execution, life imprisonment, solitary confinement, or even very long periods of incarceration. If so, then these rights could generate a limit on the use of the criminal law without giving rise to a subject-matter-based constraint—it

45. See Christopher Wellman, *Rights Forfeiture and Punishment* (Oxford University Press 2017).

46. This presents a puzzle regarding so-called *mala prohibita* offenses; I consider Wellman's resolution of that puzzle shortly.

47. Perhaps there is a difference between threatening to impose a sanction and actually imposing a sanction. For a subtle discussion, see Warren Quinn, "The Right to Threaten and the Right to Punish," *Philosophy & Public Affairs* 14(4) (1985): 327–73. I shall leave this complication aside here.

doesn't matter *what* kind of crime you commit, the state simply cannot treat you in that way (without violating your rights.)

More generally, however, one might defend a rights-based theory that holds that people have natural rights that usually restrict the kinds of action the state can take against them, while allowing that those rights can be overridden under a wide range of conditions. Those conditions need not be interpreted, as on Wellman's approach, as generally sensitive to whether you have violated someone else's rights. For instance, one might claim that your right not to be treated in a given way can be overridden if the costs to others of not treating you in that way are sufficiently great (cross a relevant threshold), or if you have in some relevant sense consented to waive them under certain conditions (e.g., on the condition that everyone else do so as well, for the sake of securing some collective good). Claims of this sort would not necessarily generate subject-matter-based restrictions on the criminal law. After all, there may be a great diversity in the types of situations in which others will face sufficiently grave losses if the state does not invade your rights, or in which you might plausibly be said to have waived those rights for the sake of the common good. It might not be possible to further characterize those situations in advance.

The upshot is that a public law theory of criminalization does not impose subject- matter-based constraints on the criminal law unless those constraints flow from a more general theory of justice in public institutions. Some such theories, such as those that incorporate a strong public/private distinction, or those that give a decisive role to rights violations as a basis for rights forfeiture, may yield subject matter constraints on the criminal law. But they do so by appeal to the limits of public authority generally, rather than by appeal to a conception of punishment in particular.

The generality of a public law approach to criminalization—the way in which it is rooted in a general view of the political morality of public institutions—can perhaps be usefully illustrated by comparing two different interpretations of the harm principle.[48] One interpretation of the harm principle is the *harmful conduct principle* (HCP) which states:

48. My discussion of the harm principle in the following paragraphs draws from R.A. Duff and S.E. Marshall, "'Abstract Endangerment,' Two Harm Principles, and Two Routes to Criminalization," in *Bergen Journal of Criminal Law and Criminal Justice* 3(2) (2015): 131–61. For a comprehensive, sophisticated and recent treatment of the harm principle, see James Edwards, "Harm Principles," *Legal Theory* 20 (2014): 253–85.

> **HCP:** We have good reason to criminalize a given type of conduct if [and only if] it is harmful to others.

A contrasting interpretation of the harm principle is the *harm prevention principle* (HPP). This principle states:

> **HPP:** We have good reason to criminalize a given type of conduct if [and only if] doing so is the best available means of preventing harm to others.[49]

HCP and HPP are materially different, in that HCP focuses on conduct that itself causes harm, whereas HPP includes conduct that is in itself harmless so long as the failure to criminalize it would itself be harmful. In other words, HCP places a subject-matter-based constraint on the criminal law, whereas HPP does not. HCP favors criminalizing conduct in virtue of the fact that tokens of that type are harmful; it is a partial answer to the question, "what is a crime?" In contrast, HPP seeks to criminalize acts for the sake of reducing harm, and thus does not seek to limit "crime" to "acts harmful in themselves." HPP is a teleological principle, in that it views criminalization as a means to an end, namely reducing harm overall. Under HPP, there is reason to criminalize *any* type of conduct, from possessing firearms to possessing undersized lobsters to acting in contempt of court, if criminalizing that conduct would be the best available means of preventing harm to others.

The contrast between HCP and HPP can be illustrated by considering two cases. Gun possession is not harmful in itself; it is perfectly possible, indeed common, for people to possess guns without harming anyone. But it might be the case that setting up a system of licenses, permits, and registries for gun ownership would be a reasonable and effective way of protecting people from the harm that does accrue from unrestricted access to firearms, and it might also be the case that such a system would

---

49. See Duff and Marshall, "'Abstract Endangerment,'" 135; Edwards, "Harm Principles," 263–66. The bracketed "only if" distinguishes the harm principle as merely providing *a* basis for criminalization and the harm principle as the *exclusive* basis for criminalization. Mill defended the latter version; Feinberg the former. However, Feinberg does claim that preventing harm or serious offense "exhausts the class of good reasons for criminal prohibitions" from a liberal point of view: *Harm to Others*, 26. Mill's version of the harm principle is arguably ambiguous as between the harmful conduct and harm prevention interpretations.

only be workable if people who continually refuse to comply could ultimately be hauled into a criminal court to answer for themselves. These are, of course, complex and contestable empirical claims, but suppose they are true. In that case, the failure to criminalize the refusal to register one's firearms would itself be harmful because that type of conduct undermines what is—by hypothesis—a reasonable set of regulations that protect people from harm. Criminalizing the refusal to register a firearm would be permissible under HPP even though, we are assuming, in the vast majority of cases possessing firearms is a harmless activity. In contrast, HCP would forbid criminally enforcing restrictions on firearm ownership because owning a firearm is not sufficiently linked to harm to others on an individual level.[50]

Contrast the case of gun possession with that of drugs. Suppose that drug use harms others in some relevant way. If so, then criminalizing drug consumption would be consistent with HCP. Criminalizing drug consumption would be consistent with HCP even if criminalizing drugs only creates more harm on net. Under these assumptions, HPP would come to the opposite conclusion. It is not concerned with whether the targeted conduct is harmful. It is concerned with whether authorizing criminal sanctions is harmful, which it might be even if the targeted conduct is *also* harmful. In short, HCP would rule out criminally enforcing a publicly oriented regulatory scheme, even if doing so reduces harm on net, on the grounds that the targeted conduct (possessing a firearm) was not inherently harmful; and it would permit criminalizing activities that are inherently harmful, even when criminalization causes still more harm. In contrast, HPP yields the opposite pattern: it would not permit criminalization where criminalization causes more harm than it prevents, but it would permit criminally enforcing a regulatory scheme if doing so is, on balance, the best available means of preventing harm to others, even when the conduct in question is not itself harmful.

From a public law point of view, is there reason to prefer HPP or HCP? I am inclined to think we should generally prefer HPP. Both might be animated by a similar liberalism about harm, but unlike HCP, HPP integrates that concern into an overarching account of what public institutions ought to do, namely minimize harm. HCP seems dubious by comparison. Perhaps there is a theory of justice that entails that the state

50. For a recent discussion, see Tadros, *Wrongs and Crimes*, ch. 17.

has reason to minimize the harmful acts of others while lacking reason to minimize the harm caused by its own institutions. This is, on the face of it, an odd set of commitments. That said, it is not an obviously impossible one, so if it could be adequately motivated then perhaps there would be room for HCP on a public law conception.[51]

5.5 Criminalization and Anti-deference

I have thus far been using the generic language of harm, as much philosophical discussion of the limits of the criminal law has centered on that concept. There are, however, significant drawbacks to a focus on "harm." Most important, the crudeness of a generic conception of harm—already a well-recognized problem in the context of traditional criminal law subjects—would be a serious handicap when extended to the evaluation of public institutions generally.[52] A more specified approach draws on the political ideal of anti-deference considered in Chapter 3. Recall that the political ideal of anti-deference states that, subject to constraints of political equality, public institutions and policies should be designed in such a way as to maximally promote effective access to central capability for all. From the point of view of anti-deference, "criminalizing" X means authorizing the imposition of ex post sanctions on people who deliberately do X, where the sanctions in question impair a person's effective access to one or more central capabilities. Hence, from the point of view of anti-deference, one might suggest the following principle (*the anti-deference principle*) (ADP):

> **ADP:** We have good reason to criminalize X if doing so is the best available means of promoting universal and effective access to central capability on terms acceptable to social and political equals.[53]

---

51. There are, of course, many complex and difficult problems about harm—for instance, whether the proper index in any given context is aggregate harm, average harm, or some other standard; and whether the preferred treatment should focus on moderating the intensity of harm in the median case or on those cases on the right tail of the distribution. For a discussion of these issues in the context of drug policy, see Robert J. MacCoun and Peter Reuter, *Drug War Heresies: Learning from Other Vices, Times, & Places* (Cambridge University Press 2001), especially chs. 14 & 15.

52. On the crudeness of the harm principle, see Bernard Harcourt, "The Collapse of the Harm Principle," *Journal of Criminal Law and Criminology* 90(1) (1999): 109–95.

53. The "best available means" standard is meant to include all possible strategies for responding to X, including doing nothing, civil liability, regulation, changing social norms, and so forth.

As stated, ADP is consistent with acknowledging other reasons in favor of criminalization, since all ADP does is to state *a* reason in favor of criminalization without ruling out other reasons that might entitle us to criminalize X. A somewhat stricter version of ADP is:

> **ADP^{+}**: The only reasons that would make it permissible to criminalize X are those that tend to show that criminalizing X is the best available means of promoting universal and effective access to central capability on terms acceptable to social and political equals.

The principal difference between the two is that the latter rules out moral wrongfulness, standing alone, as a reason in favor of criminalizing some type of conduct. However, ADP^{+} could be made stricter still. After all, ADP^{+} is consistent with the possibility that at least sometimes even a very powerful consequentialist argument in favor of criminalizing might be defeated by other, non-consequentialist, reasons. The most thoroughly consequentialist version of ADP is therefore:

> **ADP^{++}**: It is permissible to criminalize X if and only if doing so is the best available means of promoting universal and effective access to central capability on terms acceptable to social and political equals.

The principal difference between ADP^{+} and ADP^{++} is that the latter rules out moral wrongfulness as a constraint on criminalization. Under ADP^{++}, satisfying the criterion of anti-deference is a necessary and sufficient basis for criminalization, whereas under ADP^{+} it is only a necessary condition. As I noted in Chapter 3, I do not insist that there are no relevant deontological constraints on the coercive use of state power, and indeed regard political equality and anti-subordination along those lines. Hence, although (for reasons I shall presently turn to) I am inclined to endorse ADP^{++}, I am ultimately agnostic as to whether we should accept ADP^{++} over ADP^{+}. Perhaps there are compelling rights-based arguments (beyond the ones built into anti-deference) that serve to further limit what it is permissible to criminalize; but then again perhaps not. I am, however, more persuaded that we should prefer ADP^{+} to ADP.

As indicated, the main challenge in this context is dealing with the wrongfulness principle. The wrongfulness principle operates at cross purposes to the political ideal of anti-deference, since conduct can be manifestly wrong regardless of whether sanctioning it fosters effective access to central capability for all, and since it can also be the case that sanctioning conduct protects access to central capability even when the conduct in question is not manifestly wrongful. My reasons for favoring ADP^{+} over ADP turn on my doubts about whether we have reason to criminalize acts simply because they are wrongful. Rejecting that claim makes a prima facie case in favor of ADP^{+} over ADP. However, since the wrongfulness constraint is often conceived of as not only a reason *for* criminalization (the position of Duff and other legal moralists), but also as a reason *against* it (the position of Feinberg and other liberals), it is worth considering the merits of wrongfulness in that more restrictive guise. I shall argue that understood strictly as a constraint on criminalization, wrongfulness is either empty or implausible. If so, we should be more favorably inclined toward ADP^{++}. This is because the wrongfulness constraint is the most popular deontological constraint on criminalization recognized in the literature, and rejecting it strengthens the case for ADP^{++}. Nevertheless, I do not embrace ADP^{++}, because I leave open the possibility that there might be deontological constraints on the public use of coercive power other than wrongfulness.[54]

Wrongfulness as a reason to criminalize. Should the criminal law serve to publicly condemn moral wrongdoing as wrongdoing? I don't think we should recognize any such reason. Under a fully political standard of justification, whether use of the criminal law is worth supporting depends upon whether that use would be approved by public institutions that are themselves worth supporting. Hence, the question is whether public institutions committed to the political ideal of anti-deference would approve criminalizing conduct solely because the conduct in question is morally wrongful. I think they would not, on grounds of both political and substantive equality.[55]

As to political equality, consider Lord Devlin's explanation for why the criminal law should be used to punish "sin." Not, Devlin claimed, because it was sin, but rather because punishing sin reinforces the "invisible bonds of common thought" that hold a society together.[56] Regardless of the merits

---

54. One might, for instance, endorse the prohibition on using people as a means, as defended by Victor Tadros in *The Ends of Harm* (Oxford University Press 2011).

55. For a contrary view, see Matt Matravers, *Justice and Punishment: The Rationale of Coercion* (Oxford University Press 2000), 111–21.

56. Patrick Devlin, *The Enforcement of Morals* (Oxford University Press 1965), 10.

of his rather far-fetched prediction of social calamity as a result of failing to clamp down on deviant sex, Devlin's argument fails to take seriously that justifying the existence of coercive state institutions requires showing not only that they stabilize social arrangements, but that the arrangements they stabilize are ones that free and equal citizens—including those who commit the acts Devlin would have us consider criminal—could reasonably endorse. Other versions of legal moralism—that punishment is authorized because it lowers the status of the criminal (Hampton), because people morally deserve it in some unanalyzable sense (Moore), or because it vindicates a community's thick ethical life (Kleinfeld)—seem vulnerable to versions of the same concern.[57] They do not give those who do not share the same thick comprehensive doctrine a reason that they can reasonably be expected to endorse. This is a point that Chad Flanders has recently emphasized: sincere belief in wrongdoing should not be regarded as sufficient to authorize punishment insofar as it "depends on controversial ideas . . . that people might reasonably reject."[58]

By the same token, in criminal justice as elsewhere, the flipside of a highly communtarian ethos is a highly exclusionary politics. Group members who appear to stray from the accepted dogma are punished harshly because of the challenge they present to group solidarity (a phenomenon known to social psychologists as the "black sheep effect"[59]). Remarking on the highly communitarian ethos of criminal justice in the American colonies, Samuel Walker observes that their tendency to expel people they deemed undeserving indicated that "[t]here was no concept, either in law or in common practice, that someone had a fundamental right to live in the village or town, and certainly not in defiance of community norms." As Walker notes, "colonial communities were not tolerant, liberal, and pluralist in the modern sense."[60] To be sure, not every form of legal moralism is equally subject to this concern. Duff has provided

57. Jean Hampton, "An Expressive Theory of Retribution," in *Retributivism and Its Critics*, ed. Wesley Cragg (Papers of the Special Nordic Conference held at the University of Toronto, June 25–27, 1990): 1–25 at 11–15, 21–22; Michael S. Moore, *Placing Blame: A General Theory of the Criminal Law* (Oxford University Press 1997); Joshua Kleinfeld, "Reconstructivism: The Place of the Criminal Law in Ethical Life," *Harvard Law Review* 129 (2016): 1486–565.

58. "Public Wrongs and Public Reason," *Dialogue* 1 (2016): 45–58 at 51.

59. Willem van Prooijen, *The Moral Punishment Instinct* (Oxford University Press 2018), ch. 7.

60. *Popular Justice: A History of American Criminal Justice*, 2nd ed. (Oxford University Press 1998), 20.

a characteristically thoughtful and nuanced account of the place of what he calls "dissenters and recusants" within his "modest" legal moralism.[61] Duff's attempt to reconcile equal citizenship with legal moralism remains the exception, however. By and large, this remains an issue that legal moralists have yet to fully canvass.

Criminalization of wrongdoing for its own sake can also impair substantive equality. This point can be brought out by an example. Suppose that online bullying is manifestly wrong, but that the weight of the evidence suggests that criminalizing online bullying will not protect those at risk of being bullied. Is there nonetheless good reason to criminalize online bullying, for instance to publicly denounce it as the wrong it is?

I do not think we should recognize any such reason. Criminalizing online bullying, we are assuming, does not further the ends of anti-deference because, even if online bullying jeopardizes access to central capability, criminalization is ineffective at protecting that access. But not only does criminalization fail to advance the ends of anti-deference, it in fact sets them back. This is because it jeopardizes the capabilities of those whose conduct might be swept up by an online bullying statute and will consequently get caught up in the criminal justice system and acquire criminal records. We might be tempted to discount their interests, on the ground that their conduct is morally odious, but we could not do so while respecting the principle of inclusive aggregation—the principle that people do not lose their standing to be considered as equals by virtue of their criminal acts. Hence, criminalizing online bullying under the circumstances described above would be unjust.

Of course, that doesn't end the argument. Perhaps it is not obvious that, in cases of conflict, we should generally prefer ensuring that we have just public institutions to ensuring that we have publicly condemned wrongdoing. Perhaps it is not obvious that justice is a more important value than retribution. Why shouldn't we say: so what if it's unjust? We should punish the bastard anyway—what he did was *wrong,* and we need to publicly stand up and make this clear to all the world.

Here is one argument for why we shouldn't say that. Assume, as I argued in Chapter 2, that the basic function of the criminal law is to stabilize cooperation with public institutions. Assume, further, that we

61. Antony Duff, *The Realm of Criminal Law* (Oxford University Press 2018), 127–37.

accept the fully political standard of justification: that how well or how poorly the criminal law carries out its generically coercive rule-enforcing function is determined by appeal to the same standard that applies to public institutions generally. Putting those two claims together suggests that performing its rule-enforcing function well—performing it in conformity with whatever theory of justice we endorse—is a more basic standard of success for the criminal law than advancing whatever other functions it may have. At its most basic level, what the criminal law is *for* is stabilizing the rule of law, and it only does that job well when it secures justice. The criminal law might have other functions too—functions other than supporting just institutions—but pursuing those other goals should not lead us to compromise on ensuring that the criminal law succeeds at its most basic task. As a result, the pursuit of retribution, no matter how richly deserved, is permissible only within the constraints of a broader account of the political morality of public institutions.

To be sure, this argument is not conclusive either. I can think of at least two ways of responding to it. First, one might argue that the substantive standard of justice for public institutions simply is that they vindicate people's pre-justicial claims not to be wronged, regardless of whether doing so secures any other benefit. In that case, supporting justice in public institutions will reduce to supporting public condemnation of wrongdoing qua wrongdoing. Second, one might deny that the criminal law performs its rule-enforcing function well only when the institutions it supports are just. One might claim that the criminal law performs that function well simply when it contributes to the *stability* of the institutions it supports, regardless of whether they are also just. Since it is not implausible that the criminal law can be effective at stabilizing unjust institutions, one could then conclude that there is no problem with using the criminal law to pursue public condemnation of wrongdoing even when doing so is unjust. It must only take care that in doing so it does not undermine people's willingness to go along with the condemnatory project.

These are deep challenges to anti-deference, in that they rest on a quite different picture of the political morality of public law. Since it is not my aim to defend anti-deference as the only, or even necessarily the best, account of the political morality of public law, I shall not explore these issues further. I note only that these responses essentially boil down to an argument in favor of a theocratic state, either in the sense of a state that pursues some ideal of pre-justicial morality at the expense of justice in its basic institutions, or in the sense of a state that cannot conceive of a difference between the two. Either justice is overridden in the name of interpersonal morality (the intrinsic viciousness of bullying gives us good reason to criminalize it, even if doing so is inconsistent with general principles of justice), or justice is defined in terms of interpersonal morality (just institutions are, by definition, ones that ensure people get what they deserve). Both of these views strike me as profoundly illiberal. Some—libertarians and retributivists, notably—may nonetheless find this to be an appropriate use of public authority. However, if you do not regard justice in public institutions as secondary to moral righteousness, then you should prefer that, in cases where they conflict, society's basic institutions prioritize securing justice over criminalizing wrongdoing simply because it is wrongdoing.[62]

Wrongfulness as a constraint on criminalization. Let me now consider the wrongfulness principle from a different angle. Many who endorse the wrongfulness principle do so as a *limit* on criminalization, rather than as a reason in favor of criminalization. Indeed, some go so far as to insist that it is not just desirable that only wrongs are criminalized, but that this is in some sense part of the *meaning* of criminal law.[63] The foregoing argument, however, is only targeted at wrongfulness as a positive reason to criminalize. Is the wrongfulness principle more plausible as a constraint rather than as a positive reason to criminalize?

On balance, I think we should probably reject a purely negative wrongfulness principle as well. My argument for this conclusion breaks down into two cases. Either the relevant sense of "wrongful" is strictly construed, in which case it is inconsistent with too much of the liberal welfare state; or it is interpreted more generously to include conduct that is wrongful only because prohibited by just public institutions, in which case it appears trivial. So understood, it would simply restate the claim that the offense-creating law is just, except in the language of right and wrong.[64]

---

62. My thanks to Leora Dahan-Katz and François Tanguay-Renaud for helpful discussion on this point, though I suspect neither may be convinced that there is anything much wrong with what I have called "theocracy"!

63. See, e.g., Duff, *The Realm of Criminal Law*, 19–20.

64. One way of rejecting the wrongfulness principle is to reject the idea that *types* of action, as opposed to particular *tokens*, can be wrongful. If that meta-ethical claim is true, then the wrongfulness principle as it is usually understood must be false, since it is usually understood to apply specifically to types of conduct (intentional killing, taking items of value without consent, etc.) rather than particular tokens. This has to do with wrongfulness as a constraint on legislation, rather than case-by-case adjudication. This would still leave the

Consider an example. Suppose it turns out that requiring people to pay taxes to support government services is an integral part of just public institutions. Suppose, further, that a just strategy for encouraging people to pay their taxes includes making tax evasion a crime. Plausibly, if failing to pay your taxes is wrong, it is only because a legitimate public authority has required you to do so, not because you have a pre-justicial duty to pay taxes. Nevertheless, the wrongfulness principle would prohibit criminalizing tax evasion if it is understood to prohibit criminalizing conduct that is not pre-justicially wrong, that is, wrong regardless of how public institutions are set up. This is implausibly restrictive. Intuitions about the meaning of "criminal law" seem insufficiently important to justify imposing this kind of constraint on the otherwise just operation of public institutions.

Modern administrative states require people to do lots of things that they would not be morally required to do in the absence of the relevant laws and institutions, from paying taxes to spending a dozen years or more in compulsory education to not standing in contempt of court. Solving coordination problems and enabling extended forms of cooperation beyond what would be possible by private ordering alone is a large part of why public institutions are valuable. For this reason, while it might be true that, in the absence of law or public institutions, you would not wrong anyone if you acted otherwise, that seems beside the point. In many cases, achieving cooperative aims will require the use of some quantum of coercive force (if only the coercion of threatening to revoke your driver's license if you continue to refuse to pay your outstanding speeding tickets). If the public use of coercive force could only be brought to bear against you on account of manifest wrongdoing—something that it would have been wrong to do even if the law didn't tell you not to do it—then a great deal of the administrative state would be effectively unenforceable. Consequently, if public institutions could not effect a change in what it is morally permissible to require of others, then the entire project of the modern administrative state would be cast into serious doubt. Any political theory that does not seek the dismantling of the administrative state cannot afford to draw a bright line around manifest wrongdoing in the strict sense.

Of course, a strict wrongfulness principle would be considerably more plausible if it could be applied only to the criminal law in particular, rather

---

principle that no one should be convicted of a crime if he was not culpable in acting as he did. However, culpability in this sense is a matter of fault in particular instances—mens rea and affirmative defenses—rather than criminalization.

than the administrative state generally—to (true) crimes rather than mere regulation, to punishments rather than mere penalties.[65] But this route is no longer open once we reject the idea that there is a distinctive inner morality to the criminal law. From the point of view of criminal law as public law, constraints on criminalization flow out of the ordinary principles of political morality applicable to public institutions generally, rather than criminal law specifically. Therefore, from a public law point of view, the strict wrongfulness principle stands in some considerable tension with the basic legitimacy of the administrative state.

Can the wrongfulness constraint be salvaged by interpreting it more broadly? Perhaps, for instance, willful noncompliance with a legal rule is wrong when it concerns a regulatory scheme that promotes important public values while only imposing modest and reasonable burdens. One might argue that there is a limited duty to obey the law, at least when the law in question is just. Failing to live up to that duty, one might then claim, is a wrong.[66] Hence, criminalizing that failure would be consistent with the wrongfulness principle after all, even though the conduct in question is wrong only by virtue of deviating from fair and reasonable laws. Duff, Marshall, and Wellman have all defended a weaker wrongfulness principle along these lines.

Duff and Marshall defend a broad wrongfulness principle because, on their view, the criminal law exists to publicly describe conduct as wrongful.[67] Hence, the criminal law would be saying something false if the conduct it criminalizes was not wrongful irrespective of whether it was criminalized. By insisting that there is a limited duty to obey the law, they are able to consistently claim that the criminal law speaks truthfully when it then announces breaking the law to be wrong.[68] Since I am of the view that the criminal law may, but need not, publicly describe conduct as morally wrongful, it is on my account sufficient that the law enjoining you to do (or to refrain from doing) X on pain of a criminal sanction be just.

---

65. Joel Feinberg, "The Expressive Theory of Punishment," *Monist* 49(3) (1965): 397–423.

66. Duff and Marshall, "Abstract Endangerment"; Duff, "Towards a Modest Legal Moralism"; Wellman, "Rights Forfeiture and *Mala Prohibita*." Stuart Green defends a similar claim: "Why It's a Crime to Tear the Tag off a Mattress: Overcriminalization and the Moral Content of Regulatory Offenses," *Emory Law Journal* 46 (1997): 1535–614 at 1581.

67. Or, as Doug Husak has put it, that blame is intrinsic or integral to the criminal law.

68. Duff and Marshall, "Abstract Endangerment," 138. See also Duff, *The Realm of Criminal Law*, 299–332; Wellman, "Rights Forfeiture and *Mala Prohibita*."

No additional label of "wrongful" need be applied to failure to follow that law's command. This approach is agnostic as to whether there is a moral duty to obey the law. Perhaps, as Alice Ristroph has suggested, the state is at liberty to enforce the law, and you are at liberty to resist it.[69] I take no side on this particular issue.

In any case, I do not see that very much is gained by seeking to salvage the wrongfulness principle in this way. Suppose we have established that a legal rule requiring you to pay income tax is just under your preferred theory of justice, and that we have also established that enforcing that regulation with a criminal sanction is also just under that very same theory. You can add that someone who fails to comply with that regulation acts "wrongfully" if you like, but I cannot see that doing so adds anything to what we have already established, which is that the state acts justly in imposing a criminal sanction on you if you do not pay your taxes. Labeling the conduct in question "wrongful" does not contribute to explaining why it is permissible to criminalize it. The latter is a question about the moral status of institutions; the former is a question about whether individuals are obligated to comply with what those institutions do. At best, all this strategy does is save the theory that only wrongful conduct may be criminalized by postulating a duty to comply with the law.[70] From a public law point of view, the crucial question is whether the state acts within its legitimate authority in using the criminal law to enforce that aspect of the tax code. If so, it is not obvious why it should matter whether noncompliance is also morally wrong.[71]

---

69. Ristroph, "Respect and Resistance in Punishment Theory," *California Law Review* 97 (2009): 601–32.

70. Compare Duff's suggestion that a just legal rule is one that serves the common good in a way that does not involve imposing unreasonable burdens on people, and that as a result is one that it is wrong to violate. *The Realm of Criminal Law*, 70.

71. Duff attempts to rescue a form of legal moralism from a version of this objection by distinguishing between conduct that is "pre-legally" and "pre-criminally" wrong: see "Towards a Modest Legal Moralism," 4–6 (discussing Tadros's example of criminalizing possession of a knife.) By insisting that carrying a knife becomes "pre-criminally" wrong by virtue of being prohibited by a just (non-criminal) law or regulation, the proposition that only conduct that is wrongful may permissibly be criminalized reduces to the proposition that we should not criminalize conduct when doing so is inconsistent with the operation of just public institutions. But this is just another way of stating the principle that criminalization should be subject to a constraint of justice. Because it is defined in terms of conformity with just institutions, wrongfulness no longer does independent work. For a more recent discussion, see Duff, *The Realm of Criminal Law*, 58–70.

Wellman has recently sought to defend a version of the broad wrongfulness principle on the basis of a more overtly rights-based account. For Wellman, defending an obligation to obey the law allows him to reconcile his statism—his view that we have reason to value states on account of the benefits they provide—with a rights-forfeiture view of punishment, according to which the state may only permissibly punish you if you wrong another, thereby forfeiting your claim not to be punished. On Wellman's view, there is a moral duty for each person to "obey the law as his or her fair share of the collective political task."[72] If the state enacts a legal rule that imposes a fair burden on you, then you have a moral duty to comply, and if you do not comply, you wrong your fellow citizens who depend on the state to achieve valuable public goods. Hence, Wellman argues that he can reconcile his statist preferences with his rights-forfeiture theory of punishment.

Unfortunately, even this broad account is too narrow. This emerges when we examine the role of taxation on Wellman's picture. The liberal welfare state is typically supported to a substantial degree by a variety of income and consumption taxes. These taxes apply to you simply by virtue of earning an income or consuming goods and services while in the relevant jurisdiction. Suppose that it is fair to tax people in this way, creating a moral duty to comply. Is this sufficient to explain the permissibility of punishing people who refuse to pay their taxes?

It is not so clear. After all, Wellman expressly claims that you have a moral right to your money. Hence, in taxing you, the state is invading your *rights*. Since your rights condition what it is permissible for the state to do to you, before it is legitimate for the state to take your money in the form of taxes, it must be shown that you have forfeited that right. Wellman suggests you forfeit rights by wronging others or by violating a legal rule. Plainly, however, you wrong no one, nor do you violate any legal rule, simply by virtue of earning an income or consuming goods or services. True, you violate the legal rule if you do not pay taxes despite earning an income or consuming goods or services, but this cannot be the basis for deeming your right forfeit, for then rights would do no work as a constraint on policy; your rights would be forfeit simply by legislative diktat. But if you have not forfeited your right to your money, then even if

72. "*Malum Prohibitum* and Rights Forfeiture," 84–85.

it would be very generous of you to support the state by giving it some of your money, you cannot be conscripted to do so, or punished if you do not. Otherwise put, the fairness of the tax alone cannot be a sufficient basis, on Wellman's view, to authorize the state to require you to pay it. This is because your property, like your person, is protected by a right, and rights are not defeated simply by showing that the state has a valuable aim in view, and that conscripting you to serve it would not be unfair.[73] Establishing this claim, after all, is in large part of the point of Wellman's rights-forfeiture account of punishment: even if valuable public aims would be furthered by punishing you, it is not permissible for the state to do so unless you have forfeited your right against being punished.[74] By the same token, then, even if a valuable public aim (providing valuable public goods) would be furthered by taxing you, it is impermissible for the state to do so unless you have forfeited your right to your money. But income and consumption taxes are not conditional on your forfeiture of a right. In short: if it is impermissible for the state to require you to pay taxes, and if (as seems plausible) raising revenue through taxation is a key part of how the welfare state operates, then Wellman's view casts doubt on the legitimacy of the welfare state after all.

One might respond by denying that we have a moral right to our money, but I suspect Wellman may regard this as unpalatable, as he uses that right to illustrate his claim that you have strong moral rights that limit what other people may do to you.[75] In any case, this response seems ad hoc, as it gives the appearance of redescribing the rights you have so as to accommodate the valuable public aims that one is anyway inclined to support. But that is to give up the game: it is to make rights parasitic on an account of socially valuable pursuits, rather than the other way around.

A more promising response might be to consider the fairness of the tax as a sufficient basis to obligate you to comply—whether or not you

73. Perhaps it would further some valuable collective aim for the state to twist your arm and kick your shins. Perhaps it would not be unfair for you to suffer those harms, relative to the potential benefits of securing that collective aim. However, because twisting your arm and kicking your shins violates your rights, the state is not permitted to do that unless you have in some way forfeit your right *not* to have your arm twisted and your shins kicked. It doesn't change things if the state threatens to punish you if you do not voluntarily make yourself available for such abuse.

74. Wellman, "The Rights Forfeiture Theory of Punishment," *Ethics* 122(2) (2012): 371–93.

75. Wellman, "*Malum Prohibitum* and Rights Forfeiture," 78–79; see also Wellman, *Rights Forfeiture and Punishment*, 2–3; but for evidence to the contrary, see 51–52.

have a right to your money. But what is good for the goose is good for the gander: the same reasoning suggests that if criminalizing X puts a fair burden on you, relative to some valuable social aim (for example, securing access to central capability for all), then it is immaterial whether or not X is wrongful, and, hence, whether or not you forfeit a right not to be punished if you do X. Rights drop out of the criminalization analysis: whatever your moral rights may be, they can be set aside if the goal is worthwhile, and the burden on you is fair. Again, you can *call* failure to comply with a fair public rule a moral wrong if you like, but that label does no independent work. It is entirely a matter of nomenclature rather than substance.

More generally, a broad interpretation of wrongfulness calls into question the very point of distinguishing between *mala in se* and *mala prohibita* in the first place. After all, if it is true that you act wrongfully by failing to comply with a fair scheme of cooperation that requires you to pay taxes, then it is also true that you act wrongfully in failing to comply with a fair scheme of cooperation that requires you to resolve your disputes in a court of law rather than settling them through your own force. In both cases the state acts well within the ambit of its legitimate authority in enacting such a law. The explanation for the legitimacy of criminalizing tax evasion turns on the significance of cooperation with public law, not manifest wrongdoing. If the significance of cooperation with public law is a sufficient basis for criminalization, and if ensuring that people are not murdered, raped, and so forth is in substantial part the product of cooperation with public law, then whether or not that type of conduct is manifestly wrong is an idle question on which nothing turns. The only *mala* that matter for the criminal law are the *mala* that are *prohibita*.

To sum up, the wrongfulness constraint in its strict interpretation is implausibly demanding. In its broader guise, it invites controversy about whether there is a moral duty to obey the law, while adding little to what is already required by a fully political justification of the criminal law. So I think it is probably best to drop it. Since the wrongfulness principle is a very popular deontological constraint on criminalization, rejecting it is a significant step toward endorsing ADP^{++}, which makes satisfying the antideference principle necessary and sufficient for justified criminalization. However, since I do not claim that there are no other possible deontological constraints on criminalization, I am content to endorse only ADP^{+}. Criminalizing X is only permissible if doing so would be an efficient way of promoting universal and effective access to central capability, and the fact that it would have that effect is a very good reason to do so. There may be deontological constraints on criminalization, but wrongfulness is not one of them.[76]

I conclude with one final observation. From the point of view of anti-deference, criminalizing X, in the sense of creating a criminal offense of X-ing, is only significant insofar as the existence of such an offense is expected to have an impact on effective access to central capability for real, flesh-and-blood people. Perhaps some rarely enforced crimes make no material difference to anyone's access to central capability, particularly if they are sufficiently obscure as to be unlikely to have any ex ante effect on people's behavior. From the point of view of anti-deference, those kinds of criminal laws, while perhaps unfortunate, are not of grave concern. Sometimes, however, the mere existence of some crimes matters quite a lot even if they are only rarely prosecuted. The formal existence of a crime often gives police the power to surveil, detain, and search people that they would not otherwise have. This kind of discretionary power, as I argued in Chapter 3, can have a serious impact on a person's access to central capability, such as the capability to move about in public space free of unwanted harassment. These are considerations that an application of ADP^+ must take into consideration in deciding whether criminalizing X would be an optimal way of promoting universal and effective access to central capability. There might sometimes be reason to believe that public institutions will do better at safeguarding and promoting capability if they are also empowered to interfere with them from time to time, but that case has to be made in a convincing and empirically grounded manner.

In this respect, the political ideal of anti-deference vindicates the approach common among criminologists and social scientists to "criminalization," as against more formal approaches that are focused upon the symbolic or expressive meaning of criminalization. Duff, for instance, has stressed the symbolic importance of formally criminalizing conduct, analogizing the formal criminal law to a professional code of conduct for citizens.[77] I do not dispute that designating a given type of conduct

---

76. What other deontological constraints on criminalization might be plausible? One might interpret the anti-subordination principle (sketched in ch. 3) in these terms. Even if criminalizing X would not unfairly jeopardize anyone's interests, it might still be objectionable if doing so reflected (or sustained) inequality at the level of basic social status. My thanks to Colleen Murphy for discussion on this point.

77. See Duff, *The Realm of Criminal Law*, chs. 2–4.

as "criminal" can be symbolically significant, in much the way that Duff suggests. However, from the point of view of anti-deference, criminalization in this sense—the content of the criminal code or court decisions—is of secondary importance. What is of fundamental importance is not what the criminal law *says* but what the criminal law *does,* and the most basic thing that the criminal law does is to enforce a society's rules, thereby contributing to a distribution of advantage across a population.[78]

5.6 Conclusion

In this chapter, I have defended the following claims:

(1) There is no apparent justification for construing the criminal law as consisting purely of a system of "direct prohibitions."
(2) A broader view of the criminal law undermines a subject-matter-based approach to criminalization, at least where those subject-matter constraints are not derived from more encompassing principles of political justification.
(3) From a public law point of view, the content of the criminal law should be determined by a fully political standard of justification.
(4) As one such standard, anti-deference suggests that the only reasons that would make it permissible to criminalize X are those that tend to show that criminalizing X is the best available means of promoting universal and effective access to central capability on terms acceptable to social and political equals.

78. Braithwaite and Pettit argue that an adequate theory of the criminal law should be both *comprehensive* and *consequentialist,* in that it should address the overall impact of the criminal law's interlocking institutions. See *Not Just Deserts,* chs. 2–3. Among other things, a comprehensive theory must display sensitivity to the ways in which procedure relates to substance. For instance, whether the prevailing prosecutorial norm is one of mandatory or discretionary prosecution should matter to a theory of criminalization. Insofar as discretionary prosecution enables prosecutors to make fine-grained decisions about when it is appropriate to prosecute, a procedural system of this kind would likely tend to err on the side of overinclusive liability standards since errors can be filtered out by declination. In contrast, systems that make it harder to filter out false positives, such as a system of mandatory prosecution, might be more likely to err on the side of under-inclusive liability standards. In principle, the end pattern of criminalization in practice could be the same, even if the formal content of criminal codes in those types of jurisdictions differ significantly; one system doing through discretion what the other does through law. But whether that is likely to be borne out in practice is a different question.

(5) Possibly there are further deontological constraints on criminalization, but wrongfulness is not one of them.

I recognize that these arguments have their limitations. In particular, while I have rejected certain claims about the value of retribution on the ground that they imply an overly libertarian or theocratic conception of political authority, I have not attempted to make the case that we should reject a libertarian or theocratic conception of the state in favor of an administrative state that serves liberal egalitarian aims. So in that respect at least, my conclusions are limited: *if* you accept the basic legitimacy of the modern administrative state, *then* you have reason to look at criminalization from a public law point of view.[79] It is in this respect that a public law conception provides an account of the criminal law in the age of the administrative state.

---

79. Compare Simmons, who complains that Rawlsians build statism into their very conception of reasonableness, meaning that those who reject collective political solutions to social problems are inevitably seen as unreasonable. "Justification and Legitimacy," *Ethics* 109 (1999): 739–71 at 765.

6

Formalism and Pragmatism in Criminal Procedure

6.1 Introduction

What is "criminal" law? In many contexts, this might be thought of as an idle question. But in at least one type of context, it is a question with significant practical repercussions. This is the context of procedure. Many jurisdictions define a special procedural regime for people facing criminal charges. For instance, if a person is being criminally prosecuted, typically the state bears the burden of proving guilt beyond a reasonable doubt, may be required to subsidize his or her defense, and is barred from imposing a sanction on a retroactive basis. None of this is typically true outside the criminal process. If, for instance, you are being sued for negligently damaging someone's car, no one—neither the plaintiff nor the state—needs to provide you with a lawyer; nor must your liability be proven beyond a reasonable doubt; nor, for that matter, is the court prohibited from being persuaded to recognize a novel cause of action in the case against you. Hence, in any jurisdiction that maintains a distinctive type of legal process for criminal as opposed to non-criminal matters, answering the question, "what is 'criminal' law?" takes on practical significance.

To be sure, in most cases, the answer to this question will not be controversial. However, in some cases the answer is not clear, and in those cases it will be important to have a principled way of deciding which procedural regime should apply. In the United States, the Supreme Court has regularly had to decide when a borderline case qualifies as a criminal case and when it does not. With some qualifications, the approach the Supreme Court has taken has been to define the criminal law by reference to the state's intention to condemn (through punishment) rather than merely regulate (through generic sanctions). Under a formalist approach of this kind, if you are unsure whether you are involved in a criminal case, you should ask whether the state is trying to punish you, in the sense of: is intending to express moral condemnation of your actions. If so, chances are you are dealing with a criminal case. If not, then probably not.

In this chapter, I shall explore an alternative basis for deciding how to allocate procedural rights. I first consider the Supreme Court's formalist model of rights allocation, and some of its more troublesome implications. These include difficulties in establishing what the state intended in enacting a law, as well as the problematic status of the so-called collateral consequences of the criminal process. I then sketch a contrasting model of rights allocation. Drawing upon the capabilities approach literature, I suggest a model that is sensitive to the potential impact on central capability, regardless of whether the action in question qualifies as "punishment." I refer to this approach as "due process pragmatism."

6.2 Pragmatism and Formalism in Defining "Criminal" Law

In Chapter 5, I defended the following principle:

> **ADP^{+}**: The only reasons that would make it permissible to criminalize X are those that tend to show that criminalizing X is the best available means of promoting universal and effective access to central capability.

This principle is meant to provide a framework for thinking about whether to criminalize a given type of conduct. However, it is silent as to what it *means* to criminalize conduct. One of the aims of this chapter is to spell that idea out more concretely.

In part, a conception of criminalization is implicit in the account of criminal law as public law: criminalization is a matter of attaching a sanction to defection from a shared rule of conduct. But that is only part of the answer. There are many occasions on which legal rules are enforced by attaching sanctions to noncompliance. Typically, only some of them are considered to establish "criminal" offenses. The question is how to determine which ones those are, having in mind that functionally this determines the type of procedure that applies. The answer to this question flows out of the account of anti-deference sketched in Chapter 3: criminal offenses are those whose enforcement is likely to result in a serious sanction being imposed on those against whom they are enforced. When is a sanction sufficiently "serious" to warrant the procedural safeguards of "criminal" procedure? When it can be expected to undermine a person's effective access to central capability, where a central capability is one standardly required to ensure basic equality in a give social context. This is the gist of due process pragmatism.

This approach is pragmatic in that it is more sensitive to what is concretely at stake in a legal dispute than how that dispute is traditionally categorized. The job of the ADP⁺ principle is to determine when it is permissible to impose such costs on people. Under that principle, adopting such a criminal enforcement policy may be permissible when it is the best available means of protecting effective access to central capability overall. However, because the effect of enforcing a criminal law is to concentrate the costs of obtaining that social good on discrete individuals, there is reason to be particularly guarded about how such a law is enforced. If we have reason to be concerned about the erroneous or abusive infliction of sanctions, it seems sensible to attend to just how serious those sanctions are likely to be for the parties. When an individual has a lot at stake, the cost of a false positive is high. Even if society has a significant interest in the outcome of the dispute, society's interest is likely to be relatively more diffuse, moderating the cost of a false negative for any given individual.[1]

More complicated considerations arise in areas of litigation where the interests of the parties are more evenly balanced, as in child custody or domestic-violence-type cases. In those types of cases, an adverse finding will have serious consequences for both parties. In such cases, the same

1. Due process pragmatism bears some resemblance to Glanville Williams's proposal to define substantive criminal law by reference to criminal procedure, rather than the other way around: see Williams, "The Definition of Crime," *Current Legal Problems* 8(1) (1955): 107–30 at 123–25. More recently, Issacar Rosen-Zvi and Talia Fisher have developed a sophisticated analysis that considers both what is at stake in a given case and the identity of the litigants—individuals (one-shotters) or institutions (repeat players). See Rosen-Zvi and Fisher, "Overcoming Procedural Boundaries," *Virginia Law Review* 94(1) (2008): 79–155. David Ball has also proposed replacing the formalistic civil-criminal distinction with a more flexible due process analysis centered on the notion of stigma: see David Ball, "The Civil Case at the Heart of Criminal Procedure," *American Journal of Criminal Law* 38(2) (2011): 117–80. See also Charles Reich, "The New Property," *Yale Law Journal* 73 (1964): 733–87 at 784.

sensitivity to expected loss arguably counsels providing equal rights to both parties—including requiring proof to a balance of probabilities rather than beyond a reasonable doubt—on the ground that the costs of error are evenly distributed.[2]

Due process pragmatism stands in sharp distinction to the formalistic way in which many legal theorists, as well as the Supreme Court of the United States, are inclined to define "criminal" law. In a line of cases stretching back well over a century, the Supreme Court has consistently held that the rights the government is obligated to respect in imposing a deprivation on a person is a function of whether that deprivation is plausibly construed as "punishment," in the sense of being imposed as a means of condemning some aspect of that person's prior conduct. If the government is not trying to punish you, then it is not moving against you criminally, and hence there is no reason to treat your case as if it were a criminal matter. Call this "criminal law formalism."

The argument for criminal law formalism is disarmingly simple. It starts with the observation that the Constitution creates special procedural rights for people accused of "crimes." The next step is to draw a sharp distinction between "criminal" law and other types of law (tort law, regulatory law, and so forth). The distinctive hallmark of the criminal law is that it seeks to condemn perceived wrongdoing through punishment; if a sanction is not punishment, then the law authorizing it cannot be "criminal" law. The final step is to observe that "punishment" means more than merely imposing a deprivation on someone. In addition, the deprivation must be intended as condemnation for perceived wrongdoing. It follows that if the state does not act with the requisite condemnatory intent, then whatever else it is doing it is not prosecuting someone under a "criminal" law. Accordingly, the various procedural protections reserved for criminal procedure do not apply.[3]

---

2. My thanks to Talia Fisher and Jakob Holtermann for discussion of this important point.

3. The Supreme Court's reliance on a formal conception of "punishment" in this context has been frequently noted. See Rosen-Zvi and Fisher, "Overcoming Procedural Boundaries"; Alice Ristroph, "State Intention and the Law of Punishment," *Journal of Criminal Law & Criminology* 98(4) (2008): 1353–406; Kenneth Mann, "Punitive Civil Sanctions: The Middleground between Criminal and Civil Law," *Yale Law Journal* 101 (8) (1992): 1795–873; Mary Cheh, "Constitutional Limits on Using Civil Remedies to Achieve Criminal Law Objectives: Understanding and Transcending the Criminal-Civil Law Distinction," *Hastings Law Journal* 42(5) (1991): 1325–413; Aaron Xavier Fellmeth, "Civil and Criminal Sanctions in the Constitution and the Courts," *Georgetown Law Journal* 94(1) (2005): 1–66; William Stuntz, "Substance, Process and the Civil-Criminal Line," *Journal of Contemporary Legal*

The formalist argument can be represented as follows:

1) "Criminal" proceedings are entitled to special procedural protections.
2) A proceeding is "criminal" if and only if the sanction that the state is seeking to impose qualifies as "punishment."
3) Generally speaking, a sanction qualifies as "punishment" only if it is intended as condemnation of a prior wrong believed to have been committed by the defendant.
4) Hence, whether you are entitled to the special protections of criminal procedure depends on whether the state is seeking to condemn you for wrongdoing, rather than (for instance) regulating in the name of public safety.

I shall not have much to say about the first premise, although it certainly has not gone unchallenged. Issachar Rosen-Zvi and Talia Fisher, for instance, have challenged the idea that procedural law should draw a categorical distinction between civil and criminal cases. "There is," they write, "no necessary correlation between the logic underlying the classification of a certain sanction as punitive (that is, criminal) or nonpunitive (that is, civil) and the rationale for the use of the more restrictive criminal procedure or the less restrictive civil procedure."[4] They propose, instead, allocating procedural rights based upon both the identity of the parties (individuals or institutions) and the expected severity of the consequences. In a similar vein, the overlap between criminal law and immigration law has in recent years drawn increasing scrutiny from legal scholars.[5]

Issues 7(1) (1996): 1–42; Wayne Logan, "The Ex Post Facto Clause and the Jurisprudence of Punishment," *American Criminal Law Review* 35(4) (1998): 1261–318; Ball, "The Civil Case at the Heart of Criminal Procedure."

4. Rosen-Zvi and Fisher, "Overcoming Procedural Boundaries," 130.

5. There is a sizable literature on this topic. For an overview, see Juliet Stumpf, "The Crimmigration Crisis: Immigrants, Crime and Sovereign Power," *American University Law Review* 56(2) (2006): 367–419; Stephen Legomsky, "The New Path of Immigration Law: Asymmetric Incorporation of Criminal Justice Norms," *Washington & Lee Law Review* 64(2) (2007): 469–528; David Sklansky, "Crime, Immigration, and Ad Hoc Instrumentalism," *New Criminal Law Review* 15 (2) (2012): 157–223. Perhaps emblematic of this trend, the Antiterrorism and Effective Death Penalty Act of 1996, § 435, Pub. L. No. 104–132, 110 Stat. 1214, made a crime of "moral turpitude" into grounds for removal, although what constitutes a crime of moral turpitude—pre-justicial wrongdoing?—is apparently so obvious that it does not require statutory clarification: see Stumpf, "The Crimmigration Crisis," 383; Sklansky, 176–77.

This is perhaps unsurprising, as approximately half of all federal law enforcement—arrests and referrals for prosecution—are for immigration offenses, far outstripping any other category of federal crime.[6] While this line of scholarship does not suggest that criminal offenses should *not* be given heightened procedural safeguards, it does suggest that not *only* criminal offenses should be; in particular, it suggests that immigration offenses should be treated in a somewhat parallel manner. However, as a matter of law, the unique status of criminal procedure seems well entrenched. In American law, for instance, the Constitution's Article I ex post facto and bill of attainder bans, as well as some of the rights contained in the Fifth, Sixth, and Eighth Amendments apply only to criminal cases.[7]

The third premise has mostly been discussed in the context of efforts by philosophers and legal theorists to provide a definition of punishment. In that literature, the significance of condemnatory intent as a defining feature of punishment is widely accepted.[8] John Gardner provides a representative statement. "There are," Gardner writes, "many possible reasons for punishing people, but the fact that a wrong was (supposedly or actually) committed is the only reason for punishing people of which it is true that one is not punishing people unless one acts for this reason."[9] Or

6. M. Motivans, "Federal Justice Statistics, 2013—Statistical Tables," tables 1.1 and 2.1, U.S. Bureau of Justice Statistics, https://www.bjs.gov/content/pub/pdf/fjs13st.pdf.

7. The Fifth Amendment grand jury right is predicated on "capital, or otherwise infamous crime," the Sixth Amendment is by its own terms limited to "criminal prosecutions," and the Eighth Amendment provides a right against cruel and unusual "punishment." See also United States v. Ward, 448 U.S. 242, 254 (1980) (self-incrimination); Selective Service System v. Minnesota Public Interest Research Group, 468 U.S. 841, 851 (1984) (bill of attainder); *United States v. One Assortment of 89 Firearms*, 465 U.S. 354, 362 (1984) (double jeopardy); Kansas v. Hendricks, 521 U.S. 346, 369 (1997) (double jeopardy and ex post facto); Smith v. Doe, 538 U.S. 84, 92–95 (2003) (ex post facto). The exclusionary rule is also limited to criminal trials: see Pennsylvania Bd. of Probation and Parole v. Scott, 524 U.S. 357, 363–64 (1998); Lingo v. City of Salem, 832 F.3d 953, 958 (9th Cir. 2016).

8. See, e.g., David Boonin, *The Problem of Punishment* (Cambridge University Press 2008), 12–17 (2008); Doug Husak, "The Costs to Criminal Theory of Supposing That Intentions Are Irrelevant to Permissibility," *Criminal Law & Philosophy* 3 (2009): 51–70 at 57; John Gardner, "Introduction" to H.L.A. Hart, *Punishment and Responsibility*, 2nd ed. (Oxford University Press 2008), xxx; Alan Brudner, *Punishment and Freedom* (Oxford University Press 2009), 21; Zach Hoskins, *Beyond Punishment* (Oxford University Press 2018), ch. 2. For doubts, see Adam Kolber, "Unintentional Punishment," *Legal Theory* 18(1) (2012): 1–29, and Alice Ristroph, "State Intention and the Law of Punishment," *Journal of Criminal Law & Criminology* 98(4) (2008): 1353–406.

9. Gardner, "Introduction," xxx.

as Holmes more pithily put it: even a dog knows the difference between being kicked and being tripped over.[10]

I shall not have much to say about either the first or third premises. For my purposes, the central premise is the second one, linking the criminal law to a moralized conception of punishment. Doug Husak has recently articulated a version of this claim, insisting that "the *criminal* law is that domain of law that subjects offenders to state punishment," where punishment is understood as intentional imposition of hard treatment and stigma. Husak, however, does not purport to defend the claim, instead stating that it is true "[b]y definition."[11] Defining "criminal law" by reference to "punishment" is, according to Husak, the "orthodox" view, both in the sense that it is accepted by the majority of theorists and in the sense that it is the most likely to be correct.[12] This view implies that you cannot understand what criminal law is without understanding what punishment is.

It is telling that the idea that criminal law is centrally concerned with a moralized conception of punishment has not seemed worthy of philosophical defense. After all, one might think that what we conventionally consider to be "criminal law" is a matter of historical contingency rather than conceptual necessity.[13] One might similarly wonder whether conceptual analysis of the concept of "punishment" is a reasonable means for resolving basic questions in procedural justice.[14]

Philosophers are sometimes accused of constructing elaborate theories with no "real world" ramifications. Criminal law formalism provides a counterexample to that complaint. Criminal law formalism rationalizes certain features of the status quo in American constitutional law, including a number of its pathologies. The prevailing legal standard in this area derives from *Kennedy v. Mendoza-Martinez*, in which the United

10. Oliver Wendell Holmes, *The Common Law* (Little, Brown & Co. 1945), 3.

11. Doug Husak, *Ignorance of Law: A Philosophical Inquiry* (Oxford University Press 2016), 35.

12. "Retribution in Criminal Theory," *San Diego Law Review* 37 (2000): 959–86 at 960.

13. Looking beyond delinquency proceedings, over the course of the twentieth century, spousal support proceedings have gone from being understood as civil or equitable, to criminal, and then back again, reflecting differing views about modes of enforcement— extradition and probation, notably— as much as opinions about whether men who failed to support their spouses deserved censure. See Elizabeth D Katz, "Family Law as Criminal Law: The Forgotten Criminal Origins of Modern Family Laws and Courts," University of Chicago Law Review, (forthcoming 2019).

14. Marie Newhouse, for instance, has defended the view that there is a fundamental moral distinction between civil and criminal wrongs on the basis of a reading of Kant's Universal Principle of Right. "Two Types of Legal Wrongdoing," *Legal Theory* 22 (2016): 59–75.

States sought to automatically strip Americans of their citizenship if they were caught evading the draft.[15] The Supreme Court held that the constitutionality of the impugned sections of the Immigration and Nationality Act (INA) rested on whether automatic denaturalization imposed "punishment." Finding that it "plainly" did, the court held that forfeiture of citizenship for draft evasion "cannot be imposed without a prior criminal trial and all its incidents, including indictment, notice, confrontation, jury trial, assistance of counsel, and compulsory process for obtaining witnesses."[16] Without giving the impression of establishing a rigid doctrinal formula, the court then went on to enumerate factors that would bear on the determination of whether any particular sanction qualified as "punishment":

> Whether the sanction involves an affirmative disability of restraint, whether it has historically been regarded as a punishment, whether it comes into play only on a finding of scienter, whether its operation will promote the traditional aims of punishment—retribution and deterrence, whether the behavior to which it applies is already a crime, whether an alternative purpose to which it may rationally be connected is assignable for it, and whether it appears excessive in relation to the alternative purpose assigned.[17]

The Court then noted that "[a]bsent conclusive evidence of congressional intent as to the penal nature of a statute, these factors must be considered in relation to the statute on its face."[18] Since in this case there was conclusive evidence of Congress's punitive intent (derived from an extensive review of the INA's legislative history), those other factors proved to be immaterial. However, in the years since *Mendoza-Martinez*, the court has taken a more restricted view of legislative intent, insisting that absent the "clearest proof" of a punitive intent, a statute should be classified "on its face."[19] Consequently, unless a legislature clearly articulates that a statute

---

15. Kennedy v. Mendoza-Martinez, 372 U.S. 144 (1963).

16. *Mendoza-Martinez*, 372 U.S. at 167.

17. *Mendoza-Martinez*, 372 U.S. at 168.

18. *Mendoza-Martinez*, 372 U.S. at 169.

19. Seling v. Young, 531 U.S. 250, 262–63 and 269 (2001); see also Hudson v. United States, 522 U.S. 93, 100 (1997) (noting that the *Mendoza-Martinez* factors can only be considered in relation to the statute on its face, and that only the clearest proof "will suffice to override legislative intent and transform what has been denominated a civil remedy into a criminal

is intended to punish, it will almost always be deemed "civil." A paradigm case is *Kansas v. Hendricks*, in which the government's reasons for detaining a habitual sex offender past the expiration of his criminal sentence were viewed as non-punitive, namely preventing future offenses, rather than further condemning past ones.[20] As a result, even though Hendricks would likely remain confined for the rest of his life under conditions that approximate those of imprisonment, neither the prohibition on retroactive punishment nor double jeopardy applied, as they are reserved specifically for criminal—that is, punitive—matters.

There are well-known costs to concentrating so exclusively on whether a statute is intended to be punitive. For instance, many have noted that important as it is to have access to counsel in criminal cases, there are other areas of law in which an adverse outcome could be equally, if not more, devastating—disputes over child custody and access to housing come to mind. But from a formalist perspective, however devastating loss of custody over a child or loss of housing may be, as a general matter those types of cases are not plausibly interpreted as cases in which the state is trying to punish you for some prior wrongdoing. Those cases are therefore categorically excluded from the criminal process.

Conversely, because the formalist framework is sensitive to intent rather than substance, it extends procedural rights even in contexts where the defendant is not vulnerable to the same kinds of losses as an individual would be. Consider the treatment of criminal liability for corporate entities. As long as the state is in the punishment business, then the full panoply of procedural rights applies—proof beyond a reasonable doubt, the presumption of innocence, counsel of choice, anti-retroactivity, and so forth—even though corporate entities cannot suffer the same kinds of harms that natural persons can. Criminal law formalism thus provides relatively lower protection for natural persons facing devastating outcomes than it does for corporate entities that are facing significantly less devastating outcomes, on account of the view that the former are not being "punished" whereas the latter are. Perhaps nowhere else is the privileging of form over substance quite so stark.

---

penalty."). Other courts have recognized, however, that a formalistic way of drawing the civil-criminal distinction need not be quite so deferential to legislative labeling. See, e.g., App. No 8544/79 *Özturk v Germany* (1984) 6 EHRR 409 at para. 53 (rejecting Germany's argument that a traffic offense was merely regulatory on grounds that, despite the minor sanctions involved, it was nevertheless of a "punitive character").

20. Kansas v. Hendricks, 521 U.S. 346 (1997).

Another challenge for formalism concerns the so-called collateral consequences of a criminal conviction.[21] These consequences are often the result of specific laws and policies that place additional restrictions on what a person who has been convicted of a crime is allowed to do. They include prohibitions on convicted drug offenders living in public housing, restrictions on eligibility for student loans, loss (sometimes permanent) of the franchise, ineligibility for public office, deprivation of accrued government benefits, loss of the right to adopt or retain custody of children, restrictions on employment in a wide array of public and private settings, requirements that sex offenders keep officials apprised of their whereabouts, prohibitions on residing within a certain distance of schools, and so forth. The number of collateral consequences can be extensive. An online database recently set up by the American Bar Association to track collateral consequences in the United States currently reports over 45,000 separate state and federal laws that impose collateral consequences.[22] A misdemeanor conviction in New York gives rise to 354 distinct collateral consequences pertaining to government benefits, employment and occupational licensure, immigration status, family and domestic rights, housing eligibility, civic participation, and so on. A felony conviction results in 555 collateral consequences.[23]

The Supreme Court has regularly noted that these consequences are not strictly intended as punishment—that is why they are "collateral"—and it has consequently concluded that the laws and policies authorizing them are not truly criminal law. This sweeping view of the civil-criminal distinction's significance has been instrumental in a wide array of cases, dealing with matters as disparate as civil forfeiture orders; registration as a sex offender; removal (i.e., deportation); the revocation of old-age,

21. "So-called" because they are only collateral relative to the punishment that is specifically intended, and hence secondary to punishment only if you accept the relevance of the intending/foreseeing distinction in this context.

22. National Inventory of Collateral Consequences of Conviction, http://www.abacollateralconsequences.org/map/.

23. National Inventory of the Collateral Consequences of Conviction, http://www.abacollateralconsequences.org. (Search terms are "any misdemeanor," "any felony," and "New York," searched May 17, 2017.) The mean number of collateral consequences for a misdemeanor conviction in the fifty-four jurisdictions currently tracked on the database is 166. Texas reports 318, whereas Vermont reports 75. The mean number for a felony conviction is 351, with Texas reporting 813 distinct collateral consequences and the federal government reporting 423.

survivor, or disability benefits; and denial of federal educational loans.[24] Since none of these consequences are considered "punishment," the state need not respect the usual panoply of procedural rights that apply in the context of true criminal law. After all, no one is being punished. This line of reasoning is supported by criminal law formalism, whether in the abstract form favored by legal philosophers or in the doctrinally grounded form favored by judges.[25]

6.3 The Case for Capabilities

Evidently, due process pragmatism sorts cases differently from a more traditional interpretation of the civil-criminal distinction. It lumps some areas of family law and immigration law together with most, but probably not all, of what is traditionally considered criminal law. Some areas of traditional criminal law—most plausibly, cases of corporate crime and regulatory offenses where only minor financial penalties are at stake—might be treated as not that different from civil regulatory actions, at least where those actions do not threaten to bankrupt or seriously stigmatize someone. Due process pragmatism's revisionary character may be off-putting to theorists who view the proper role of legal theory as providing a "rational reconstruction" of the law.[26] Rational reconstruction has its merits, but for better or worse, it is not the aim of this book. Rather than seeking to recover some latent understanding of the civil-criminal distinction, my aim is to suggest how we might transcend that distinction in the name of more general due process values.

More specifically, I propose an interpretation of due process values drawn from the capabilities literature. Much of that literature is devoted to

24. See, e.g., United States v. Ursery, 518 U.S. 267 (1996) (civil forfeiture); Smith v. Doe, 538 U.S. 84 (2003) (sex offender registry); INS v. Lopez-Mendoza, 468 U.S. 1032 (1984) (removal); Flemming v. Nestor, 363 U.S. 603 (1959) (termination of government benefits); Selective Service System v. Minnesota Public Interest Research Group, 468 U.S. 841 (1984) (denial of federal student loan assistance).

25. Other legal systems have been more direct in acknowledging the significance of "collateral" consequences. A basic principle of sentencing under German law is that "[t]he effects which the sentence can be expected to have on the offender's future life in society shall be taken into account." ("Die Wirkungen, die von der Strafe für das künftige Lebens des Täters in der Gesellschaft zu erwarten sind, sind zu berücksichtigen.") § 46 StGb.

26. The most sophisticated proponent of rational reconstruction in the criminal law remains Antony Duff: see his recent book, *The Realm of Criminal Law* (Oxford University Press 2018).

assessing the consequences of different types of social policy on people's lives, and measuring the relative seriousness of outcomes for individuals. In the capabilities literature, the issue is typically framed as a metric (or index) of well-being, rather than a standard of fair distribution per se.[27] Regardless of which standard of distributive justice you are most drawn to—prioritarianism, utilitarianism, sufficientarianism, and so forth—you will require some index for comparing how policy A does relative to policy B in affecting how peoples' lives go. This index could be expressed in a variety of ways, for instance in terms of wealth, happiness, preference satisfaction, social primary goods, or capabilities. In the present context, the question we are concerned with is how to determine when a litigant's potential losses are sufficiently severe to warrant a more cautious procedure biased against false positives. Like the broader question of well-being, whatever theory of due process one endorses, nevertheless some framework for assessing the "severity" of the potential losses is required. The proposal here is to apply the established framework of capabilities to this problem.

The capabilities approach has been applied in areas as diverse as health policy, education, and gender.[28] Perhaps surprisingly, neither criminal justice, nor legal process more generally, appear to have figured significantly in the discussion about the capabilities approach, even though both criminal acts and the punishment imposed by public institutions in response to them often directly affect what most people would consider to be centrally important capabilities. My discussion here can only begin to fill that gap in the literature in a very initial and impressionistic way.[29]

---

27. Elizabeth Anderson, "Justifying the Capabilities Approach to Justice," in *Measuring Justice: Primary Goods and Capabilities*, ed. Harry Brighouse and Ingrid Robeyns (Cambridge University Press 2010), ch. 4; Amartya Sen, *The Idea of Justice* (Harvard University Press 2011), 232; Flavio Comim, "Measuring Capabilities," in *The Capability Approach: Concepts, Measures and Applications*, ed. Flavio Comim, Mozaffar Qizilbash, and Sabina Alkire (Cambridge University Press 2008), 157–200 at 162–63.

28. See the papers collected in Brighouse and Robeyns, eds., *Measuring Justice*.

29. My approach builds on the pioneering work of Andrew von Hirsch and Nils Jareborg, who drew upon Sen's work in estimating crime severity: see "Gauging Criminal Harm: A Living-Standard Analysis," *Oxford Journal of Legal Studies* 11(1) (1991): 1–38. Von Hirsch has recently suggested extending this approach to the topic of this chapter, namely punishment severity: *Deserved Criminal Sentences* (Bloomsbury 2017), 67–69. Hamish Stewart is, to the best of my knowledge, the only other legal theorist who has suggested applying the capabilities approach to problems in criminal justice. See Stewart, "The Limits of Consent and the Law of Assault," *Canadian Journal of Law & Jurisprudence* 24 (2011): 205–23.

(a) What is a "capability" and when is it "central"? The capabilities approach has given rise to a quite extensive literature.[30] I shall not try to do justice to the extensive literature on the capabilities approach here, but will limit myself to some of the main points. Capabilities represent functionings that are available to a person, where a functioning is a state or activity that contributes to a person's well-being: for instance, to move about, to be well-nourished, to work, to maintain family and personal relationships, or to the capabilities constitutive of healthy functioning. As Sen has put it, a capability represents the "actual freedom of choice a person has over alternative lives that he or she can lead," where an "alternative life" is represented in terms of sets of "functionings."[31] A functioning, in turn, is an actual state of doing or being—holding a job, walking through a neighborhood, staying well fed, and so forth.

Why focus on capabilities rather than achieved functionings? Here, I draw on Pettit's suggestion that a person's freedom should be assessed by her ability to do or achieve X free from interference, rather than whether she actually decides to do or achieve X.[32] A slave may have the opportunity to enjoy bodily integrity if he acts in an appropriately servile way toward his master. Even though the slave enjoys the relevant functioning, he does not do so on his own terms, as his bodily integrity is conditioned on the noninterference of the master. His enjoyment of that functioning could

---

30. Here is a very selective sampling: Amartya Sen, "Equality of What?," in *Tanner Lectures on Human Values*, ed. M. McMurrin (Cambridge University Press 1980), 197–200; Sen, "Capability and Well-Being," in *The Quality of Life*, ed. Martha Nussbaum and Amartya Sen (Oxford University Press 1993), 30–53; Sen, *The Idea of Justice*, especially part III; Nussbaum, "Constitutions and Capabilities: 'Perception' against Lofty Formalism," *Harvard Law Review* 121(1) (2007): 4–97; and Nussbaum, *Creating Capabilities* (Harvard University Press 2011). See also the contributions by Philip Pettit, Elizabeth Anderson, T.M. Scanlon, and Amartya Sen to a symposium on the capabilities approach: *Economics and Philosophy* 17(1) (2001): 1–66; Norman Daniels, "Equality of What: Welfare, Resources, or Capabilities?," *Philosophy and Phenomenological Research* 50 (1990): 273–96; Gerald Cohen, "Equality of What? On Welfare, Goods, and Capabilities," in *The Quality of Life*: 30–53; Elizabeth Anderson, "Justifying the Capabilities Approach to Justice," in *Measuring Justice: Primary Goods and Capabilities*, ed. Harry Brighouse and Ingrid Robeyns, eds. (Cambridge University Press 2010), 81–100; Erin Kelly, "Equal Opportunity, Unequal Capability," in *Measuring Justice*, 61–80; and Ingrid Robeyns, "The Capability Approach: A Theoretical Survey," *Journal of Human Development* 6(1) (2005): 93–117.

31. Amartya Sen, "Justice: Means versus Freedoms," *Philosophy & Public Affairs* 19(2) (1990): 111–21 at 114.

32. Philip Pettit, *Republicanism: A Theory of Freedom and Government* (Oxford University Press 2000); and, more recently, Pettit, *On the People's Terms: A Republican Theory and Model of Democracy* (Cambridge University Press 2012).

hardly count as a state of freedom. Although this thought is arguably implicit in the idea of a capability, it can be emphasized by stressing that what is being secured is *effective* access to capability: access that is reasonably robust against the most significant sources of interference with one's ability to choose whether to exercise a given capability. A person has "effective" access to a capability if his or her decision to act on it is reasonably free from unwarranted interference, whether actual or threatened, from others.

There is a connection between the conception of freedom implicit in the capabilities approach and an ideal of social equality. If each of the members of a group of people enjoys effective access to a set of capabilities, then they stand in a relation of social equality relative to each other. Each is an independent agent who is not required to bow and scrape as a condition of securing basic prerogatives of equal membership, and is in that respect a peer among peers. Each person has decisive control over how his or her life goes with respect to at least some important range of functioning, not in the sense of absolute control, but in the sense that the most probable sources of interference are kept in check up to the point where they cease to be objectively credible, and kept in check in a way that is consistent with each person's status as an equal.

Which capabilities are "central"? A capability is "central" insofar as it is required, within a given social context, to secure a life without shame.[33] Plausibly, this will include the ability to move about freely, to obtain a decent education, to speak freely, and to have one's voice heard on matters of public importance, to stay nourished and maintain one's health, to live and work in safe and sanitary conditions, and so forth. Which capabilities are central in this sense will presumably vary with context. But while the list is surely open-ended, not every capability will be included. For instance, while traveling the world may be important to a person's self-conception, it does not plausibly qualify as a central capability, even though a more limited ability to move about one's environment without fear of assault or harassment plausibly does.[34] That said, a full list of

33. Compare the concept of a central capability to Daniels's conception of the "normal opportunity range for a given society" as the "array of life plans reasonable persons in it are likely to construct for themselves." In this parlance, a central capability would be one that is required to keep open a person's fair share of the normal opportunity range, given his or her skills and talents. See Daniels, "Equality of What," 281.

34. As Daniels puts it, "[w]hat is of urgent moral concern to us is not assuring equality of capability in some global way, in all of its dimensions, but the more modest goal of protecting

central capabilities is likely to be highly variable and culturally relative. Hence, while I am broadly sympathetic to Nussbaum's universal account of the central capabilities, ranging from life and health to affiliation, play, and control over one's environment, ultimately the equal-opportunity-for-influence principle suggests political rather than philosophical resolution of questions of this kind.[35]

In contrast to single-valued theories of well-being, the capabilities approach is pluralistic. A person's capability set encompasses all the sets of functionings that are possibly realizable by that person, and hence has as many dimensions as there are distinct types of functionings. A strong version of this claim is that the central capabilities are non-fungible: having less of one is not adequately compensated for by having more of another.[36] This view is attractive because it is plausible that the grounds of social equality are diverse, and that having more of one cannot make up for having less of another. The well-being of someone who earns a healthy income but is constantly harassed as she moves around the city differs meaningfully from that of someone who earns a more modest income but is able to move around the city without being harassed. Protecting central capability means protecting a person's ability to exercise each of these functionings to an appropriate degree, without being forced to compromise on one in order to secure another.

On the other hand, as a practical matter, most policies will involve trade-offs across different central capabilities—more reliable trials might mean less privacy, better access to education might mean less access to healthcare, and so on—and people are likely to vary in how securely and consistently they have access to the central capabilities over time. Hence some method for comparing and aggregating the different types of central capability is probably inevitable. The particular form that this

---

individuals from certain impairments of their capabilities. The reference to a normal range of functioning is crucial . . . [w]e have special claims on others only when our functioning falls short of the normal range (remember, *normal* is not a statistical notion.)" "Equality of What," 283.

35. Nussbaum, *Creating Capabilities*; see also Sabine Alkire, *Valuing Freedoms: Sen's Capability Approach and Poverty Reduction* (Oxford University Press 2002), 78–82 (table 2.12) (collecting information on thirty-nine different accounts of dimensions of human development drawn from a range of disciplines).

36. On non-fungibility, see Jonathan Wolff and Avner de-Shalit, *Disadvantage* (Oxford University Press 2007), ch. 1. Anderson stresses non-fungibility as well: see Elizabeth Anderson, "What Is the Point of Equality?," *Ethics* 109(2) (1999): 287–337.

aggregation should take remains an open and difficult question for capability theorists.[37]

One way of gaining at least some traction on these issues draws on forms of disadvantage that have systematic impact on other aspects of well-being. Wolff and de-Shalit have proposed an approach that is deliberative, consensus-oriented, and pragmatic. If disadvantage clusters around certain key indicators—for example, if people who do poorly on health also tend to do poorly on education, housing, and so on—that would provide a reason to prioritize those capabilities, even if it is not possible to specify a precise ordering of central capabilities.[38] In any case, for my immediate purposes, it is not necessary to settle on a particular method for comparing capabilities against each other. For the purposes of a due process analysis, the question is simply whether a defendant is exposed to the possibility of a nontrivial impairment on his or her effective access to a central capability. Answering that question does not require comparing capabilities against each other.

(b) Why not subjective experience? As an index of well-being, the capabilities approach enjoys advantages relative to both objective resources and subjective welfare. The problem with objective resources is, as Sen has pointed out, that people vary in how effectively they are able to convert resources into welfare.[39] Some people require more resources than others to achieve a parallel level of welfare. Conversely, the problem with a purely subjective index is that it is unable to deal with problems of adaptive preference on the one hand, and expensive tastes on the other. While a purely objective index is insufficiently sensitive to how ostensibly

---

37. For an overview of some of the critiques of the capability approach on this score, and some lines of response, see Ingrid Robeyns, "The Capability Approach in Practice," *Journal of Political Philosophy* 14(3) (2006): 351–76, especially 356–58; Wolff and de-Shalit, *Disadvantage*, ch. 5; Enrica Chiappero-Martinetti, "Complexity and Vagueness in the Capability Approach: Strengths or Weaknesses?," in Comim, Qizilbash, and Alkire, eds., *The Capability Approach*, 268–309; and (in the same volume) Comim, "Measuring Capabilities," 157–200, especially 181–85.

38. Wolff and de-Shalit, *Disadvantage*, ch. 5. Relying on qualitative interviews with individuals in the UK and Israel, Wolff and de-Shalit report a tentative convergence on the categories of life, bodily health, bodily integrity, affiliation, and control over one's environment and the category of sense, imagination, and thought as central capabilities deemed to be of particular salience. If validated more broadly, that finding would provide a way of meliorating some of the practical challenges posed by indexing under a pluralistic conception of advantage, although it leaves unresolved the precise relation among these clustered forms of disadvantage.

39. Sen, "Justice: Means versus Freedom," 115–16.

similar levels of resources can affect people in different ways, a purely subjective index is so sensitive that it is unable to take a sufficiently critical stance toward patterns of revealed preferences.[40]

In a provocative paper, Adam Kolber has critiqued sentencing practices that focus solely on the duration of the sentence and fail to take into account how that incarceration concretely affects those who suffer them.[41] The "subjective disutility of punishment," Kolber writes, "is not some mere aftereffect of punishment. Rather, it is largely or entirely the punishment itself."[42] Just as the felt impact of a $100 fine varies with the wealth of the individual defendant, a set term of years in prison can be expected to have a differing impact on the happiness of differently situated individuals, some of whom have a harder time adapting to prison than others. To nevertheless insist that equality in punishment is measured by the amount of time spent idling in prison is to ignore the obvious: people vary in how they respond to punishment, and this variation is of moral significance insofar as it results in widely varying, and potentially quite cruel, experiences for those affected.[43] This variability in how punishment is actually experienced is rendered invisible by what Kolber, in a subsequent paper, refers to as the "duration fetish" of our sentencing practices.[44]

Kolber's challenge to punishment theory parallels familiar debates in distributive justice as to whether public institutions should operate over means (primary goods) or ends (welfare). Kolber is, in effect, challenging the prevailing approach of defining punishment by reference to the means to subjective utility, rather than subjective utility itself. If punishment is meant to impose subjective disutility, then why not measure sentences

40. See Cohen, "Equality of What?"

41. Adam Kolber, "The Subjective Experience of Punishment," *Columbia Law Review* 109(1) (2009): 182–236. Kolber's focus on the experiential quality of punishment, as opposed to more spare representations of preference, would appear to rely on the interpersonal comparability of those experiences. See also John Bronsteen, Christopher Buccafusco, and Jonathan Masur, "Happiness and Punishment," *University of Chicago Law Review* 76(3) (2009): 1037–82 at 1065.

42. Kolber, "The Subjective Experience of Punishment," 212–13.

43. Kolber, "The Subjective Experience of Punishment," 213.

44. Adam Kolber, "The Comparative Nature of Punishment," *Boston University Law Review* 89 (2009): 1565–608 at 1606. Kolber's claim here parallels Sen's claim that Rawlsians "fetishize" primary goods by attending to "good things rather than with what these good things *do* to human beings." See Sen, "Equality of What?," 218 and 216 ("Rawls takes primary goods as the embodiment of advantage, rather than taking advantage to be a *relationship* between persons and goods.")

with reference to subjective utility itself, rather than with reference to obviously imperfect indicia such as sentence length?[45]

A capabilities approach shows both what is appealing and what is implausible in Kolber's argument. Kolber is surely right to point out that superficially equivalent sanctions may have dramatically different impacts on people's lives for a host of reasons, such as age, health, job prospects, and familial or citizenship status. Although the duration of a custodial sentence is clearly related to its impact on a person's capability set, there is little reason to think that duration alone is a particularly good proxy. It is clear that the consequences of, say, a six-month period of incarceration on a middle-income offender with no dependents are likely to be less devastating than they would be for an impoverished offender with substantial childcare obligations. The variability in the suffering inflicted by an equivalent period of incarceration exemplifies Sen's point that a purely objective approach will fail to take into account potentially quite significant differences in how peoples' lives go, even when they have equal resources at their disposal. As a result, Sen has argued, simply tracking the distribution of resources will systematically disadvantage people who have relatively low "conversion rates"—that is, those who have a more difficult time converting resources into functioning, who experience incarceration as unusually disabling.[46] An exclusive focus on the amount of time someone is likely to spend in custody, or the face value of a monetary fine, has much the same effect, and a capabilities-based approach joins Kolber in rejecting it.

However, I would not go as far as Kolber in sliding all the way from objective goods to subjective utility. The capabilities approach provides a stopping point between the two, one that is sensitive to what goods and resources enable people to do without being beholden to how people happen to feel about those abilities.[47] A capabilities approach does not conceive of

45. Alon Harel has argued that Kolber's critique of duration as a metric of sanction severity "is based on a misunderstanding of retributivism," insofar as retributivism "is not about subjective disutility but about the communicative and expressive significance of punishment." See Alon Harel, "Economic Analysis of Criminal Law: A Survey," in *Research Handbook on the Economics of Criminal Law,* ed. Alon Harel and Keith Hylton (Edward Elgar 2012), 10–50 at 46. However, even if you think that the reason we punish is to censure, you will nevertheless require some kind of index for assessing whether the severity of a given punishment adequately conveys the intended degree of censure.

46. Sen, "Justice: Means versus Freedom," 115–16.

47. On this point, see Cohen, "Equality of What?," at 30–53.

sanctions as equivalently harsh simply because they are equivalently long, but it also does not conceive of them as equivalently harsh because they are experienced as equivalently painful. The relative severity of state-imposed sanctions is, instead, assessed through the impact those sanctions have on a person's ability to achieve important functionings. By this metric, detention for a few days could be considered cruel if the detainee suffers from a serious illness that will be left untreated while he is detained, even if it would not be cruel in other cases, and even if the illness is not especially painful. If someone is the primary breadwinner or childcare provider, then a custodial sanction will be worse for him (and not just worse for family members) than if he had no such obligations. This is not because he experiences the period of incarceration as worse—indeed, maybe he would enjoy the break—but because it amounts to a greater restriction on his capability set.[48]

While Kolber is of course right that sadistically imposing minor nuisances or causing a person pointless anxiety requires justification, that doesn't show that the severity of the sanctions imposed by public institutions should be expressed in terms of subjective experience.[49] The question is not whether all else being equal it is worse to be unhappy; it is whether subjective experience is a good way of assessing the relative severity of a sanction. I have suggested that it is not, because the sanction may bear upon well-being in a way not captured by subjective experience.

Another reason to doubt subjective experience in this context is that how one experiences a punishment may itself be determined by background social conditions. Kolber's emphasis on subjective experience runs into a version of the problem of expensive tastes. People tend to adapt to harsh conditions, meaning that a two-year term of imprisonment may not be experienced as twice as adverse as a one-year term. But it is not plausible to maintain that a person has no legitimate complaint if he is acclimated to harsh conditions, and thus requires *extra* harsh treatment to be brought to an equivalent level of subjective utility. A person whose punishment is served under dangerous and brutalizing conditions has a legitimate complaint regardless of whether he has adapted to living under them. "If," as Elizabeth Anderson puts the point, "people find happiness

48. Plausibly, a limitation on satisfying counterfactual family obligations is a lesser incursion on a capability set than a limitation on satisfying *actual* family obligations. If so, then while imprisonment in some sense prevents the unattached offender from conjointly having family obligations and discharging them, that amounts to a lesser incursion on capability than in the case of the offender with actual familial obligations.

49. See Kolber, "Unintentional Punishment."

in their lives despite being oppressed by others, this hardly justifies continuing the oppression."[50] The same point applies, as Kolber acknowledges, to people whose baseline condition is unusually high or low. Replacing a wealthy offender's satin sheets with cotton ones does not raise the same concerns as replacing a poor offender's bedroll with a concrete slab, even if the change in subjective utility is the same.

The choice between subjective utility and capability is not purely theoretical. A clear example of the unequal impact of apparently identical punishment on differently situated people is the use of fixed-rate fines. Plainly, a $1,000 fine will affect a prince differently than a pauper. Fixed-rate fines are inevitably crude: too lenient for the wealthy, too harsh for the poor. Day fines, in contrast, are more likely to equalize the actual impact of the fine. These fines impose equivalent "days" of punishment on equivalent crimes, but rather than assess those days in terms of fixed dollar amounts, they do so relative to a person's income or wealth, meaning that the face value of the fine imposed on a wealthy person will be substantially higher than that imposed on a poor person.

Should we prefer day fines to fixed-rate fines? From the point of view of subjective utility, it is unclear whether the substitution of a day fine for a fixed-rate fine is an improvement, since it may well be that a miserly prince is more upset about the loss of even a trivial percentage of his wealth than a carefree pauper.[51] In contrast, the capabilities approach clearly suggests a preference for day fines. The calculation of day fines typically exempts some basic level of income for subsistence and support of dependents, thus recognizing the relative priority of central capabilities. Beyond those central capabilities, by siphoning a person's income relative to his wealth, day fines do better than fixed-rate fines at imposing at least roughly equivalent restrictions on each person's capability set, and they are not affected by how their subjects feel about those restrictions.[52]

---

50. Anderson, "What Is the Point of Equality?," at 304. Sen makes a similar point: "[o]ur reading of what is feasible in our situation and station may be crucial to the intensities of our desires, and may even affect what we dare to desire. Desires reflect compromises with reality, and reality is harsher to some than to others." "Well-Being, Agency and Freedom," *Journal of Philosophy* 82(4) (1985): 169–221 at 191.

51. For Kolber's discussion of these types of cases see Kolber, "The Comparative Nature of Punishment," 1588–89.

52. For background on the use of day fines in Europe versus the United States, see Elena Kantorowicz-Reznichenko, "Day Fines: Reviving the Idea and Reversing the (Costly) Punitive

Felon disenfranchisement is another context where the choice between subjective utility and capability matters. As I noted in Chapter 3, many people in the United States—perhaps 5 to 6 million individuals—are politically disenfranchised as a result of a criminal conviction.[53] Are these people unhappier as a result? And if not, does that give the state license to continue disenfranchising them? (What if *most* people, ex-felon or not, would not be made unhappy by being politically disenfranchised?) Suppose they are unhappy about losing the vote. Would a legitimate response be to pay them off, up to the point where their levels of subjective welfare were just as they were before?

Unlike a subjective metric, a capabilities approach can represent political exclusion as a distinctive form of inequality, rather than just another way in which the law makes people more or less happy. On a capabilities approach, the judgment that people who are politically excluded are treated unfairly does not depend on the thought that people are thereby made less happy. Perhaps the disenfranchised sometimes become happier, for instance because they no longer feel compelled to keep up with politics. Moreover, even if they do experience disenfranchisement as upsetting, its exclusionary effect would not be remedied if the law were to compensate the disenfranchised with some other benefit (a better apartment or a warmer coat) that they would prefer. Participation in collective self-government is a central capability—a capability constitutive of equal status in a democratic society—rather than merely a source of subjective utility.[54]

That said, a focus on capabilities does not categorically exclude consideration of psychological states in the assessment of sanction severity. After all, some of the central capabilities—notably, those having to do with self-respect and the ability to live publicly without shame—are in large

---

Trend," *American Criminal Law Review* 55(2) (2018): 333–72. Day fines are also prevalent in Latin America; see Edwin Zedlewski, "Alternatives to Custodial Supervision: The Day Fine," U.S. Department of Justice (2010), available at: https://www.ncjrs.gov/pdffiles1/nij/grants/230401.pdf.

53. Jeff Manza and Christopher Uggen, *Locked Out: Felon Disenfranchisement and American Democracy* (Oxford University Press 2006), 76.

54. See Niko Kolodny, "Rule over None I: What Justifies Democracy?," *Philosophy & Public Affairs* 42(3) (2014): 195–229 and "Rule over None II: Social Equality and the Justification of Democracy," *Philosophy & Public Affairs* 42(4) (2014): 287–336. Admittedly, the contrast with a Rawlsian approach is less sharp here, in that restrictions on the franchise and the ability to hold public office impair the basic rights and freedoms secured under the first principle of justice as fairness.

part grounded in a person's psychology. However, the focus on capability emphasizes that what is important in this context is not that you enjoy this or that psychological state, but that the psychological state be objectively well grounded. Self-respect is important not because it is an agreeable psychological state, but because it is the usual outcome of social and political relationships of equality. In other cases, psychological states may figure more directly in the evaluation of sanction severity. It may be that much of the harm of extended periods of solitary confinement or harsh interrogation practices—regardless of whether they amount to "torture"—is to undermine a person's psychological integrity. Since to undermine a person's capacity for ordered thought and feeling is to undermine a capability necessary for the effective enjoyment of other central capabilities, these practices are fully cognizable within a capabilities framework.

In short, Kolber is right to challenge the "duration fetish" of contemporary sentencing law and policy. I agree with Kolber that we have reason to question the default position that punishments are to be ranked according to how long they are (in the case of custodial sanctions) or their face value (in the case of monetary fines). These are proxies that, while easy to observe, are insensitive to individual variability in how punishments bear upon well-being. However, we need not adopt a purely subjective account of well-being in order to accommodate individual variability. The capability approach is sensitive to how a sanction affects differently situated individuals, but assesses that impact on what a person is objectively able to do and achieve. For some people, a shorter sentence will have a greater impact than a longer sentence would for others. Not because some people are happier in prison than others, but rather because people vary in how imprisonment affects their real freedom, both on account of who they are, as well as on account of the circumstances in which they find themselves.

(c) Pragmatism in practice. What might due process pragmatism look like in practice? Contrast the formalism of *Mendoza-Martinez*—focused on whether the statute in question imposed "punishment"—with the well-known due process cases, *Goldberg v. Kelly* and *Mathews v. Eldridge.*[55]

---

55. Goldberg v. Kelly, 397 U.S. 254 (1970); Mathews v. Eldridge, 424 U.S. 319 (1976). *Goldberg* and *Mathews* both involved judicial review of administrative decisions, and both came shortly after the end of the Warren Court, which significantly expanded procedural rights in criminal cases. Some have argued that the flexibility of administrative due process norms paved the way for watering down stricter criminal procedure norms: see Rosann Greenspan, "Criminal Due Process in the Administrative State," in *Studies in Law, Politics and Society, Vol. 14*, ed. Susan Silbey and Austin Sarat (JAI Press 1994), 169–211, especially 183–87.

Goldberg was a case in which the state sought to terminate an individual's welfare benefits without first providing an evidentiary hearing. The Court held that due process required a pre-termination hearing, and rejected the government's argument that public assistance was merely a "privilege" rather than a "right."[56] For people in Kelly's position, the majority reasoned, "welfare provides the means to obtain essential food, clothing, housing, and medical care," and hence denial of benefits in advance of a hearing would deprive someone in fact entitled to those benefits "of the very means by which to live" while he attempted to clear up the mistake, rendering his situation "immediately desperate."[57] Welfare is a means of ensuring that even the poor could access "the same opportunities that are available to others to participate meaningfully in the life of the community," and should for that reason not be regarded as "mere charity."[58]

In *Mathews*, the government sought to terminate an individual's disability (rather than welfare) benefits without a prior evidentiary hearing. This time, the majority held that due process did *not* require a prior evidentiary hearing, distinguishing *Goldberg* by reasoning that an erroneous interruption of disability benefits was less likely to be devastating than a similar interruption in welfare benefits. Whatever the (somewhat dubious) merits of that conclusion, at no point in the analysis did the court pause to consider whether the harm imposed by an interruption in government benefits was intended by the state as punishment, or merely foreseen as a "collateral consequence" of the enforcement of the agency's eligibility rules.[59] Instead, in *Mathews* the court articulated its well-known tripartite scheme for adjudicating due process claims: the defendant's interests affected by state action, the risk of an erroneous invasion of that interest under both extant and proposed procedural regimes, and the state's interest in proceeding.[60] For my purposes, however, the point is that under *Mathews*, the focus is

---

56. *Goldberg*, 397 U.S. at 262.

57. *Goldberg*, 397 U.S. at 264.

58. *Goldberg*, 397 U.S. at 265.

59. Jerry Mashaw suggested reasons to doubt the specific conclusion in *Mathews*; see Mashaw, "The Supreme Court's Due Process Calculus for Administrative Adjudication in *Mathews v. Eldridge*: Three Factors in Search of a Theory of Value," *University of Chicago Law Review* 44(28) (1976): 28–59 at 39. More generally, the contrast I draw between formalism and pragmatism has echoes of the Mashaw's discussion of the "model of appropriateness" and the "model of competence." See *Due Process in the Administrative State* (Yale University Press 1985).

60. *Mathews*, 424 U.S. at 335.

squarely on the overall impact of enforcing the law, not on whether that burden was intended, much less whether it is punishment.

Goldberg and *Mathews* are of particular interest from the point of view of the capabilities approach. In those cases, the Supreme Court did not focus simply on the sheer dollar value of the petitioners' loss, but rather on what that loss would *mean* for people situated in the relevant social and legal context. One might disagree with the court's concrete judgment distinguishing between welfare and disability benefits while accepting the broader point, which is that what matters for purposes of due process is not the specific dollar amount at issue, but rather the significance of that loss in terms of a petitioner's access to central capability. The principle that procedural fairness should be sensitive to what is at stake for the litigant is, after all, hardly an idiosyncratic view of due process.[61]

Unlike *Mendoza-Martinez*, and the Supreme Court's other civil-criminal cases, neither *Goldberg* nor *Mathews* suggested that the kind of process to which a petitioner is entitled is sensitive to whether the state's motivation is condemnatory in nature. Due process pragmatism suggests extending that approach to the allocation of rights in criminal cases as well. For purposes of determining what kind of process is fair and appropriate in a given context, the focus should be, as in the normal case of due process adjudication, more squarely on how the proposed mode of enforcing the rule will affect individual interests as against social ones. Whether a given law is classified as "criminal" is, from this point of view, a question on which nothing of substance turns.

This is of course only the barest sketch of an approach, and there are many unanswered questions. As I have noted, there are important questions about its application to contexts where there are roughly equivalent interests on both sides rather than, as is more commonly the case in criminal law, the urgent interests of a specific individual versus urgent, but much more diffuse, interests of a larger public. In those cases, symmetrical rights (rather than the more typical asymmetrical rights in criminal procedure) might well be defended. Second, should the analysis be concerned with potential or expected outcomes? The argument for potential rather than expected outcomes, as for categorical rather than case-by-case assessment, rests largely on information costs. Accurately

61. See, e.g., *Kane v University of British Columbia*, [1980] 1 SCR 1105, para. 31 (noting that "a high standard of justice is required when the right to continue in one's profession or employment is at stake.").

estimating expected outcomes requires more information than estimating potential outcomes, as it requires knowledge of prosecutorial and judicial preferences with respect to charging and bargaining matters, and hence case-specific knowledge. On the other hand, arguably the same sensitivity to real freedom that is the hallmark of the capabilities approach would weigh in favor of a case-by-case, rather than categorical, approach to assessing outcomes.[62] Hence, one might argue that due process should be sensitive to case-specific vulnerabilities, rather than limited to inevitably crude generalizations. Finally, one might well wonder how significant procedural rights are when they are waivable—and standardly waived—in the course of plea negotiations. This, of course, raises deep and unresolved questions about waiver, coercion, and institutional oversight in litigation in which the public has an interest.[63]

These are important questions that a fuller account of due process pragmatism would need to consider. Rather than pursue them further, however, I shall turn to considering the practical upshot of the contrast between due process pragmatism and criminal law formalism with respect to the so-called collateral consequences of a criminal conviction.

(d) Collateral consequences. The forms in which discrimination against people with criminal records can occur are multifarious, broadly applied, and often permanent; their cumulative impact can be severe.[64] The exclusionary impact of these types of restrictions would appear to amount to a form of social subordination, and to that degree inconsistent with the ideal of status equality embodied by the political ideal of anti-deference. In addition to being antidemocratic, one might also question the policy wisdom of obstructing a person's ability to access educational loans, housing, or employment on account of that person's criminal record. It is probable that many of the formal restrictions that legislatures in the United States have placed upon people with criminal records are unjustifiable and should be repealed, and it is also probable that more efforts should be made to limit the reach of informal discrimination against people with criminal records.

62. See, e.g., *Lassiter v Department of Social Services*, 452 U.S. 18, 32 (1981) (applying case-by-case approach to assistance of counsel in parental rights termination context).

63. A theme in the work of Talia Fisher; see "The Boundaries of Plea Bargaining: Negotiating the Standard of Proof," *Journal of Criminal Law & Criminology* 97(4) (2007): 943–1008.

64. See Bruce Western, *Punishment and Inequality in America* (Russell Sage Foundation 2007); Marc Mauer and Meda Chesney-Lind, eds., *Invisible Punishment: The Collateral Consequences of Mass Imprisonment* (New Press 2002); James Jacobs, *The Eternal Criminal Record* (Harvard University Press 2015), ch. 13; Hoskins, *Beyond Punishment.*

Earlier, I criticized formalist conceptions of the criminal law for failing to attend adequately to the full range of consequences of a criminal conviction. They fail to attend to these consequences because they are not motivated by a punitive intent. (That is why they are "collateral.") Due process pragmatism, however, is not sensitive to whether collateral consequences are or are not punishment. It is focused on their foreseeable impact on central capability. This distinguishes due process pragmatism from other reform-minded theorists. Zach Hoskins, for instance, argues that we should decide whether collateral consequences constitute "punishment" on a case-by-case basis, with (presumably) criminal procedure protections only required in those cases where they are established to be punishment.[65] In contrast, due process pragmatism suggests that the foreseeable impact of creating a criminal record should be taken into account at all stages of the criminal process, whether or not they are punishment.[66] The more relevant questions are: How does that law affect how people's lives go? Does it impair effective access to central capability? If it does, what should count as a fair procedure in deciding whether to impose X in a particular case?

Due process pragmatism also does not draw a sharp line between a burden that is formally imposed by law, and a burden that is merely foreseen as the highly likely side effect of a legal judgment. Often, for instance, the criminal law has downstream effects on a person's life that are not formally imposed by law, as when a person's friends and family become more reluctant to associate with him after he has been convicted of a crime, or when employers, landlords, and universities discriminate against applicants with criminal records. As Bruce Western has shown, the fact of having served a custodial sentence produces significant and persistent effects on lifetime earnings, employability, and marital status.[67] This approach stands in contrast to that of the American Bar Association, which construes "collateral consequences" as "penalties, disabilities, or disadvantages imposed upon a person as a result of a criminal conviction,

65. Hoskins, *Beyond Punishment*, ch. 2.

66. See Alessandro Corda, "More Justice and Less Harm: Reinventing Access to Criminal History Records," *Howard Law Journal* 60(1) (2016): 1–60.

67. See Western, *Punishment and Inequality in America*; Jacobs, *The Eternal Criminal Record*, ch. 14.

either automatically by operation of law or by authorized action of an administrative agency or court on a case by case basis."[68] From the point of view of due process pragmatism, the allocation of procedural rights should not be limited to officially imposed restrictions or disabilities, but should take into account expected social stigma, even of an informal nature.[69]

While estimating the impact of informal social stigma can be difficult, it is hard to see why public institutions should be entitled to ignore these downstream effects. True, these effects do not amount to officially imposed punishment. But *DeShaney* notwithstanding, the responsibilities of public institutions are not limited to keeping their own hands clean. Given their foreseeability, it seems arbitrary to ignore the broader social consequences of a criminal conviction simply because others are their more proximate agents. Public institutions do not act in an informational void, and it would be odd to insulate the evaluation of their decisions from readily accessible facts. For one thing, public institutions play a large role in shaping the actions of those agents. Access to a person's criminal history reflects specific decisions and policies adopted in a particular jurisdiction at a particular time, with jurisdictions varying in how much access they grant to the public to criminal history records.[70] Public law determines whether it is permissible for private employers and landlords to discriminate against people with criminal records, how long one has a criminal record, how readily available they are to third parties, whether a record can be expunged, and if so, under what conditions.[71] In the United States, fingerprint-based background checks for non-criminal justice purposes have become routine, and indeed outnumber such checks for criminal justice purposes.[72] Surveys of employers have revealed that over two-thirds perform criminal history checks on job applicants, with the most commonly cited reason "to reduce legal liability for negligent

---

68. See: http://www.abacollateralconsequences.org/user_guide/#q01.

69. I thank Francesco Vigano for discussion of this point.

70. Jacobs, *The Eternal Criminal Record*, especially ch. 9 (comparing the American emphasis on public access to records to a European norm of restricted access); Corda, "More Justice and Less Harm," 26–41, 46–52 (comparing open access to criminal history records in the United States to restricted access in Europe).

71. See James Jacobs and Tamara Crepet, "The Expanding Scope, Use, and Availability of Criminal Records," *New York University Journal of Legislation and Public Policy* 11(2) (2008): 177–213.

72. U.S. Department of Justice, Attorney General's Report on Criminal History Background Checks (2006), https://www.bjs.gov/content/pub/pdf/ag_bgchecks_report.pdf, at 3.

hiring."[73] Similarly, federal law practically requires states to create sex offender registries or face loss of federal funding; many state registries make offenders' identities, personal information (including photographs), and offense of conviction publicly available.[74] Since these types of practices influence the likelihood that private parties will react in discriminatory ways toward people with prior convictions, it seems reasonable to include foreseeable private discrimination as a possible input into the due process calculus.[75]

It is worth noting that, for all the attention given to mass incarceration, vastly more people's lives are negatively affected by restrictions related to their criminal records. By some estimates, almost one out of five Americans has a criminal record of some sort.[76] Discounting collateral consequences on the ground that they are not intended by the state as punishment has the effect of relegating much of the criminal justice system's impact on people's lives to the shadows. The formalistic impulse to distinguish sharply between intended punishment and merely foreseen knock-on effects has given a philosophical imprimatur to public indifference toward the broader consequences of criminal convictions. Egalitarian values should lead us to question that indifference. From political disenfranchisement to formal restrictions on housing, education, and employment to informal stigmatization in social, familial, and community relations, the overall impact of the criminal law is often to impair

---

73. Society for Human Resource Management, *Background Checking: Conducting Criminal Background Checks* (2012), available at https://www.shrm.org/hr-today/trends-and-forecasting/research-and-surveys/pages/criminalbackgroundcheck.aspx (slides 2 and 6); Jacobs, *The Eternal Criminal Record*, 5.

74. Jacobs and Crepet, "The Expanding Scope, Use, and Availability of Criminal Records," 203–8.

75. See Devah Pager, *Marked: Race, Crime and Finding Work in an Era of Mass Incarceration* (University of Chicago Press 2007).

76. Bureau of Justice Statistics, Survey of State Criminal History Information Systems (2012), available at https://www.ncjrs.gov/pdffiles1/bjs/grants/244563.pdf, at 3, (reporting that state-level criminal history repositories hold criminal records—including arrests and subsequent dispositions—of over 100 million people); Michelle Navidad Rodriguez and Maurice Emsellem, "65 Million Need Not Apply: The Case for Reforming Criminal Background Checks for Employment" (National Employment Law Project 2011), available at http://www.nelp.org/content/uploads/2015/03/65_Million_Need_Not_Apply.pdf (estimating that, after discounting for people with records in multiple states, that 65 million Americans have a criminal record).

the ideal of a society of peers.[77] Even when incarceration is not (or is no longer) at issue, the criminal law often embodies an exclusionary judgment: those who commit crimes are no longer one of us, and neither their interests nor their opinions are worthy of consideration, especially when compared to those of us who are unblemished by crime.

6.4 The Priority of Due Process

The "pragmatic" spirit of my proposal is perhaps reasonably clear. What may be less clear is why I refer to it as *due process* pragmatism. As I have noted, the United States Supreme Court has unequivocally embraced criminal law formalism. These types of claims arise in manifold contexts, from professional disbarment to regulatory fines to contempt of court. People facing such sanctions have raised a host of legal claims. They have argued that the state should be required to prove its case to the beyond-a-reasonable-doubt proof standard, or should be forced to respect the ban on double jeopardy and retroactive legislation, or that it should be required to fund their legal defense. For over a century—going back to its early deportation cases—the Supreme Court has repeatedly denied such claims on the basis that the petitioners were not being "punished," and hence could not avail themselves of the prerogatives of criminal procedure.

However, even as the Supreme Court relied on formalist reasoning to block attempts to categorize this or that type of action as a criminal action, it has nevertheless kept open the possibility that special procedural rights might be appropriate even for non-criminal matters. Not, of course, because the state is seeking to punish, but rather on the basis of a broader conception of due process. In this way, due process values have played a critical role in allocating rights in cases that lie on the civil-criminal boundary. A particularly clear example of this interplay is the Court's approach to punitive damages in tort. Despite its clearly articulated view that the Eighth Amendment is limited to criminal punishment rather than civil damages, within a few years the Court came around to the view that punitive damage awards would be subject to (admittedly, rather light)

77. See Pager, *Marked*, ch. 4 (finding that a criminal record causes a substantial decrease in callbacks from employers, particularly for African-American jobseekers); Gabriel Chin, "The New Civil Death: Rethinking Punishment in the Era of Mass Conviction," *University of Pennsylvania Law Review* 160(6) (2012): 1789–833 at 1790–91.

regulation by means of the Fourteenth Amendment's due process clause.[78] This is not an isolated case; the same pattern can be found in a wide range of other substantive areas. The Court subjects an entire substantive area of law to a sweeping, formalist analysis—usually deeming it to be "not punishment," and hence categorically excluded from criminal procedure—while nevertheless allowing piecemeal due process challenges in response to the particular interests at stake.[79] Consider the following cases.

(a) Deportation. In *Fong Yue Ting v. United States,* the appellants contested their deportation under the Geary Act, the successor to the Chinese Exclusion Act of 1882.[80] The Court rejected their due process claims, reasoning that because the federal government is entitled to exclude whomsoever it wishes from entry it followed that it could similarly deport unnaturalized foreigners whose presence on American soil was purely at the grace of the government.[81] Although the proceeding establishing the appellants' deportability did not comply with the usual standards of criminal trials—the act placed the burden on the alien to establish the lawfulness of his residence and made deportation the default outcome—it nevertheless provided all the process that was due because deportation, unlike transportation and extradition, did not amount to punishment for a crime.[82] Because deportation "is but a method of enforcing the return to his own country of an alien who has not complied with the conditions upon the performance of which the government . . . has determined that his continuing to reside here shall depend," the majority held that the stripped-down procedure established by the Geary Act did not deprive the appellants of life, liberty, or property without due process of

78. Compare Browning-Ferris Indus. of Vermont, Inc. v. Kelco Disposal, Inc., 492 U.S. 257, 262 (1989) (Eighth Amendment applies "primarily, and perhaps exclusively, to criminal prosecutions and punishments") with BMW of North America v. Gore, 517 U.S. 559 (1996) (relying on Fourteenth Amendment's due process clause to impose a "grossly excessive" standard on punitive damages awarded by a jury).

79. For these reasons, I suspect that the "punishment" label need not be quite as material as Hoskins suggests. See *Beyond Punishment,* ch. 2.

80. Fong Yue Ting v. United States, 149 U.S. 698 (1893); see also INS v. Lopez-Mendoza, 468 U.S. 1032, 1038 (1984) (stating that a deportation proceeding is a "purely civil action to determine eligibility to remain in this country, not to punish an unlawful entry.").

81. *Fong Yue Ting,* 149 U.S. at 724.

82. *Fong Yue Ting,* 149 U.S. at 730. "Transportation" was the practice of sending convicted criminals to labor in remote colonies for a set number of years. For an account of the origins and uses of transportation, see J.M. Beattie, *Crime and the Courts in England, 1660–1800* (Oxford University Press 1986), ch. 9.

law, and that Fourth, Fifth, and Eighth Amendment rights did not apply.[83] The Court has not retreated from its view that deportation (now known as "removal") is not punishment, even in the face of statutes that make deportation a consequence of a criminal conviction.[84] Indeed, it has extended this line of reasoning to permit the introduction of illegally obtained evidence in removal hearings, ex parte proceedings, adverse inferences drawn from the potential deportee's silence, proof below the beyond-a-reasonable-doubt standard, and the introduction of statements that were made without the benefit of *Miranda* warnings, all of which are prohibited in a typical criminal trial.[85]

Yet, while the Court has never retreated from its view that deportation is not punishment, it has at the same time insisted on stricter procedural safeguards in deportation cases than would apply in normal civil litigation.[86] The Court has, for instance, held that the minimum standard of proof required at a deportation hearing is "clear, unequivocal and convincing" evidence—higher than the civil preponderance standard, even if not as demanding as the beyond-a-reasonable-doubt standard in criminal trials.[87] The Court justified this elevated standard by referring to the "drastic deprivations" that flow from deportation.[88] More recently, in *Padilla v. Kentucky*, the Court rejected the government's suggestion that deportation is merely a "collateral" consequence of conviction and hence does not fall within the Sixth Amendment right to counsel. Instead, the Court held that the failure of Padilla's lawyer to inform him that pleading guilty made him subject to automatic deportation violated his right to effective assistance of counsel, despite acknowledging that deportation is not

---

83. *Fong Yue Ting*, 149 U.S. at 730. Each of the three dissenters insisted that the Geary Act in fact imposed punishment and, as such, required more substantial procedural protections than the Geary Act provided. See *Fong Yue Ting*, 149 U.S. at 740 (Brewer, dissenting); 759 (Field, dissenting); 763 (Fuller, dissenting).

84. Loh Wah Suey v. Backus, 225 U.S. 460 (1912); Mahler v. Eby, 264 U.S. 32 (1924); Carlson v. Landon, 342 U.S. 524 (1952); Harisiades v. Shaughnessy, 342 U.S. 580 (1952); and Galvan v. Press, 347 U.S. 522 (1953).

85. *Lopez-Mendoza*, 468 U.S. at 1039 (exclusionary rule, ex parte, proof beyond a reasonable doubt and *Miranda*) and 1043 (adverse inferences).

86. For a brief synopsis comparing the procedural rights in the immigration and criminal contexts, see Stumpf, "The Crimmigration Crisis," 390–95.

87. Woodby v. INS, 385 U.S. 276, 286 (1966).

88. *Woodby*, 385 U.S. at 285.

in the "strict sense" a true criminal punishment.[89] Citing the increasingly automatic removal of noncitizens found guilty of a broad range of crimes, Justice Stevens expressly noted the "dramatically raised" stakes of a criminal conviction, and stated that these changes "confirm [the Court's] view that, as a matter of federal law, deportation is an integral part—indeed, sometimes the most important part—of the penalty that may be imposed on noncitizen defendants who plead guilty to specified crimes."[90] While *Padilla* was not expressly decided under the due process clause, in effect—as Justice Scalia noted in his dissent—it imported due process concerns into the Fifth and Sixth Amendment contexts.[91]

(b) Pretrial detention. Pretrial detention resembles incarceration, our paradigmatic form of legal punishment. However, were it to actually *be* punishment, then the usual restrictions of criminal procedure would apply, making pretrial detention a dead letter. After all, the entire point of pretrial detention is to hold someone before a trial at which the state proves that person's guilt beyond a reasonable doubt. Requiring the state to prove guilt beyond a reasonable doubt before it is allowed to detain the person prior to trial would defeat the purpose of pretrial detention. In *United States v. Salerno*, the Supreme Court considered a challenge to pretrial detention under the Bail Reform Act, and emphasized that the process that was due to pretrial detainees depended crucially on whether their detention amounted to "punishment."[92] Perhaps unsurprisingly, the Court demurred, distinguishing between regulatory detention and punitive incarceration.

Again, however, although in *Salerno* the Supreme Court rejected the claim that pretrial detention should be granted the full panoply of rights available to people facing punishment, it acknowledged that the deprivation of liberty—whether through punishment or otherwise—must be consistent with prevailing due process standards. The Bail Reform Act

---

89. Padilla v. Kentucky, 559 U.S. 356, 365–66 (2010).

90. *Padilla*, 559 U.S. at 364.

91. *Padilla*, 559 U.S. at 391.

92. United States v. Salerno, 481 U.S. 739 (1987); see also Bell v. Wolfish, 441 U.S. 520, 537 (1979) (recognizing "a distinction between punitive measures that may not constitutionally be imposed prior to a determination of guilt and regulatory restraints that may."). The Supreme Court of Canada has been more willing to admit that pretrial detention amounts to punishment, although it has been unwilling to require the standard set of procedural safeguards that punishment typically entails; see *R v Wust*, 2000 SCC 18, [2000] 1 SCR 455.

satisfied those standards because, among other things, it required the government to "convince a neutral decision maker by clear and convincing evidence that no conditions of release can reasonably assure the safety of the community or any person."[93] Whether or not this is an adequate standard, in light of the very severe deprivation inflicted by pretrial detention, it is surely noteworthy that the Supreme Court took for granted that the Bail Reform Act was subject to evaluation under the due process clause. This is particularly noteworthy given the lengths to which the Court went to characterize the Bail Reform Act as non-punitive and hence not truly criminal law. The inference is clear: whether or not the Bail Reform Act qualified as "criminal law," it still had to satisfy established standards of due process.

(c) Involuntary commitment. More recently, in *Kansas v. Hendricks*, a majority of the Court held that the retroactive character of a state law authorizing the potentially indefinite civil commitment of a dangerous sex offender did not amount to either ex post facto punishment or double jeopardy, constitutional principles that apply specially to criminal cases. The Court accepted Kansas's stated intent that it was trying to protect the public from dangerous individuals, rather than attempting to deter or provide just deserts to sex offenders through punishment. For that reason, under formalist principles it followed that the proceedings against Hendricks were not criminal in nature, and hence neither the ex post facto nor double jeopardy clauses were available to him.[94]

Significantly, although the Court suggested in *Hendricks* that both retribution and deterrence were "punitive" purposes, it has since rejected deterrence as a sufficient basis for attributing a punitive purpose, on the ground that considering deterrence to be a punitive purpose would "severely undermine the Government's ability to engage in effective regulation."[95] In *Hudson*, the Court noted, plausibly enough, that "all civil penalties have some deterrent effect," meaning that taking deterrence as a sufficient basis for establishing a punitive purpose would have the effect of transforming all civil penalties into criminal punishments. Consequently, in disputed cases certain procedural rights are available only if the petitioner can demonstrate that the state's motives are retributively motivated;

---

93. *Salerno*, 481 U.S. at 750–51 (balancing, under the due process clause, the government's interest in preventing crime against the individual's interest in liberty).

94. Kansas v. Hendricks, 521 U.S. 346, 360–69 (1997).

95. Hudson v. United States, 522 U.S. 93, 105 (1997).

deterrence alone will not suffice. Of course, establishing a retributive rationale is likely to be difficult or impossible in many cases.

Although *Hendricks* is largely remembered for its highly formalistic interpretation of the civil-criminal distinction, it is important to recall that the case was decided against a backdrop of existing law that had established relatively strict procedural requirements for civil commitment on due process grounds. By the time *Hendricks* was decided, it had already been resolved that a state cannot commit someone unless that person is *both* mentally ill *and* a danger to himself or others.[96] In addition, commitment proceedings require, at a minimum, proof by a heightened clear and convincing standard.[97] Moreover, the procedure provided in *Hendricks* was in fact rather extensive: a prosecutor was required to file a petition in state court seeking involuntary commitment, at which point the court was required to determine whether sufficient grounds existed to support classifying the individual as a "sexually violent predator." The individual in question was to be provided with a "professional evaluation," followed by a trial in which the burden of proof was on the state to prove beyond a reasonable doubt that he met the legal definition of a sexually violent predator. Indigent persons were provided with state-funded counsel and mental health examinations, as well as liberal adversarial and disclosure rights at trial. Once committed, the individual had a right to annual review and the right to petition for release; if the state was at any point unable to establish that the individual continued to be a sexually violent predator beyond a reasonable doubt, the individual was entitled to release.[98]

(d) Delinquency. Juvenile justice presents a particularly interesting episode in the Court's oscillation between formalism and pragmatism. Juvenile delinquency hearings were specifically designed as a non-punitive alternative to the criminal process. They were intended to be procedurally less demanding than a typical criminal case.[99] Since the juvenile

---

96. Foucha v. Louisiana, 504 U.S. 71, 77 (1992) (a person acquitted by reason of insanity can be civilly committed "as long as he is both mentally ill and dangerous, but no longer"); *Hendricks*, 521 U.S. at 358 (involuntary commitment generally requires proof of mental illness or abnormality).

97. Addington v. Texas, 441 U.S. 418, 433 (1979).

98. *Hendricks*, 521 U.S. at 352–53. See also Stephen Schulhofer, "Two Systems of Social Protection: Comments on the Civil-Criminal Distinction, with Particular Reference to Sexually Violent Predator Laws," *Journal of Contemporary Legal Issues* 7(1) (1996): 69–96.

99. "The idea of crime and punishment was to be abandoned. The child was to be 'treated' and 'rehabilitated' and the procedures, from apprehension through institutionalization,

delinquency regime was specifically intended to be non-punitive, formalism does not support anything approximating regular criminal procedure in these cases. Justice Stewart defended this austere position in his dissent to *Gault*, a landmark delinquency case involving a boy who made a lewd telephone call to a neighbor.[100] In that case, the boy was subjected to a custodial term thirty-six times longer than the maximum available for an adult, a sentence under an astonishingly casual process.

Notwithstanding the non-punitive origins of juvenile delinquency, however, the Court has gradually come to insist on heightened safeguards in juvenile proceedings—perhaps unsurprisingly, given the kinds of sentence that were being imposed.[101] In *Gault*, the Court acknowledged that juvenile proceedings are not intended to punish and should be treated as a distinct, non-criminal procedural regime. Under a purely formalist framework, that should have been the end of the story. However, while the Court was careful not to import criminal procedure wholesale into the juvenile justice context, it nevertheless insisted that due process required notice, provision of counsel in custodial cases, a privilege against self-incrimination, and sworn testimony subject to cross-examination.[102] The Court rejected the state's argument that the Fifth Amendment's right against self-incrimination was expressly limited to "criminal" cases, remarking that "commitment is a deprivation of liberty" and "is incarceration against one's will, whether it is called 'criminal' or 'civil.'" "To hold otherwise," Justice Fortas insisted, "would be to disregard substance because of the feeble enticement of the 'civil' label-of-convenience which has been attached to juvenile proceedings."[103]

It is worth recalling in this connection that the most iconic of rights in criminal procedure—the right to an acquittal absent proof of guilt "beyond a reasonable doubt"—was in fact established as a constitutional right in the context of juvenile delinquency proceedings; that is in an expressly

---

were to be 'clinical' rather than punitive." *In re* Gault, 387 U.S. 1, 15–16 (1967). This feature of juvenile justice stretches back to the Progressive era: see Samuel Walker, *Popular Justice: A History of American Criminal Justice*, 2nd ed. (Oxford University Press 1998), 114.

100. *Gault*, 387 U.S. at 78 (Stewart, dissenting).

101. See, e.g., McKiever v. Pennsylvania, 403 U.S. 528 (1971) (refusing to extend right to jury trial to juvenile delinquency proceedings, and discussing the court's incremental approach under the due process clause).

102. *Gault*, 387 U.S. at 34, 41, 55 and 57, respectively.

103. *Gault*, 387 U.S. at 49–50.

non-criminal context. *Winship* established the beyond-a-reasonable-doubt standard on the basis of a basic norm of due process. It did not base the beyond-a-reasonable-doubt standard on the allegedly special morality of the criminal law.[104] Indeed, the *Winship* Court expressly rejected the relevance of the civil-criminal distinction: "civil labels and good intentions do not themselves obviate the need for criminal due process safeguards in juvenile courts," since the loss of liberty that followed a finding of delinquency was "comparable in seriousness to a felony prosecution."[105]

What these cases suggest is that even while the Supreme Court has regularly relied on formalist reasoning to restrict access to procedural rights, it has at the same time regularly relied on broader conceptions of due process pragmatism to justify heightened procedural safeguards in high-stakes decisions. Even as the Court has sought to keep criminal procedure pure by restricting it to truly punitive laws, it has at the same time recognized that the classification of a law as "civil" or "criminal" does not dispose of more substantive questions of procedural justice. When it has turned to address those questions, the Court has often acted under the auspices of due process pragmatism, even while superficially proclaiming allegiance to criminal law formalism.

This feature of the Court's jurisprudence should not come as a surprise. After all, the concept of due process is arguably a more basic constitutional value than the classification of a law as "civil" or criminal." This suggests that, as a jurisprudential matter, nothing prevents federal courts from using the due process clause to extend procedural rights beyond formalist limits. Doing so would not require courts to overturn settled case law on whether a given deprivation counts as "criminal." All it would require is for federal courts to reframe disputes about whether a deprivation is "civil" or "criminal" as disputes about whether deprivation, if imposed, would invade a sufficiently important interest to justify subordinating it to stricter due process scrutiny. This would have the effect of bringing many

---

104. *In re* Winship, 397 U.S. 358, 368 (1970).

105. *Winship* at 365–66. In *Breed v. Jones*, a unanimous court relied on *Winship* and *Gault* in holding that a juvenile delinquency adjudication is sufficient to trigger the double jeopardy clause, rejecting attempts to limit the reach of the double jeopardy clause to strictly "criminal" cases. Breed v. Jones, 421 U.S. 519, 529–31 (1975). In a similar vein, David Ball has stressed that although *Apprendi* is widely understood as a Sixth Amendment case about the centrality of the jury in criminal prosecutions, its insistence that sentencing facts be proven beyond a reasonable doubt actually derives from *Winship*, a non-criminal case. Ball, "The Civil Case at the Heart of Criminal Procedure," 121.

of the legally imposed collateral consequences of a conviction under more effective constitutional scrutiny, without insisting that those consequences amount to punishment. So far as I can see, there is nothing inconsistent in observing that (for instance) although the double jeopardy clause does not prohibit the state from pursuing a second prosecution, the due process clause does.[106]

Admittedly, it would be more elegant if there were a single jurisprudential basis for deciding such matters, rather than achieving this end partially through the civil-criminal distinction and partially through due process. But perhaps inelegance of this sort is only to be expected when it comes to an old, intensively interpreted and exceedingly hard-to-modify constitutional instrument.[107] Be that as it may, the more important point is that the concept of due process is sufficiently flexible to permit the development of a functionally equivalent body of jurisprudence, without upsetting the criminal law formalism that the Supreme Court has so long endorsed. Maybe there are procedural entitlements that become

---

106. For a brief period in the 1990s, it seemed as if the Supreme Court was poised to shift course. See United States v. Halper, 490 U.S. 435, 447 (1989) (noting that the scope of the double jeopardy clause "can be identified only by assessing the character of the actual sanctions imposed on the individual by the machinery of the state"); overruled by *Hudson*, 522 U.S. at 101–3 (returning to a framework based largely on legislative intent).

107. As it happens, the Canadian *Charter of Rights and Freedoms*—a newer and less intensively interpreted constitutional instrument—provides this kind of conceptual framework. Section 7 of the *Charter* protects rights in "life, liberty and security of the person" against incursions that are inconsistent with "principles of fundamental justice." See *Canadian Charter of Rights and Freedoms*, s 7, Part I of the *Constitution Act, 1982*, being Schedule B to the *Canada Act 1982* (UK), 1982, c 11. In a landmark case involving a provincial statute that made it an absolute liability offense to drive on a suspended license—a law that probably lay closer to the regulatory rather than punitive end of the spectrum—the Supreme Court of Canada insisted that if the state is trying to put someone in prison, it must at a minimum offer that person the possibility of establishing her lack of fault. *Re B.C. Motor Vehicle Act*, [1985] 2 SCR 486, 24 DLR (4th) 536. In sharp contrast to the formalism of the American Supreme Court, the Supreme Court of Canada did not regard the province's intent in enacting such a law as relevant to determining whether the *Charter*'s guarantee, under s.7, of "fundamental justice" applies. The Court reaffirmed this view in a case that rejected the government's claim that deportation and detention in the immigration context are immune from s.7 scrutiny because immigration law is not genuine criminal law. In response, the Supreme Court observed that s.7 "appl[ies] in criminal proceedings, not *because* they are criminal proceedings, but *because the liberty interest is always engaged* in criminal proceedings." *Charkaoui v Canada*, 2007 SCC 9, at para 18, [2007] 1 SCR 350, (italics modified; citing Hamish Stewart, "Is Indefinite Detention of Terrorist Suspects Really Constitutional?," *University of New Brunswick Law Journal* 54 (2005): 235–50 at 242). Though see *Medovarski v Canada*, 2005 SCC 51, at para 46, [2005] 2 SCR 539 (holding that the "deportation of a non-citizen in itself cannot implicate the liberty and security interests protected by s.7 of the *Canadian Charter of Rights and Freedoms*.").

appropriate when the state is trying to punish you. And maybe deportation, disbarment, asset forfeiture, denial of government benefits, public registration of ex-offenders, and so forth are not truly punishment, and hence not truly criminal law. But so what? From the point of view of due process pragmatism, the question is whether they engage constitutionally protected interests, not whether they are truly criminal law.

6.5 Conclusion

When are you entitled to the procedural rights specially reserved for criminal defendants? Criminal law formalism says: whether you are entitled to those rights depends upon whether the state is out to get you or whether, as Holmes put it, it is merely tripping over you. This is because criminal law is the law of punishment, and punishment in turn is constituted by the punisher's motives—in particular, the state's motive in vindicating a wrong that it believes you committed.

In contrast, due process pragmatism says: whether you are entitled to those rights depends upon whether enforcing the law has the potential to impair your effective access to central capability. The state's intentions in enforcing the law are not to the point. This is because, on the account of social equality I favor, effective access to central capability is constitutive of equal civic membership. In sketching this argument, I defended a capabilities-based interpretation of due process values against more subjectivist approaches, and considered its application in the context of the so-called "collateral consequences" of a criminal conviction. To be sure, due process pragmatism is at odds with the widely-held view that the criminal law is the law of punishment, a view well rooted in the precedents of the United States Supreme Court. However, even that Court has consistently recognized that the basic values of due process have a significance that transcends any merely formal distinction between "civil" and "criminal" law.

7

Responsibility without Resentment

"We must re-establish the principle that men are accountable for what they do, that criminals are responsible for their crimes, that while the youth's environment may help to explain the man's crime, it does not excuse that crime."[1]

"The sympathy toward the boy he was is at odds with outrage toward the man he is . . . In fact, each of these responses is appropriate, but taken together they do not enable us to respond overall in a coherent way."[2]

7.1 Introduction

Lindsay Farmer has recently remarked that "for many—whether analysing the law from a conventional or a critical perspective—responsibility, and in particular individual responsibility, is foundational to the modern criminal law." The concept of responsibility, Farmer writes, "precedes and structures any theoretical account of the criminal law."[3] Contrast Farmer's observation with one made by Samuel Scheffler, nearly a quarter century ago. Remarking on the conflict between the tenets of political liberalism with everyday moral sentiments, Scheffler observed that "none of the most

1. Platform statement of the 1968 Republican Party (Nixon versus Humphrey); cited in Elizabeth Hinton, *From the War on Poverty to the War on Crime: The Making of Mass Incarceration in America* (Harvard University Press 2016), 139.

2. Gary Watson, "Responsibility and the Limits of Evil," in *Responsibility, Character, and the Emotions: New Essays in Moral Psychology*, ed. Ferdinand Schoeman (Cambridge University Press 1988), 266–96 at 275.

3. Lindsay Farmer, *Making the Modern Criminal Law* (Oxford University Press 2016), 16; see also David Garland, *Punishment and Welfare* (Gower Publishing 1985), 185–9; Nicola Lacey, *In Search of Criminal Responsibility* (Oxford University Press 2016).

prominent contemporary versions of philosophical liberalism assigns a significant role to desert at the level of fundamental principle." Liberalism as a philosophical doctrine, Scheffler claimed, gave desert "no role whatsoever to play in the fundamental normative principles that apply to the basic social, political, and economic institutions of society."[4] Why has desert, and its closely related concept, responsibility, played such a central role in philosophical thinking about the criminal law, whereas those concepts—desert especially—have come to occupy (luck egalitarianism aside) such a marginal role in mainstream forms of political liberalism?

This chapter is devoted to exploring a range of answers to that question. Perhaps the criminal law has a special relationship to responsibility because blame and punishment are central to our sense of ourselves as responsible agents. Perhaps when we are face to face with actual criminal wrongdoing, we are called upon to respond with blame and punishment, no matter how much we are invested in other means of dealing with crime. Maybe we should try to prevent crime from happening. But when it happens, as it inevitably will, treating its perpetrators as responsible agents requires responding appropriately. Perhaps responsibility means that people can be liable to punishment in ways that have nothing in particular to do with equality and other liberal values, for instance if someone, without lawful excuse, wrongfully threatens another.

I shall suggest reasons to be skeptical of each of these answers. Blame and punishment may indeed be central to our sense of ourselves as responsible agents, but they are far from the exclusive manner in which moral engagement manifests. Whatever reasons we have to blame and punish people who commit crimes can be weighed against our reasons to respond in other ways, whether through compassion and repair, or through efforts to ensure that similar acts are not committed in the future. The ex post perspective of the criminal law is functionally continuous with the ex ante perspective of crime prevention, meaning that under conditions of scarcity, whatever reason we have to respond to actual instances of wrongdoing is to be weighed against our reason for investing more heavily in preventive measures. Finally, although it may be true that people who commit crimes render themselves liable to defensive harms that they would not otherwise be subject to, that is consistent with insisting that everyone's rights and interests—guilty and innocent alike—are due

4. Samuel Scheffler, "Responsibility, Reactive Attitudes and Liberalism in Philosophy and Politics," *Philosophy & Public Affairs* 21(4) (1992): 299–323 at 304.

equal consideration. Indeed, egalitarian values suggest that administrative states should often favor crime prevention over punitive response.

7.2 Equality and Responsibility

Farmer's observation reflects an important feature of contemporary normative theorizing about punishment. Although retributive theories differ amongst themselves as to what punishment consists in (censure, suffering, community sentiment, and so forth), and although they differ as to why we should impose it (vindicating rights, upholding law, communicating social disapproval, and so forth) they are unified by a basic intuition about responsibility. This intuition might be expressed somewhat as follows: what you deserve depends, to some significant degree, upon the choices you make. Part of being a responsible agent is that your normative status can be affected by your choices, and hence your choices shape how it is appropriate for others to relate to you. The shared concern among retributivists with pre-politically, pre-legal, individual desert might, in this way, be traced back to a more basic concern about responsibility. From this perspective, giving up on desert of punishment is giving up on treating people as responsible agents.[5]

Gary Watson expresses this thought eloquently. Commenting on Strawson's suggestion that making moral demands of others—and resenting them when those demands are ignored—is constitutive of treating others as part of a moral community, Watson writes:

> If holding one another responsible involves making the moral demand, and if the making of the demand *is* the proneness to such attitudes, and if such attitudes involve retributive sentiments and hence a limitation of goodwill, then skepticism about retribution is skepticism about responsibility, and holding one another responsible is at odds with one historically important ideal of love.[6]

---

5. Peter Ramsay connects the modern criminal law's focus on responsibility—exemplified in categories of subjective mens rea—to the universalization of civil rights. "The Responsible Subject as Citizen: Criminal Law, Democracy and the Welfare State," *Modern Law Review* 69 (2006): 29–58 at 41.

6. Gary Watson, "Responsibility and the Limits of Evil," 286. In this passage, Watson is examining, not endorsing, the Strawsonian idea.

My main concern in this chapter is the contrast Watson draws in this passage between responsibility and love. While the evaluative principles I have sketched flow out of an ideal of democratic equality rather than love, surely it ends up (one might suspect) in the same place: an attitude of moral detachment that is humanitarian, objectifying, and a little condescending—one more concerned with assuaging suffering than with making moral demands of each other. The virtues of democratic equality, one might object, are not *so* important that they would entitle us to give up on practices of responsibility altogether. Whatever else the criminal law is, one might continue, it is a bedrock form of accountability. We cannot give up on the criminal law without doing serious damage to our sense of ourselves as responsible agents, even in the name of a political value as important as democratic equality.

Recall that on the account I have sketched, status as an equal is not waived in virtue of even serious crime, which is to say that status equality is not choice-sensitive. Moreover, I have interpreted equal status to mean that a person's basic rights and interests—represented as effective access to an array of central capabilities—are not discounted in public deliberation about crime policy, even for people guilty of serious crimes. Murderers and rapists, no less than their victims, are due equal concern and respect in public law. I have also argued that culpable wrongdoing is neither necessary nor sufficient to justify criminalization. And I have claimed that even when conduct is properly criminalized, a commitment to democratic equality may prohibit punishing each of its instances, no matter how culpable those instances may be. More generally, I have emphasized that protection from crime is a socially provided good, and that public institutions should be expected to allocate it on terms that respect each person's status as an equal. This includes not relying on criminal sanctions when less invasive means of encouraging cooperation will do, quite independent of whether those who commit crimes are to blame for doing so. All of this may seem to imply that people should not be held responsible for what they do. And what could be the basis for such a judgment, other than skepticism that people truly are responsible agents?

This is a serious challenge. It provides a plausible answer to the question with which I started: why has responsibility been so central to philosophical thinking about the criminal law? The answer it suggests is that criminal law, unlike other areas of public law, manifests our concern to treat each other as responsible agents. To give up on punishment for crime is to give up on engaging with each other as responsible agents, perhaps in favor of humanitarian moral detachment.

7.3 Prevention, Quarantine, and "Social Hygiene"

The label "preventive justice" has acquired a rather poor reputation because it is often associated with policies such as indefinite civil commitment, broken windows policing, and other forms of draconian social policy. This is an unfortunate association, if for no other reason than that many of the policies characteristic of the welfare state, starting with the earliest initiatives in social security and unemployment insurance, are obviously meant to prevent foreseeable social ills and are, in that respect, accurately described as forms of "preventive justice."[7] (The basic failure in *DeShaney* was, after all, a failure of preventive justice.) However, as a result of these associations, theories that focus on preventing crime ex ante rather than punishing it ex post are often associated with skepticism that people are truly responsible agents, and with the idea that crime policy should be one of "social hygiene" focused on the detention of dangerous persons.

This association is consequential. Retributivists get some mileage out of the thought that the alternative to holding people's feet to the fire for the bad choices they make is subjecting them to paternalistic and authoritarian social engineering that completely ignores responsibility and agency. As Alexander and Ferzan have put it, treating people as able to choose whether to comply with the law "involves as its corollary" blaming and punishing them when they choose instead to break the law.[8] This association lends credence to the thought that we must choose between punishment and moral detachment.

What makes it seem that we cannot give up on our practices of blame and punishment without giving up on our self-conception as responsible agents? I suspect that the imagination of criminal law theorists

---

7. On this point, see Fred Schauer, "The Ubiquity of Prevention," in *Prevention and the Limits of the Criminal Law*, ed. Andrew Ashworth, Lucia Zedner, and Patrick Tomlin (Oxford University Press 2013), 10–22; Matt Matravers, "Is Twenty-First Century Punishment Post-Desert?," in *Retributivism Has a Past: Has It a Future?*, ed. M. Tonry (Oxford University Press 2012), 30–44 at 41–42.

8. Larry Alexander and Kimberly Ferzan, with Stephen Morse, *Crime and Culpability: A Theory of Criminal Law* (Cambridge University Press 2009), 6.

here is unduly influenced by popular, but exaggerated, tropes: from the brainwashing of Anthony Burgess's *A Clockwork Orange* to the punishment of "pre-crime" in Philip K. Dick's *Minority Report* to Barbara Wootton's suggestion that the criminal law's mens rea and excuse doctrine should be allowed to "wither away" and be replaced with estimations of a person's future dangerousness. If you believe that the main alternative to a traditional conception of the criminal law is the indefinite detention of the dangerous, the medicalization of the idiosyncratic, and aggressive policing and mass surveillance for everybody else, then retributive punishment will seem appealing by comparison.[9] For unlike punishment, those other types of policies do not treat people as the authors of their own lives. Rather, they treat people as potential vectors of social harm. Plausibly, however, public institutions should treat you as a responsible moral agent, whether or not you are also a potential vector of social harm. After all, there are worse things than punishment—pity, for instance.[10]

Consider Derk Pereboom and Gregg Caruso's defense of a "quarantine" model of criminal justice, a defense that they ground in their skepticism about free will.[11] Given that skepticism, Pereboom and Caruso suggest that responding to wrongful acts with resentment, blame, and

9. For instance, see David Hoekema's defense of a system of ex post punishments compares ex ante prevention to the mass surveillance and policing of a "kindly totalitarian state." "The Right to Punish, and the Right to Be Punished," in *John Rawls' Theory of Social Justice*, ed. H. Gene Blocker and Elizabeth Smith (Ohio University Press 1980), 239–69 at 256. For a rather more nuanced account of mid-century criminology, see David Garland, *The Culture of Control* (University of Chicago Press 2001), ch. 2.

10. To say nothing of the cruelty and sadism that can be disguised as well-intentioned and humane "treatment." Although I have been critical of modern retributivism in this book, it is important to acknowledge that doctrine's roots in concern over the many abuses of mid-century criminal justice. Modern administrative states have created new avenues for subordination and domination, and skepticism about their claims that they are acting in the public interest is often compelling. This is the context for the agonized turn away from mid-century rehabilitationism to fin de siècle retributivism lucidly captured in Willard Gaylin and David J. Rothman's introduction to Andrew von Hirsch, *Doing Justice: The Choice of Punishments* (Hill & Wang 1976).

11. See Gregg Caruso, "Free Will Skepticism and Criminal Behavior: A Public Health-Quarantine Model," *Southwest Philosophy Review* 32(1) (2016): 25–48 at 26–27; Derk Pereboom, "Free Will Skepticism and Criminal Punishment," in *The Future of Punishment*, ed. Thomas Nadelhoffer (Oxford University Press 2013), 49–78. See also Ferdinand D. Schoeman, "On Incapacitating the Dangerous," *American Philosophical Quarterly* 16(1) (1979): 27–35.

punishment would be inappropriate.[12] On the quarantine model, instead of blaming and punishing people for their bad choices, criminal justice institutions contain and treat people as a means of preventing harm going forward.[13] Anxieties about the quarantine model do not depend on the idea that quarantine is inhumane. For all we know, it could be quite comfortable. Anxieties about quarantine rest on the thought that it treats people in ways that are not linked to their choices.[14] Consequently, it is perhaps not surprising that to some even a highly retributive criminal law seems like an exercise in human liberation by comparison.

In my view, a focus on ex ante prevention should be sharply distinguished from the idea that people are not responsible agents. Skepticism about responsibility is, to be sure, one reason for supporting ex ante prevention. However, there are other reasons that do not presuppose skepticism about responsibility. Indeed, respect for responsibility can sometimes support a preference for ex ante prevention over ex post punishment, particularly when we take a less dystopian view of crime prevention. Recall an example I first discussed in Chapter 3: the choice between *schools, now* or *prisons, later*.[15] There is substantial evidence that high quality early childhood education can prevent criminal offending in the future. This evidence suggests that there are young children who, if we do nothing, will go

---

12. Derk Pereboom, *Living without Free Will* (Cambridge University Press 2001), 158; Caruso, "Free Will Skepticism and Criminal Behavior," 33–35. Some version of this dialectic has been unspooling for over a century: for a detailed account, see Thomas Andrew Green, *Freedom and Criminal Responsibility in American Legal Thought* (Cambridge University Press 2014).

13. Pereboom, "Free Will Skepticism and Criminal Punishment," 72–74; Caruso, "Free Will Skepticism and Criminal Behavior," 32–36.

14. See Saul Smilansky, "Pereboom on Punishment: Funishment, Innocence, Motivation and Other Difficulties," *Criminal Law and Philosophy* (May 2016), doi 10.1007/s11572-016-9396-3; John Lemos, "Moral Concerns about Responsibility Denial and the Quarantine of Violent Criminals," *Law and Philosophy* 35 (2016): 461–83; Michael Corrado, "Two Models of Criminal Justice," UNC Legal Studies Research Paper No. 2757078 at 1, available at https://papers.ssrn.com/sol3/papers.cfm?abstract_id=2757078 (accessed May 15, 2018) (linking Pereboom and Caruso's quarantine model to Wootton's proposal to do away with mens rea and focus instead on dangerousness).

15. See Chapter 3, Section 3.3, for references to the empirical literature. These choices arise repeatedly in criminal justice. In the 1970s, the residents of Washington, DC, then in the grip of a heroin epidemic, had to decide whether to enact harsh mandatory minimum sentences for drug offenses. As James Forman Jr. observes, at the time the city's drug treatment facility "was equipped to treat just one-tenth of the addicts who needed help." The decision about whether to enact harsh mandatory sentences was, in effect, a choice between hospital beds and prison cells. See *Locking Up Our Own: Crime and Punishment in Black America* (Farrar, Straus and Giroux 2017), ch. 4.

on to commit crimes later in life that they would not commit if provided with better education than they currently receive. Suppose the evidence is sound. That presents us with a choice. From the point of view of crime policy, we can choose to invest in a strategy of *schools, now*. Or we can forgo that investment, investing instead in a strategy of *prisons, later*. The choice between *schools, now* and *prisons, later* is a choice between ex ante prevention and ex post punishment: prevent kids from committing crimes as they grow up, or wait for them to commit the crimes and punish them for doing so. As I suggested in Chapter 3, I think we have reason to prefer *schools, now* over *prisons, later*. From the point of view of protecting each person's effective access to central capability, *schools, now* plainly outperforms *prisons, later*. *Schools, now* yields less crime and less punishment than *prisons, later*. Moreover, under the principle of inclusive aggregation, the punitive impact of *prisons, later* cannot be discounted on the basis that those who are punished are responsible for their wrongful acts.[16]

To be sure, the manner in which we engage with people as responsible agents in educational and punitive settings differs. In the former, we respect agency by promoting the conditions under which it is robustly exercised, whereas in the latter we respect it by acknowledging the moral significance once it has been exercised. However, the crucial point for my purposes in this chapter is that the preference for *schools, now* over *prisons, later* does not presuppose that disadvantaged children, or the adults they become, are not fully responsible agents. To the contrary: in large part, the appeal of early childhood education (as with many other forms of parenting, educational, health, and employment initiatives) is that those types of programs serve to promote the emotional, psychological, and social capacities that undergird responsible agency. A plausible interpretation of investment in educational, social, and employment programs of this kind is that they enable people to develop the emotional and social skills that enable them to exercise a greater degree of independent judgment and to be less prone to impulsive behavior in life.[17] Responsible agency,

---

16. Does the appeal of *schools, now* over *prisons, later* rely on the fact that we only know that some of today's children will subsequently commit crimes, but not which ones specifically? That seems doubtful. Suppose we were to learn which children specifically will grow up to become criminals absent some intervention on our part. If anything, that would seem to strengthen our reasons for intervening now.

17. J. Heckman, R. Pinto, and P. Savelyev, "Understanding the Mechanisms through Which an Influential Early Childhood Education Program Boosted Adult Outcomes," *American Economic Review* 103(6) (2013): 2052–86 at 2053.

after all, is not an all-or-nothing affair, but rather comes in degrees. Hence, the choice between *schools, now* and *prisons, later* is not a choice between treating people as potential vectors of harm and as responsible agents. It is a choice between two different ways of respecting people as responsible agents: strengthening capacities for moral deliberation and choice, or responding to poor exercises of that agency with official forms of censure, blame, and punishment.

A further line of argument, drawing upon recent work by Erin Kelly, bolsters this conclusion.[18] Kelly argues that there is a substantial gap between acknowledging that someone is responsible for a wrong, and responding with blame or resentment. We may hold someone responsible for a wrong in that we judge that person to have intentionally acted in a way that violates the moral expectations that apply in a given case, and to have had at least some capacity to have recognized reasons that favor a better course of conduct than the one she did choose. But, Kelly argues, although there is substantial value in relating to people through universal moral expectations of this kind, people sometimes violate those expectations because their moral competence—their capacity to grasp and to feel motivated by moral reasons to act in a better way—was strained under the circumstances; not necessarily because they were insane or in some way not really acting at all, but rather because they acted under limitations or hardships that made moral action difficult. People are subject to a wide range of cognitive, emotional, and psychological traits over which they have, at best, only limited control, even when their behavior satisfies minimal standards of rationality. Fear and anger, a desire to fit in, impulse control, and a lack of attention to long-term consequences can make it difficult for a person to act morally, without making it the case that they do not act at all, or that what they did was not wrong.

Kelly concludes, plausibly in my view, that recognizing that people are limited, or have faced challenges that make morality difficult, should lead us to question the appropriateness of blame in some cases. At the very least, such cases indicate that blame is not inevitably morally required.

18. See Erin Kelly, *The Limits of Blame: Rethinking Punishment and Responsibility* (Harvard University Press, forthcoming), chs. 2–4. See also Nicola Lacey and Hanna Pickard, "From the Consulting Room to the Court Room? Taking the Clinical Model of Responsibility Without Blame into the Legal Realm," *Oxford Journal Of Legal Studies* 33(1) (2013): 1–29 (discussing "clinical model" of responsibility, which both emphasizes a person's choices and control over her conduct, while forgoing "affective blame" in favor of "concern, respect and compassion").

Responsible wrongdoing can be addressed through a variety of non-retributive responses—disappointment, sadness, sympathy, or compassion, for instance—that do not amount to taking an objectivizing, condescending, or otherwise non-agential attitude toward the wrongdoer. These responses take seriously, Kelly has pointed out, that the person at whom they are addressed is responsible for wronging another. Responses that stop short of resentment or blame can be grounded on an appreciation that although a person could have chosen differently than she did, doing so would have been unusually difficult for her. Under those circumstances, we can acknowledge her responsibility for the wrong without blaming or condemning her for it. Kelly's argument lends support to my claim that, in choosing between *schools, now* and *prisons, later*, we are not choosing between ignoring versus respecting responsible agency. Rather, we are choosing between two different ways of respecting responsible agency. We are choosing between strengthening the constitutive elements of responsible agency and resenting people for their choices, including when those choices were made under conditions under which anyone would likely have faltered.[19]

I do not want to give the impression that the main reason people commit crimes is because of their own lack of moral development (nor is this Kelly's view). To the contrary, poverty, social exclusion, and oppression only serve to further complicate the relation between responsibility and resentment. People living under such conditions may well have a claim that justice requires favoring *schools, now* over *prisons, later*. What I draw from Kelly's argument is that, in addition to possible claims of injustice, there are also distinct responsibility-related reasons for opting out of blame. Not because people growing up under conditions of serious deprivation are not responsible agents (surely they are), or because the state lacks standing to punish them given its own injustice (though it might), but rather because consistently choosing to refrain from crime can be particularly difficult for people grappling with impulse control, social exclusion, and other barriers to the effective exercise of responsible agency.

The upshot is that the choice between *schools, now* and *prisons, later* is a responsibility-responsibility trade-off. Indeed, it is entirely possible

19. Judges might address issues of this kind at sentencing. The point I am emphasizing is that the same choice is reflected in social policy more generally. Sentencing discretion is at most a small part of an overall social choice about how public institutions best respect responsible agency. My thanks to Veenu Goswami for discussion on these points.

that non-punitive, preventive means can potentially be superior to punitive ones at fostering responsible agency. Giving people a decent education may better develop responsible agency than blaming, resenting, and punishing them for the bad choices they make. To be sure, punishment ex post might be characterized as respecting responsible agency, whereas ex ante social programming might be characterized as promoting it. But this seems beside the point, which is that in either case we are choosing between different ways of responding to people as responsible agents. Hence, we can doubt whether it is appropriate to resent, blame, or punish someone without calling into question his status as a responsible agent rather than a human-shaped piece of nature, a vector of potential injury to be controlled rather than reasoned with. We can have responsibility without resentment. We should reject the thought that the alternative to retribution is humanitarian detachment, and that the alternative to punitive just deserts is medicalized social hygiene.

7.4 Can the Criminal Law Be Purely Remedial?

Proposals to invest more heavily in early childhood education, youth employment, and other such programs may seem independently attractive. They are ways of managing the social risk of crime that are neither punitive nor Woottonite, and one might concede that we have a variety of reasons to invest in programs of that kind in preference to an exclusively ex post system of punishment, including reasons grounded in democratic equality. But, or so you might think, this does not yet reach the heart of the matter. The fact is that no society has completely eradicated crime, and probably none ever will. That means that there will always be an ex post problem; whatever steps we take to minimize it, there will always be crime. And what are we supposed to do about it once it *does* happen? Surely, the fact that A has culpably victimized B requires a public, and indeed, punitive, response.[20]

Call this the purely remedial thesis, or the PRT for short. The PRT amounts to this: if someone commits a crime, then we are morally called upon to respond to that person with blame, resentment, or punishment. Since this proposition is conditional on a crime being committed,

20. See Andreas von Hirsch, *Deserved Criminal Sentences* (Bloomsbury 2017), 122–25.

it is entirely consistent with favoring policies that prevent crimes from occurring in the first place. This is why it is purely remedial. It does not tell us that the only thing we ought to do about crime is punish it. Rather, it tells us that we have a distinctive kind of reason to respond to crimes once they have happened, whether through punishment or some other blaming response.

What is the nature of that reason? There are many possible answers to that question, but one influential line of thought goes as follows: one might argue, in a Strawsonian spirit, that to *be* a responsible agent is to be *treated* as one. To treat someone as a responsible agent consists, in part, in responding to wrongdoing with a demand for justification, and with resentment, condemnation, even punishment, if the justification falls short. After all, one way of disregarding someone's status as a responsible agent is to replace resentment with pity. Pity can be more degrading than resentment; it is certainly more condescending.[21]

Half a century ago, Herbert Morris made a similar argument. He claimed that to treat a human as a person requires "permit[ting] the person to make the choices that will determine what happens to him," as well as formulating responses that "are responses respecting the person's choices."[22] In a similar spirit, Stephen Morse once defended a "law and order" approach to crime over a "social justice" approach on the ground that "poor criminals can and should be held accountable for law violations."[23] For this reason, Morse suggested limiting the range of "nonresponsibility defenses" in order to "make clear to individuals that society views them as responsible persons who are in control of their lives and who are accountable for their actions." To treat people otherwise, Morse concluded, "is to treat them as less than human."[24] A similar thought also seems to underpin Alexander and Ferzan's claim that respecting your ability to obey the law entails blaming and punishing you when you do not. Von Hirsch's "censure" theory similarly stresses punishment's role in "addressing the

21. See Michael Moore, "Causation and the Excuses," *California Law Review* 73 (1985): 1091–149 at 1145–47 (comparing our sympathy for disadvantaged offenders to the optical illusion of a stick bent in water, and suggesting that those attitudes are based on "elitism" and "condescension").

22. "Persons and Punishment," *Monist* 52(4) (1968): 475–501 at 492.

23. Stephen Morse, "The Twilight of Welfare Criminology: A Reply to Judge Bazelon," *Southern California Law Review* 49 (1976): 1247–68 at 1265.

24. Morse, "Twilight of Welfare Criminology," 1267–68.

offender as a moral agent," as a "person capable . . . of evaluating the propriety of his conduct."[25] Finally, Duff has recently suggested that wrongdoers have a categorical "right to be prosecuted," on the ground that prosecuting someone "is to address her as a responsible member of the political community": responsibility positively requires calling wrongdoers to account through the criminal process.[26]

What does the PRT suggest for the choice between *schools, now* and *prisons, later*? As I have stressed, it is surely not the case that you need early childhood education or a summer job to qualify as a responsible agent. Hence, one might argue, regardless of whether we invest in *schools, now*, we always still have reason to invest in *prisons, later*. No matter what we do, some people will commit crimes. Often, those who commit crimes will be responsible for doing so. Under the PRT, we consequently have reason to set up a social institution of blame and punishment to deal with those cases. But, one might suggest, this is not so troubling: the state has lots of reasons to do lots of different things. Perhaps it should *also* invest in preventing crime ex ante. All that the PRT claims is that for the crime that does happen, blame and punishment are appropriate. What is troubling about this? Some degree of investment in punishment does not seem obviously out of line.

The idea that the criminal law can be purely remedial in orientation may go some way toward accounting for the overwhelmingly individualistic orientation of normative criminal law theorizing. A preoccupation with responding to crimes after they happen is, ultimately, a preoccupation with responding to discrete actions by particular individuals. If you are only concerned with responding to bad acts after they occur, the moral sentiments that those bad acts engender—directed at specific, discrete individuals—will naturally take center stage, rather than more abstract concerns about social policy. How public institutions should manage the risk of crime in the aggregate is just a different type of question: institutional and forward-looking, rather than individualistic and backward-looking. Early childhood education, summer employment, rectification of background injustice, and so forth: all great ideas, you might say. But they have nothing to do with *criminal law*. Criminal law is, by definition, a matter of responding to wrongs after they occur. Hence, the PRT

25. von Hirsch, *Deserved Criminal Sentences*, 18; and ch. 3 generally.

26. Antony Duff, *The Realm of Criminal Law* (Oxford University Press 2018), 211.

underwrites a very traditional understanding of the difference between criminal law and criminal justice policy. As Farmer once put it, "[t]o the criminal lawyer, the question of enforcement is seen as something beyond the law, to be carried out by agencies and institutions of criminal justice. The law stands above and beyond the sphere of public debate and policy."[27] From this (the traditional) point of view, the criminal law is an "autonomous philosophical system," for which moral philosophy provides "the only legitimate mode of analysis."[28]

But if the PRT is to be more than just definitional fiat, it must do more than provide a plausible account of the kind of reason that we collectively have to respond to actualized wrongdoing with blame and punishment. It must also explain how that reason relates to the other things we have reason to want public institutions to do. Backward-facing, retributive theories of punishment have mostly focused on the first issue: explaining, for instance, why we have reason to call wrongdoers to account, to censure them, and perhaps to express that censure through punishment. But we should also inquire into the second issue: assuming that we do have a good reason to respond to instances of culpable wrongdoing with blame and punishment, how does that reason relate to the other reasons that apply to public institutions?

It is important to first clarify what it would take to vindicate the PRT. There are two possibilities here. One is very robust, and the other very weak. If responding to actualized wrongdoing with blame and punishment is constitutive of responsible agency, then the PRT provides an overwhelmingly strong reason for setting up a system of prosecutions and punishment, given how central responsible agency is to our sense of ourselves. (Duff, recall, defends a *categorical* obligation to prosecute.) Hence, on this interpretation, the PRT says that we fail to treat people as responsible agents unless we blame and punish them for their culpable wrongdoing. It does not say that we should blame and punish them unless we have some other, better, use for the time, energy, and resources that doing so would consume. Conversely, if that were all it said, then the significance of the PRT would be greatly diminished. It would amount to the claim that blaming and punishing culpable wrongdoing is of *some* positive value.

27. Lindsay Farmer, *Criminal Law, Tradition and Legal Order* (Cambridge University Press 2005), 8. See also Ramsay, "Responsible Subject as Citizen."

28. Farmer, *Criminal Law, Tradition and Legal Order*, 7–8.

That version of the PRT would be entirely consistent with never punishing anyone for anything. Perhaps there are more important things for the state to expend its limited time and resources on. Other activities might be of much greater value than punishing people—for instance, educating them, providing them with healthcare, building subways, and so forth. Interpreted in this way, the PRT boils down to the claim that censuring and punishing people for their wrongdoing is not entirely without value—plausible, but anodyne. Certainly, it would appear, not strong enough to play a significant load-bearing role in justifying a social institution of censure and punishment.[29]

What makes this second interpretation of the PRT anodyne? Consider three policy regimes: (a) the state fully enforces the criminal law, giving it lexical priority over other public aims; (b) the state partially enforces the criminal law, sometimes preferring the pursuit of other public aims over prosecuting and punishing criminals; and (c) the state never enforces the criminal law, always preferring to pursue other public aims instead. Must a proponent of any of these regimes deny that prosecuting and punishing wrongdoers is of some positive value? No. Even a state that never prosecutes and punishes anyone for anything can acknowledge the value in doing so, but hold that it has other, morally more urgent, aims that take priority. Specifying the PRT in a more concrete way, so that it rules out (c), would require some account of why responding to wrongdoing punitively on this or that occasion takes precedence over other important public aims, and it is hard to see how that can be done without some set of covering principles that adjudicate conflicts between important public aims. Ultimately, then, going beyond an anodyne interpretation of the PRT requires an account of the aims and limits of public power—that is, a theory of justice appropriate to public institutions. However, simply acknowledging a moral connection between responsibility and ex post prosecution and punishment does not on its own determine the content of a theory of justice. Hence,

29. This is one way of interpreting Duff's discussion of why we might sometimes "do nothing" rather than criminalize: *The Realm of Criminal Law*, 280–82. A yet more anodyne interpretation might be: in deciding whether to prosecute and punish someone we believe to be guilty of a crime, we ought not base our decision on a degrading belief, such as the belief that he (or people *like him*) are incapable of autonomous choice. That interpretation of the PRT is consistent with choosing not to prosecute and punish for other reasons, and is simply an instance of what I described, in Chapter 3, as the anti-subordination principle. My thanks to Mark Dsouza for discussion of this point.

under this interpretation, the PRT is anodyne, and no threat to a fully political conception of criminal law.[30]

In contrast, if we take seriously the categorical rhetoric in which the PRT is typically defended, then the claim is not just that punishing people is of some positive value, but rather that punishing people for their culpable wrongdoing is intrinsic to (constitutive of) treating them as responsible agents. Failing to prosecute and/or punish people for their criminal acts just is to fail to respect them as responsible agents; it is to fail to respond to them in the way as we morally ought to, given that they are responsible agents. Taking seriously the categorical rhetoric in which defenses of the PRT are typically couched suggests, in short, that prosecuting and punishing wrongdoers is in an important sense non-optional. It is sufficiently weighty that we have decisive reason to set up public institutions to adjudicate, blame, and punish people, despite the time, energy, and resources in doing so.

But this interpretation of the PRT faces the inverse problem from the former interpretation. It suggests that our reason to punish culpable wrongdoing is very strong: so strong that it resists being traded off against other costly activities that public institutions may have reason to pursue. (After all, what other priorities could take precedence to treating people as responsible agents?) No matter what other uses we may have for the resources consumed by a system of ex post punishment, taking people seriously as responsible agents positively demands that we allocate those resources toward a system of punishment. Consider what this implies for conditions of scarcity where every dollar spent on prosecution and punishment is a dollar not spent on social welfare. *Schools, now* or *prisons, later*? Rigorism about prosecution and punishment points in an unappealing direction.

Once we appreciate just how strong a claim the PRT actually is, it becomes easier to appreciate why it is so profoundly implausible. My argument begins with a very simple observation, which is that it does not seem to jeopardize your status as a responsible agent if you are clever or lucky enough to get away with committing a crime. There are lots of reasons people might not be held accountable for their crimes. Most of them (insufficient evidence, for instance) do not have anything much to do with whether we consider the perpetrator to be a responsible agent. It

30. My thanks to James Edwards and Simon Palmer for discussion of these points.

is surely relevant to recall that for most crimes, most of the time, people do in fact "get away with it." If it were really true that being a responsible agent requires being called to account and facing blame for every instance of culpable wrongdoing, that would imply that there are an awful lot of people who turn out *not* to be responsible agents because they have never been called to account for some crime they have committed in the past. This seems improbable.

Admittedly, this is a simple-minded thought. On any reasonable interpretation, the PRT does not claim that people who get away with culpable acts are not responsible agents. More plausibly, the claim is: conditional on the authorities having sufficient evidence establishing a person's guilt in a particular case, they should respond with some appropriate form of public blame or punishment.[31]

However, what the simple-minded thought emphasizes is that there is a difference between committing a culpable wrong and being known to have committed a culpable wrong. I have focused on this point because acquiring such knowledge is not costless. It is a function of how much we have invested into investigating crime. But how much *should* we devote to investigating crime? There does not appear to be an obvious answer to that question. We could, for instance, decide to station a police officer on every street corner for the exclusive purpose of gathering evidence of criminal conduct. On the opposite end of the spectrum, we could return to a system of privatized criminal law, in which the burden of investigating and prosecuting crimes is exclusively a matter of private initiative. Would either be a justifiable allocation of resources? That is hard to say in the abstract, but it seems unlikely that it could be decided simply by further analysis of the concept of responsibility. It would seem, among other things, to require some account about what other activities the state should be engaging in, and how much it is worth investing in those activities rather than investigating crime. After all, under conditions of scarcity, investigating crime is ultimately in competition with everything else the state does that consumes resources. That includes investing

31. Arthur Ripstein's position runs along these lines. Ripstein suggests that the state has an obligation to punish all those who it believes to have committed crimes, but also suggests that the state has no determinate obligation to find out who has, in fact, committed a crime. *Force and Freedom: Kant's Legal and Political Philosophy* (Harvard University Press 2009), 320–21. This suggests that the state that investigates and punishes each and every wrong is morally on par with the state that never investigates, and hence never punishes, anyone for anything.

in public education, healthcare, environmental regulation, employment supports, and other programs that promote the development of the emotional, cognitive, and social capacities that underpin responsible agency.[32] There will inevitably be more people who we could hold to account and punish, if only we invested more in law enforcement. But by the same token, there will inevitably be people who, if only we invested more in early childhood education, healthcare, and so forth, could see their capacity for responsible agency improved, perhaps substantially. Insofar as both forms of responding to people as responsible agents consume time, energy, and resources, then the question is which one we should prefer. The PRT provides exactly zero guidance on that question.

Hence, once we interpret the PRT—as we surely must, if we are to avoid the simple-minded objection—as conditional on our acquiring the knowledge that someone has committed a culpable wrong, then we have given up the game. We have conceded that the reason the PRT gives us to punish people for their culpable wrongdoing in fact *is* assessed against the other activities we have reason to collectively pursue. Indeed, unless we are meant to punish every wrongdoer who comes to our attention, it is inevitably the case that sometimes we punish the guilty and sometimes we do not. It seems overwhelmingly plausible that the decision about when to punish is responsive to a wide range of reasons, including those having to do with (for instance) resources, knock-on effects, opportunity costs, and policy priorities. Consequently, the PRT does not support the idea that whatever else we do, we must prosecute and punish wrongdoers whenever we can. That is a contingent question, dependent upon a wide range of other variables.

In short, defenders of the PRT face a dilemma: either it is interpreted robustly, in which case it turns out that responsible agency is jeopardized simply because people often do get away with their crimes, or it is interpreted to accommodate the other claims on public attention and resources, in which case it boils down to the plausible, but uninteresting, claim that punishing people who break the law may be of independent value.[33]

---

32. Jonathan Wolff and Avner de-Shalit have argued, persuasively in my view, that setting priorities under conditions of scarcity requires comparing the value of competing goods against each other, rather than placing them in silos of "local justice." See *Disadvantage* (Oxford University Press 2007), ch. 5, especially 94–95.

33. My argument here is similar to Murphy and Nagel's argument that fairness in tax policy is best assessed with respect to the operation of just social institutions, and the kinds of

The intuition underlying the PRT is that, no matter what we do by way of crime prevention, the fact that A has culpably victimized B calls out for a response. However, because blame and punishment are not self-executing, it turns out that it is impossible to cash out that thought in a way that vindicates its allegedly acontextual and pre-emptory claim upon us. Whether we have reason to do anything at all after A culpably victimizes B depends on what else we have reason to do, and the value of pursuing those ends relative to that of holding A accountable. But I have suggested that this is a completely anodyne observation, robbing the PRT of much of its apparent significance. The apparent significance of the PRT was that appeal to responsibility could provide a basis for deciding, at least in some range of important cases, whether public institutions have an obligation to punish. However, once the applicability of the PRT is understood as conditional on the other expectations we might have regarding the priorities of public institutions, it is no longer evident that the PRT can do what we had hoped for it. It fails to explain why responsibility has a specially powerful role in the context of criminal justice policy. Instead, it only provides an account of a type of value that a theory of justice, applicable to public institutions, might or might not treat as urgent under certain conditions. When the value of prosecution and punishment is of such urgency that it takes priority over other public aims, and when the converse, is resolved not by the PRT but by an overarching theory of justice.[34]

To be sure, you might be inclined to defend a theory of justice that gives the PRT greater weight in navigating the *schools, now* and *prisons, later* trade-off than the account I favor. Here, I reiterate that anti-deference is meant to illustrate how one might go about giving normative content

---

outcomes they generate, rather than with respect to the alleged baseline of each person's natural right to property in an imagined pre-tax world. Fairness in criminal justice, I have been claiming, is best assessed with respect to the operation of just social institutions rather than with respect to the alleged natural rights of victims to vindication in some imagined pre-politically setup. *The Myth of Ownership* (OUP 2002) esp. 175–6.

34. Alex Sarch has suggested that the PRT might be regarded as part of a rational reconstruction of the criminal law as we know it, rather than as a contribution to a critical morality of criminal justice. The PRT is undoubtedly more plausible if its significance is cabined in this way: the sort of thing that, upon reflection, we are inclined to say about the way we have, more or less, been doing things around these parts. I certainly have no quarrel with rational reconstruction in this sense; my point is only that the PRT is of limited significance when our objective is not rationalizing the status quo but considering its justifiability from the ground up.

to a conception of criminal law as public law. It is not the only possible way, and indeed you may reject anti-deference because you think it gives insufficient weight to holding people's accountable for their poor choices. My claim is that defending that preference requires going beyond punishment's significance to interpersonal morality, and must instead be based upon an account of justice in public institutions.

In Chapter 5, I rejected "subject matter" approaches to the theory of criminalization, on the ground that they sought to treat the criminal law as a moral subsystem whose principles and values are detached from a more general theory of justice applicable to public institutions.[35] The argument I have sketched against the PRT comes to a similar conclusion, although by a different route. A purely remedial approach to punishment, like a subject-matter approach to criminalization, carves out a special morality for the criminal law. Just as one might think that the criminal law has an intrinsic subject matter (pre-justicial wrongs), one might similarly think that it has an intrinsic mode of response (condemnatory punishment). We should resist both of these thoughts. Just as subject-matter approaches to criminalization ignore broader debates about the appropriate uses of state power more generally, a purely remedial conception of punishment suggests that whatever else we do, we *always* have a reason to respond to actualized wrongdoing with prosecution and punishment. However, the significance of that punitive reason should be determined by ordinary principles of political justification, not putatively special principles intrinsic to the criminal law.

7.5 Ex Ante, Ex Post

Although I have been focusing on responsibility-related reasons for endorsing the PRT, there are other reasons as well, which are not related to responsibility. The appeal of the PRT (or something close to it) is sufficiently broad that even legal theorists who are at pains to insist upon the political dimensions of the criminal law have defended it in one or another form. What explains the broad intuitive appeal of the PRT? Here is one possibility: when someone commits a criminal act, we cannot just let that go by without doing *something*, and indeed something punitive in

35. Chapter 5, Sections 5.2–5.3.

nature. That would amount, precisely, to impunity.[36] What this intuition suggests is that my claim that ex post punishment and ex ante prevention are functional substitutes is wrong. There is something that ex post punishment does that ex ante prevention does not. It vindicates our desire to ensure that people do not commit crimes with impunity. The value of ensuring that people do not act with impunity is not limited to those with retributivist inclinations. Even non-retributivists can get behind it.

Consider Duff's suggestion that we think of the criminal law as an authoritative, public statement of our shared civic values. On Duff's depiction, the criminal law is something like a code of conduct for a profession, only instead of applying to people qua doctors or lawyers or architects, it applies to them qua members of a particular polity.[37] That polity will reflect a civil order, constituted out of formal rules, informal expectations, roles, routes of salience, emotional pathways, and so forth. The criminal law helps sustain that civil order by establishing publicly shared values and calling people to account when they act in ways that depart from those values. This is why, on Duff's account, the criminal law is suffused with moral content: it is fundamentally about people giving and asking each other for reasons for what they have done, although—unlike expansive Moorean moralism—the demand for reasons is limited to public wrongs, that is, attacks on a polity's civil order.[38] Unlike most retributivists, for Duff those reasons are socially and culturally conditioned, as they are reasons drawn out of a particular polity's conception of civil order at a particular time, rather than intuited a priori by some recumbent moral philosopher. Nevertheless, for Duff regarding ex post and ex ante measures as functionally equivalent distorts the basic function of ex post response: when someone flouts our shared civic values, we necessarily have reason to call her to account, conveying to her our disappointment at what she did, encouraging her to reform, and reassuring ourselves of our commitment to those values. Ex ante measures may be worthy endeavors too, but they

36. Igor Primoratz, "Punishment as Language," *Philosophy* 64 (1989): 187–205, 200; John Kleinig, "Punishment and Moral Seriousness," *Israel Law Review* 25 (1991): 401–21, 417–18; Jean Hampton, "Correcting Harms Versus Righting Wrongs: The Goal of Retribution," *UCLA Law Review* 39 (1992): 1659–702, 1686–87. For an effective rejoinder, see Nathan Hanna, "Say What? A Critique of Expressive Retributivism," *Law and Philosophy* 27(2) (2008): 123–50.

37. Duff, *The Realm of Criminal Law*, 80–91.

38. Duff, *The Realm of Criminal Law*, 87–88.

cannot discharge this essentially retrospective function. The criminal law, on Duff's account, has a "distinctive function" that cannot be replaced by any other practice that does not "focus on moral wrongdoing."[39]

Malcolm Thorburn has also defended an essentially retrospective account of the criminal law, but on Kantian rather than communitarian grounds. Recall that Thorburn defends a conception of "robust authority," whereby one person is empowered to make rules for another. Thorburn's preferred example is of a parent standing in a relation of robust authority to his minor child: it is the parent's role to make decisions on behalf of the child, setting rules of conduct, ensuring compliance, and punishing willful noncompliance. This last part, punishment, is important to robust authority because willful noncompliance constitutes a challenge (a "direct attack") to the authority's figure status as an authority. Hence, while the authority may seek to prevent disobedience, once it materializes he must be empowered to respond with punishment. Punishing the disobedient child, Thorburn concludes, is necessary to make it the case that the child's disobedience "is no longer a genuine threat to the parent's claim of robust authority over the child."[40] Controversially, Thorburn suggests that his characterization of the parent-child relation also applies to the citizen-state relation—citizens stand to the state as children stand to parents. As a result, when someone commits a crime, punishment is required "in order to vindicate the king's claim of robust authority over the matter."[41]

For both Duff and Thorburn, the criminal law is not merely some generically coercive system for enforcing rules and fostering cooperation. The criminal law is essentially retrospective: calling someone to account for her crime, and imposing condemnatory punishment, are part of the inner morality of the criminal law. Other measures for managing crime may be valuable and worth pursuing, but they cannot be equated with the criminal law. Although Duff and Thorburn have different reasons for thinking so, they would presumably both regard an account of criminal

---

39. Duff, *The Realm of Criminal Law*, 151.

40. Malcolm Thorburn, "Punishment and Public Authority," in *Criminal Law and the Authority of the State*, ed. Antje du Bois-Pedain, Magnus Ulväng, and Petter Asp (Hart 2017), 7–33 at 21.

41. Thorburn, "Punishment and Public Authority," 25. I share Shachar Eldar's skepticism that "robust authority" is attractive either as an account of the parent-child or of the state-citizen relation: see Eldar, "Criminal Law, Parental Authority and the State," *Criminal Law and Philosophy* (forthcoming 2018), https://doi.org/10.1007/s11572-017-9452-7.

law that fails to accommodate its essentially retrospective character as departing too radically from traditional notions of crime as wrongdoing and punishment as retrospective censure for that wrongdoing. On both Duff and Thoburn's accounts, it is crucial that there is *some* system in place for retrospective punishment; they are comparatively less concerned to adjudicate the degree to which such a system should be relied upon rather than more forward-looking interventions.

There is obviously something to the intuition that crimes cannot go unpunished. Where I part company with Duff and Thorburn is that I do not seek to defend the intuition on its own terms. Rather, I think the intuition can be explained as adaptive along the lines I sketched in Chapter 2: insofar as punishment helps sustain cooperation, then it is perhaps not so surprising that humans would have come to have developed quick, emotionally-laden blaming and punitive responses when confronted with antisocial, norm-violating conduct, particularly when it comes from another group member with whom further cooperation might otherwise have been expected.[42] I have argued that the basic function of enforcing legal rules is to stabilize broad social cooperation over the long haul. If people observe deliberate rule violations repeatedly going unpunished, it will seem less and less rational to comply with the rule, at least when compliance involves costs of any kind. Reaffirming the authority of the law is, on this account, a matter of ensuring the stability of a particular type of cooperative endeavor, namely organized social life under legally constituted institutions. It would impair the cooperation-reinforcing role of law if it is widely perceived that people can defect without consequence. From this point of view, the value of the criminal law lies largely in its status as a body of authoritative, public statements about socially agreed conduct rules. To be authoritative, those rules obviously need to be enforced when they are flouted, at least to some suitable degree of probability.

Although a public law conception of criminal law is centrally concerned with a forward-looking account of what the criminal law does for people—enabling sustained social cooperation—this does not require ignoring the significance of the expressive function of the criminal law in announcing binding conduct rules and condemning deliberate violations.

---

42. The adaptive significance of the retributive sentiments is by now a familiar theme in social psychology. For accessible overviews, see Jonathan Haidt in *The Righteous Mind: Why Good People Are Divided by Politics and Religion* (Pantheon 2012), and Willem van Prooijen, *The Moral Punishment Instinct* (Oxford University Press 2018).

Indeed, precisely because the criminal law is able to sustain cooperation over the long haul by publicly establishing rules of conduct that are widely regarded to be legitimate, the criminal law's expressive function is likely to be of crucial importance.[43] To this degree, the idea that some system of ex post punishment is a stable feature of legal systems is quite plausible. This is not, however based upon an abstract conception of civic order or the political authority. Rather, it is based upon a judgment about what, given humans as they are, and social conditions as they are likely to be, is required to sustain ongoing social cooperation. There is indeed value in responding to deliberate rule-violations, perhaps by communicating censure and imposing punishment. However, this value is not distinct from the prospective value of social cooperation. To the contrary, the urge to condemn and punish those who do wrong is itself grounded in its ability to sustain social cooperation. Seen from an "internal" point of view, punishment looks fundamentally different from prevention. Seen functionally, however, ex post is ex ante: they differ in their means, not in their ends.[44]

As it happens, there is evidence that ex post punishment and ex ante prevention are indeed functional substitutes, in that less of one can be made up for by more of another. Criminologists have found evidence suggesting that there is an inverse relationship between spending on social welfare and punishment: states that spend less on the former tend to spend more on the latter.[45] In addition, there is evidence to suggest that people are more likely to comply with rules when they regard those rules as legitimate.[46] More generally, it seems likely that social cooperation is

43. What I have in mind here by "expressive" is the criminal law's function in, as Sugden puts it, making salient certain conventions of reciprocity that have come to command broad adherence in a given society, and for which people are prepared to endure some level of sacrifice in order to punish defectors. See Robert Sugden, *The Economics of Rights, Co-operation and Welfare* (Palgrave Macmillan 2004), ch. 8.

44. My difference from Duff on this point flows out of differing objectives: Duff's aim is to provide a "rational reconstruction" of the criminal law. My aim is to provide an evaluative framework appropriate for our existing institutions. See Duff, *The Realm of Criminal Law*, 11–13.

45. See Tapio Lappi-Seppälä, "Trust, Welfare and Political Culture: Explaining Differences in National Penal Policies," *Crime and Justice* 37(1) (2008): 313–87 at 356 (finding an inverse relation between spending on social welfare and imprisonment); Katherine Beckett and Bruce Western, "Governing Social Marginality," *Punishment & Society* 3(1) (2001): 43–59 (finding similar results across American states).

46. Tom Tyler, *Why People Obey Law* (Princeton University Press 2006).

more stable the more those subject to the justice system believe that it will protect their interests and resolve their disputes fairly, providing them with a compelling reason to forgo self-help. It may also be the case that stable cooperation requires the law to not depart too notably from the principles and values that are broadly understood, in that society, to be worthy of support.[47]

A public law conception can, to this extent, vindicate Duff's concern that the criminal law should reflect widely shared social values, and should be used in ways that garner the respect of polity members. It is also consistent with Thorburn's suggestion that we have a reason to care about responding to actualized rule violations, and that this reason has to do with the stability of public authority. What it cannot vindicate, however, is a freestanding moral obligation—one untethered to a more comprehensive account of public law, and social cooperation more generally—to punish wrongdoers once they have become wrongdoers. Our reason for responding to actualized crimes with condemnatory punishment are not distinct from our reasons for seeking to prevent people from committing those acts in the first place: they make it harder to achieve the ends that public institutions (and social cooperation more generally) ought to achieve.

You might think that this has all been far too abstract and is of little consequence for "real world" criminal justice. If you are tempted by this thought, consider James Forman's account of the ballot initiative that instituted mandatory minimum sentences for drug and gun offenses in Washington, DC.[48] Forman observes that although they disagreed about whether harsh mandatory minimums would stem the tide of drugs and violence, no one thought to inquire whether drug and gun crime was, in effect, a criminal law problem rather than (say) a public health or public education or labor market problem. Why not? The PRT suggests an answer: if crimes such as trafficking in drugs and guns violate a community's civic values, and if they flout the legal system's authority to make rules for citizens, then we should respond with ex post sanction. To do otherwise would be to ignore our civic values and undermine the law's authority. Responding to crime with public health initiatives rather than punishment amounts to ignoring our civic values and undermining respect for

47. See Paul Robinson, "Empirical Desert," in *Criminal Law Conversations*, ed. Paul Robinson, Stephen Garvey and Kimberly Kessler Ferzan (Oxford University Press 2009), 29–38.

48. Forman, *Locking Up Our Own*, ch. 4.

the authority of the law. So, the only real question is how much to punish, not whether to punish. That is what it takes to "re-establish the principle that men are accountable for what they do."[49]

Of course, this is just one example of a familiar phenomenon, in which familiar labels ("health," "crime," "education") create policy silos that are then guarded by dense thickets of conceptual analysis pertaining to the meaning of those terms. If we take for granted that crime is a problem for the criminal law—that those who violate widely shared values must be held to account through some condemnatory, punitive process—we will tend to ignore the other possibilities that are open to modern administrative states for heading off crime by addressing its underlying causes. This is unfortunate, as modern administrative states create new, and more sophisticated, means of addressing crime and victimization that do not, in the final analysis, boil down to pounding on conduct that angers us. Traditional legal categories—tort, crime, regulation—should either keep up or get out of the way.

7.6 Responsibility and Fair Distribution

I have argued that a robustly egalitarian attitude toward the criminal law does not depend on skepticism about individual responsibility. Preventing crimes ex ante is desirable on both egalitarian and responsibility-promoting grounds. We might forgo blaming and punishing people who commit crimes not because we view them from a condescending and objectifying moral perspective, but because we consider investment in social welfare to be morally more urgent than blaming them for their transgressions. We would have good reason to regard ex ante measures as more urgent if the evidence suggests that they prevent crime by building, rather than impairing, effective access to central capability.

However, the suspicion that equality and responsibility are at odds with each other in the criminal law might have a different source. Taking responsibility seriously, you might think, is not just a matter of responding to people in a certain way when they wrong others. Taking responsibility seriously also requires according guilt and innocence an important role in the distribution of harm. Those who are guilty of aggressing against

49. Platform statement of the 1968 Republican Party (Nixon versus Humphrey); cited in Elizabeth Hinton, *From the War on Poverty to the War on Crime: The Making of Mass Incarceration in America* (Harvard University Press 2016), 139.

others should bear the costs of repelling their criminal acts, not those who are innocent, and especially not their innocent would-be victims. Hence, taking responsibility seriously entails accepting a non-egalitarian distributive principle for punishment.

The moral significance of guilt in the distribution of harm seems deeply entrenched. For one thing, it seems to lie at the heart of self-defense. Suppose A culpably attacks B. B can repel A's attack, but only by imposing a proportionate harm on A. May B do so? Plausibly, she may. But this judgment is not grounded on an idea of political equality. After all, B may repel A's attack regardless of whether they are equals. Rather, the judgment that B may defend herself seems to be grounded on the principle that it is fairer for harms to fall on aggressors (especially, if not only, culpable aggressors) than on innocent victims.[50]

This line of thought can be traced back at least to Locke. Locke suggested that it is a "fundamental law of nature, man being to be preserved as much as possible, when all cannot be preserved, the safety of the innocent is to be preferred."[51] More recently, Daniel Farrell has made a similar argument.[52] Farrell defends a non-retributive theory of punishment grounded on a right to self-defense, the idea being, roughly, that if B may permissibly shift the harm onto A, then she may also permissibly warn A that she will do so if A attacks her. Perhaps an intuition along these lines underlies Tadros's "duty" account of punishment, whereby those who wrongfully attack others acquire a duty to make themselves available to protect others going forward.[53] Why shouldn't the harm lie where it falls? Because, one might think, it seems more equitable to shift it onto the shoulders of those who culpably create the danger in the first place.

Is the Lockean principle plausible? It seems to me that it is. In any case, it is so deeply entrenched that a theory that denies it is unlikely to win much support. Hence, it is incumbent on me to explain how it can be

50. See J.J. Thomson, "Self-Defense," *Philosophy & Public Affairs* 20(4) (1991): 283–310.

51. John Locke, *The Second Treatise of Government*, ch. III, s. 16, Peter Laslett, ed. (Cambridge University Press 1988).

52. Daniel M. Farrell, "Deterrence and the Just Distribution of Harm," *Social Philosophy and Policy* 12(2) (1995): 220–40; see also Farell, "The Justification of General Deterrence," *Philosophical Review* 94(3) (1985): 367–94 at 378–80; Warren Quinn, "The Right to Threaten and the Right to Punish," *Philosophy & Public Affairs* 14(4) (1985): 327–73.

53. Victor Tadros, *The Ends of Harm: The Moral Foundations of Criminal Law* (Oxford University Press 2011); see also Erin Kelly, "Criminal Justice Without Retribution," *Journal of Philosophy* 106(8) (2009): 440–62, 449.

accommodated within the framework of anti-deference—and, in particular, how it can be consistent with the principle of inclusive aggregation.

The first step is to highlight Locke's (other) proviso, namely that the safety of the innocent is to be preferred "when all cannot be preserved." One might interpret that proviso strictly, as a necessary condition: the rights of the innocent take precedence over the rights of the guilty *only* when it is impossible to protect the rights of all. Does this interpretation of the Lockean principle unsettle popular intuitions about self-defense? It seems to me that it does not. Suppose that when A attacks B, C could intervene and stop A's attack without causing harm to anyone. How should we rank possible outcomes? Perhaps: that no one is harmed is preferable to A being harmed, which is preferable to B being harmed. Defensive harming is permissible, but it is a second-best to alternatives that do not harm anyone, including culpable aggressors.[54]

Understood in this way, however, the Lockean principle is rather less damaging to an egalitarian theory of criminal law than it might appear. The moral position of public institutions parallels that of C, the good Samaritan in my example. They are in a position to intervene to prevent harm from materializing in the first place. Arguably, preventing foreseeable harms is part of the basic morality of the social welfare state. Public institutions in developed administrative states have a wide range of options for mitigating the risk of criminal victimization that go beyond threatening and imposing punishment on people who hurt other people. Preventive policing is only the most obvious example. More importantly, social welfare states minimize the risk of criminal victimization by creating universal access to education, employment, and healthcare, each of which may be expected to have a negative impact on criminal offending. This is obviously not the *only* reason to invest in such programs, but it is enough that it is *a* reason.[55]

Recall *DeShaney*, in which the Supreme Court rejected a claim by a boy's mother that the state's child protective services failed to adequately protect the boy from his abusive father. The petitioner's claim was grounded on the idea that public institutions have a duty to protect. Insofar as the state could have intervened without harming anyone—for instance, by

---

54. See Pereboom, *Living Without Free Will*, 172–73.

55. Nathan Hanna has similarly emphasized the importance of non-punitive alternatives: "Facing the Consequences," *Criminal Law & Philosophy* 8(3) (2014): 589–604.

removing the boy from the custody of his father—it was under an obligation to do so. This obligation was not defeated by the observation that the younger DeShaney, or a guardian acting in his stead, might have been justified in violently repelling the elder DeShaney's attacks. The permissibility of harming another in self-defense does not remove an obligation on the part of public institutions to prevent harm to anyone and everyone. Had the Supreme Court agreed, perhaps it would have said that when the interests of all can be preserved, the state has an obligation to do so; it cannot leave it to the victim to exercise self-defense—if he can.

Suppose that accepting the Lockean principle means that we can justify a system of public law that informs people that they can expect to be punished if they victimize others as a form of social self-defense. Is that consistent with the egalitarian approach to criminal justice that I have been proposing? Yes. I do not suggest that the criminal law must be abolished on grounds of equality. I suggest, rather, that we should limit its use to circumstances in which no less destructive means of safeguarding the public interest will do. In those cases, those who are punished do not have a complaint that they are being treated unfairly, for any other alternative would be worse from the point of view of protection of everyone's basic rights and interests. If it is the case that we cannot prevent harm from falling on someone, it may well be more equitable to shift that harm onto the shoulders of those who create the danger in the first place. Doing so, however, remains a second-best; second, in particular, to a system of institutions and policies that protect *each* person's effective access to central capability. But this is just what the Lockean principle, strictly interpreted, itself suggests. Otherwise put, the principle of inclusive aggregation is one of equal *consideration*, not of equal *treatment*. Anti-deference insists that the state's obligation to impartially weigh each person's rights and interests is not defeated or cancelled in cases where one party acts wrongfully. That is entirely consistent with the thought that it is permissible to create a system of legal rules enforced by ex post punishment when no alternative better protects effective access to central capability for all. Ex post punishment remains an option, but it is a last resort, just as the Lockean proviso suggests.

I have suggested that, strictly construed, the Lockean principle is consistent with a strong preference for ex ante prevention on the part of public institutions over ex post punishment of the guilty. But you may think that there is an important disanalogy here. Ex ante prevention is costly. Providing schools, healthcare, nutrition, policing, and so forth is expensive, and that expense is drawn out of general revenue. In effect, what it amounts to is requiring potential victims to purchase insurance from wrongful attacks by others. If you are drawn to this thought, you might think that the better illustration of the Lockean principle is not the case in which C intervenes and stops A's attack at no cost to B. The better illustration, you might think, is a case in which B could effectively and proportionately repel A's attack *either* by breaking A's leg *or* by taking one step to the right. Suppose B can break A's leg by pushing a button, so doing so comes at no cost to her. On the other hand, taking one step to the right, while not a heavy cost, is not nothing either. (Maybe B particularly enjoys the view from where she is standing.)

Would B have something to answer for if she chose to break A's leg under those circumstances? I think she would. Perhaps, however, you think that victims are not obligated to have any particular preferences about what they do to aggressors, so long as what they do is not excessive. You might think that requiring B to step aside amounts to allowing wrongdoers to inflict minor harms on victims for no good reason.

I think we should reject this austere position.[56] Even the innocent are obligated to accept some level of cost if doing so is required to prevent significantly more serious costs falling on others. First, as I have been emphasizing, a publicly administered scheme of punishment also consumes collective resources, so it's not as if we can avoid imposing costs on innocent third parties simply by focusing on punishment rather than social programming. Second, one of the basic functions of the social welfare state is to spread the cost of insuring people against risks of various kinds. As Rawls put it, part of the effect of public institutions in the social welfare state is to make it the case that we share in each other's fate, rather than simply leaving the costs to fall where they may. The principle that innocent victims cannot be asked to bear *any* portion of the social costs created by the wrongful criminal acts of others thus stands in significant tension with the basic terms of the social welfare state.

For these reasons, I would not interpret the Lockean principle to entail that potential victims can never be expected to contribute to the costs of their protection.[57] Indeed, if anything, it is the refusal to contribute that is more likely to generate relationships of inequality. Less investment ex ante

56. Though see Farrell "The Justification of General Deterrence," 389–90.

57. For a characteristically thoughtful treatment of these issues, see Victor Tadros, "Criminalization and Regulation," in *The Boundaries of the Criminal Law*, ed. R.A. Duff,

means more investment ex post; and, unlike measures funded through general revenue, the costs of criminal law enforcement are highly concentrated on discrete individuals.

What might seem controversial about this claim is that, unlike the risk that you will come down with a debilitating disease, be injured on the job, or be born with a serious disability, criminal acts are voluntary actions. By and large, people commit crimes out of choice, rather than compulsion, insanity, or mistake. Hence, assimilating criminal justice policy to social welfare policy might seem to lead back to the Woottonite thought that people are not really responsible for what they do, and are instead merely vectors of social harm to be managed rather than agents responsible for their choices. For the reasons I have sketched in this chapter, that suspicion is unfounded. Taking responsibility seriously does not uniquely require an exclusively ex post punitive response to criminal wrongdoing, much less a retributive exercise in blame and punishment. This is particularly important when ex ante measures do better at fostering the social, emotional, and cognitive capacities that undergird responsible agency. Rather than holding people's feet to the fire for the bad choices they make, it may be that we do better at treating people as responsible agents by helping them to make better choices in the first place. And it may be that egalitarian principles lead us to collectively bear the costs of doing so, rather than offloading those costs entirely onto the shoulders of people who are caught committing crimes. Just as egalitarian principles support economic redistribution, they also support incurring shared social costs to ensure that people are not abandoned to lives marked by crime, punishment, and social exclusion.

Of course, one could question whether we have reason to endorse social welfare states and the collectivization of risk. While I have been offering an egalitarian interpretation of that function, I have not endeavored to justify the social welfare state from the ground up. At most, I can point to familiar types of argument: perhaps asking potential victims (that is, everyone) to bear part of the costs associated with managing the risk posed by potential criminals (again: everyone) has something to do with the idea that whether one turns out to be a victim or a criminal is largely arbitrary from a moral point of view. Not because people do not choose to commit crimes out of their own volition, but because the factors that bear on whether one

Lindsay Farmer, S.E. Marshall, Massimo Renzo, and Victor Tadros (Oxford University Press 2010), 163–91.

will make that choice at some point in one's life are to a very significant degree not factors for which individuals are morally answerable.[58] Seen in this light, responsibility for establishing the social conditions under which people decide whether to commit criminal acts, like responsibility for protecting people from those criminal acts, is broadly shared. That said, I shall not try to convince you to accept the basic legitimacy of social welfare states if you are skeptical. My aim is to show how criminal law and criminal justice are accountable to a fully political standard of justification, not to provide a ground-up defense of the social welfare state.

7.7 Conclusion

Conditioning your access to the basic rights and prerogatives of civic membership upon an estimation of your moral worth would be an affront to widely shared liberal political values. For liberals, your right to vote, run for office, or express yourself freely, as with more tangible rights, such as social security benefits, a hospital bed, or a seat in a classroom, should not be contingent upon convincing some bureaucrat that you are morally deserving of that right. Yet the criminal law often has a direct and substantial impact on those very same rights and prerogatives. When you are convicted of a crime, important public institutions—landlords, employers, and schools, for instance—are allowed to discriminate against you. In many parts of the United States, you are stripped of the franchise, sometimes permanently. More to the point, when you are charged with a crime your very liberty is at stake. If liberals balk at making the rights and prerogatives of civic membership turn upon an official's opinion about your moral worth, how could it be appropriate to give that very same kind of judgment such weight in the criminal law? If we are resistant to giving responsibility and desert a central role in our political philosophy, why should we be so drawn to giving those concepts such a central role in our thinking about the criminal law? The political morality of the social welfare state is grounded on a sense of basic equality. Why, then, should the morality of the criminal law be so insistently individualistic?

In this chapter, I have explored three possible answers to that question. Taking responsibility seriously implies respecting the choices people make,

---

58. See Sharon Dolovich, "Legitimate Punishment in Liberal Democracy," *Buffalo Criminal Law Review* 7(2) (2004): 307–442 at 369–74; and Matt Matravers, "Political Theory and the Criminal Law" in *Philosophical Foundations of Criminal Law*, ed. R.A. Duff and Stuart P. Green (Oxford University Press 2011), 67–82 at 72–79, especially 78–79.

even when they are poor ones. That seems, in turn, to suggest that when people engage in conduct that is ill-considered, culpable, or blameworthy, we have reason to blame and punish them for doing so. We have reason to punish regardless of whether we also have reason to invest in ex ante prevention. Moreover, taking responsibility seriously means allowing that when people choose to commit criminal acts, they choose to make themselves liable to defensive harms that they would not otherwise have been liable to. In the context of the criminal law, taking responsibility seriously thus means marginalizing other important political values, such as equality. As a result, the criminal law proper is not a public institution like other public institutions. Other institutions may be evaluated in light of distributive justice, democratic equality, or other political virtues. But the criminal law is structured by individual responsibility and desert in a way those other institutions are not.

I have argued that we should reject all of these arguments. As Kelly has urged, many people find morality occasionally challenging for reasons that would make it challenging for pretty much anyone, including reasons having to do with one's emotional makeup, social exclusion, cognitive impairment, peer pressure, or a history of abuse and/or humiliation by intimates or authorities. Under these conditions, a blaming reaction seems particularly inappropriate.[59] Moreover, blame and punishment are in any case not required as part of treating people as responsible agents: investments in strengthening the capacity for responsible agency ex ante may legitimately substitute for ex post punishment. Indeed, taking responsibility (or authority) seriously does not require any particular level of investment in ex post punishment as against ex ante prevention. Public institutions respect people's choices by investing in the social conditions under which the capacity to choose is nurtured and developed. Finally, acknowledging that people can render themselves liable to defensive harm through their wrongful acts does not entail discounting the rights and interests of the guilty relative to those of the innocent.

In sum: the egalitarian's insistence that a person's status as an equal is not waived by crime does not imply skepticism about responsibility. There is no deep tension between equality and responsibility in the criminal law. We can treat people as responsible agents while also treating them as equals. Indeed, we can treat them as responsible agents precisely *by* treating them as equals.

59. See Kelly, *Limits of Blame*, ch. 3.

Conclusion

IN THEIR LANDMARK book, *Not Just Deserts,* John Braithwaite and Philip Pettit cautioned that "[w]hen you play the game of criminal justice on the field of retribution . . . you give full rein to those who play to the sense of normality of the majority, urging them to tyrannize the minority."[1] In the quarter century since *Not Just Deserts* was published, the American incarceration rate doubled from about 300 people in custody per 100,000 adults to over 600 people in custody per 100,000, with a disparate share of the burden falling on racial minorities. The United States now incarcerates over 2 million people on any given day.[2] During that time, retribution replaced rehabilitation as the prevailing attitude toward punishment among legal and moral philosophers in the United States. Ironically, the retributivist turn was, in large part inspired by a desire to limit the state's power to punish, and it was thought that making punishments proportional to moral desert might achieve that end.[3] But Braithwaite and Pettit were right: once unchained, the retributivist beast has proven difficult to domesticate.

In this book, I have endeavored to challenge the prevailing retributivist orthodoxy and, more generally, the individualistic and moralizing political morality that underpins it. The account I have articulated is one in

---

1. John Braithwaite and Philip Pettit, *Not Just Deserts: A Republican Theory of Criminal Justice* (Oxford University Press 1992), 6–7.

2. See Sourcebook of Criminal Justice Statistics 2003 (table 6.28), at 500; available at http://www.albany.edu/sourcebook/pdf/section6.pdf (accessed May 12, 2018) and http://www.prisonstudies.org/country/united-states-america (accessed May 12, 2018).

3. See Andreas von Hirsch, *Deserved Criminal Sentences* (Bloomsbury 2017), 107–8 and 115–18 (responding to Braithwaite and Pettit); David Garland, *The Culture of Control* (University of Chicago Press 2001), at 9, 60–61.

which the criminal law is fully enmeshed in a society's basic structure, and subject to the same principles of political evaluation that apply to that structure. Public institutions protect basic rights and interests for all, as a matter of right rather than charity, and they do so by aggregating and distributing the benefits and burdens of social cooperation. They achieve these objectives by promoting sustained patterns of cooperation among people who are not bound together by kinship, or communal or ideological affiliation, and yet have no realistic option but to find ways of living with each other. On the face of it, this kind of sustained cooperation across time, space, and social distance would seem rather improbable.

Punishment, in the form of public and coercive enforcement of agreed social rules, is one way of promoting that type of sustained cooperation. But punishment is a means that, as Durkheim famously argued, fades in relevance as complex and interlocking forms of social cooperation become self-sustaining. Insofar as we still have reason to rely on the criminal law as a means of sustaining social cooperation, its justification will rest on our reasons for wishing to promote a given form of social cooperation in the first place, in combination with our reasons for believing that criminal sanctions constitute a reasonable way of doing so. Consequently, the morality of the criminal law, and its associated institutions, must be consistent with the political morality of public institutions generally. In this book, I have suggested that we understand that morality as grounded in terms of democratic equality, and the kind of government that is appropriate to a society of equals.

Consider, in contrast, the conception of political morality that is implied by the kinds of individualistic and moralizing retributivism that have captured the philosophical imagination of Anglo-American legal theorists over the last half century. The retributivist's focus on substantive pre-politically moral wrongdoing as a central tenet of the criminal law is fundamentally antidemocratic, as it privileges the moral opinions of the philosopher over the process of deliberation and negotiation characteristic of democratic politics. Adopting the morality of interpersonal blame as a template for the morality of the criminal law yields an account that is fundamentally illiberal, as it boils down to a moral community roaring in indignation at someone who violates the norms of that community's thick moral life simply because they are the community's norms. This suggests a view of politics as a symbolic economy by means of which a moral majority steamrolls dissentients. Softer versions of expressivism—couched in terms of communication, education, or, as Duff once tellingly put it, "secular penance"—seem, if anything, to be even more insidious in their demand that the accused internalize the values and judgments of his jailer.[4] This brings to mind Foucault's remark that for us it is the soul that has become the prison of the body.[5] Yet if privacy means anything, it must mean that public officials are not entitled to insist, upon pain of punishment, that people inscribe the party line in their heart of hearts. More generally, by insisting that the interpersonal morality of blame takes precedence over democratic values, retributivism suggests that once you are responsible for a crime, *your interests no longer count.* Once you have become a criminal, public institutions no longer owe you an obligation of equal respect and concern. It is permissible to impair your life chances through punishment, even when doing so does nothing to make anyone better off.

The view, shared among retributivists of a Kantian spirit, that the criminal law is an exclusively backward-looking institution resembles a form of rights-besotted libertarianism, and a rather punitively-minded one at that. Morris suggested that respect for persons requires punishing them for their transgressions, Ripstein claims that punishment of those who flout the law is inherent in the very idea of the "rightful condition," and Brudner claims that we must punish the criminal to make manifest our rejection of his claim to be above the law. But perhaps Sammy Davis Jr. put it best: "don't do the crime if you can't do the time . . . don't roll the dice if you can't pay the price." Like libertarianism, the Kantian's single-minded focus on holding people's feet to the fire for the poor choices they make downplays the importance of public institutions in maintaining the inegalitarian and oppressive social relations that engender crime.[6] More generally, the moral philosopher's focus on pre-politically moral rights, especially as elicited in intuitions derived from idealized one-off transactions

---

4. R.A. Duff, *Punishment, Communication, and Community* (Oxford University Press 2001), 106, but see also 125–29. To be fair, Duff's more recent work is noticeably less moralistic, and places the question of criminal law squarely within the context of the constitution and maintenance of a polity's civil order: see, e.g., *The Realm of Criminal Law* (Oxford University Press 2018).

5. Michel Foucalt, *Discipline and Punish: The Birth of the Prison*, 2nd ed. (Vintage Books 1995), 30. As it happens, Herbert Morris once suggested that punishment could be justified by concern with the moral good of the guilty and the condition of his soul: "A Paternalistic Theory of Punishment," *American Philosophical Quarterly* 18(4) (1981): 263–71 at 268; see also Duff, *Punishment, Communication, and Community*, 81 (suggesting that punishment should ensure that people do what is right because they acknowledge it to be right).

6. A point that Jeffrie Murphy well recognized; see his "Marxism and Retribution," *Philosophy & Public Affairs* 2(3) (1973): 217–43.

between abstract individuals—"trolleyology," in Barbara Fried's trenchant characterization—blinds deontological retributivists to the social costs, uncertainties, and trade-offs that are inevitably part of a scheme of criminal justice in any moral world remotely like our own.[7] In a world of scarcity, such otherworldliness amounts to insensitivity to the claims of others to the resources consumed by a system of ex post punishment.

In short: the political morality of retributivism is antidemocratic, illiberal, resentful, and more concerned with the righteousness of those who punish than with the interests of those who are made to bear its costs. This is a harsh and unforgiving political philosophy. So much so that newcomers to this corner of the academic enterprise might be forgiven for surmising that modern forms of retributivism were, in effect, invented to rationalize the rise of the American carceral state. But perhaps it is unsurprising that Anglo-American criminal law theory would have adopted such a hyper-moralized approach to the criminal law at roughly the same time that American criminal justice institutions were undergoing a period of unprecedented growth. After all, ours is a system of criminal justice that runs on retributive emotions and the desire to exclude certain groups of people as undeserving of membership in the polity.[8] It is not in any obvious way characterized by a commitment to social and political equality, much less to the value of evidence-based policy in vindicating that commitment. Nevertheless, it would be a stretch to claim that retributivism in the philosophy of criminal law contributed to this generation of unremitting harshness. If anything, the causal direction is probably the reverse: it may be that a generation of legal theorists implicitly understood their task to be a matter of rationalizing the retributive sentiments prevalent in the culture.[9] I am not sure this should make us feel better about retributivism.

Is this an unfair characterization? Perhaps, if you think that the project of evaluating the criminal law differs fundamentally from the project of evaluating public institutions more generally. If you think that the criminal law rests on moral foundations that are fundamentally distinct

---

7. "What *Does* Matter? The Case for Killing the Trolley Problem (or Letting It Die)," *Philosophical Quarterly* 62(248) (2012): 505–29.

8. For an account of the exclusionary political origins of American mass incarceration, see Elizabeth Hinton, *From the War on Poverty to the War on Crime: The Making of Mass Incarceration in America* (Harvard University Press 2016).

9. Thomas Andrew Green, *Freedom and Criminal Responsibility in American Legal Thought* (Cambridge University Press 2014), chs. 7–9; Garland, *The Culture of Control*, ch. 6.

from those of other public institutions, then you will resist my attempt to connect the morality of crime and punishment to an overarching political morality. But from the point of view of criminal law as public law, the connection is inescapable. From a public law point of view, the principles and values that we call upon to evaluate criminal law are cut from the same cloth as those that we call upon to evaluate public institutions generally. Why? Because, at its most elemental, what the criminal law is for is stabilizing cooperation with the public institutions that facilitate our utopian future. When is the criminal law an acceptable means of pursuing that aim? When it conforms to the very same principles of political justification that make that future a utopian one. Why should the criminal law be subject to those principles? Because it too is a public institution, and stands in need of the same kind of political justification.

As I have stressed, there are many possible glosses one might give to these ideas. My preferred account is democratic, egalitarian, and capability-based. Those who are subject to the law are entitled to an equal opportunity to shape its content, and have claims against degrading or humiliating judgments about their worth. Subject to those constraints, public institutions should strive to maximally protect each person's effective access to central capabilities—the capabilities required to live in that society as an equal. Public institutions should not treat the principle of equal respect and concern as waived by participation in crime, and they should ensure that the burdens of law enforcement do not themselves further entrench patterns of status hierarchy. From this point of view, the role of the criminal law is to help public institutions create a society in which each person can live as a peer among peers.

In the face of the grim realities of contemporary criminal justice—particularly, though by no means exclusively, in the United States—it may seem that the best legal theorists and philosophers can do is rationalize what can be rationalized and bemoan the rest. But I am not so sure. I am not sure it is hopelessly utopian to think that states might eventually come to significantly scale back their reliance on incarceration, provide opportunities for meaningful democratic engagement at every level, demilitarize and diversify their police forces, decriminalize conduct where continued criminalization serves only symbolic purposes, restore rights of political participation to current and former convicts, and invest more heavily in evidence-based approaches to crime, particularly when those approaches have the effect of building human capability now rather than destroying it later. But whether utopian or not, the political ideal of anti-deference is an illustration of what it would be for the philosophy of criminal law to once again become a critical theory appropriate for the evaluation of our existing institutions and policies. It is one way of giving content to the idea that the criminal law does not stand apart from society's basic structure, but stands or falls with it. It is one way of giving content to the idea that criminal law is public law.

Index

www.ingramcontent.com/pod-product-compliance
Ingram Content Group UK Ltd.
Pitfield, Milton Keynes, MK11 3LW, UK
UKHW020924170926
475595UK00031B/67

9 780190 273941